THE NATIONAL INSTITUTE OF
ECONOMIC AND SOCIAL RESEARCH

Occasional Papers
XXIX

POVERTY AND PROGRESS
IN BRITAIN
1953-73

POVERTY AND PROGRESS IN BRITAIN

1953–73

*A statistical study of low income households:
their numbers, types and expenditure patterns*

G. C. FIEGEHEN
P. S. LANSLEY
and
A. D. SMITH

with a contribution by
N. C. GARGANAS

CAMBRIDGE UNIVERSITY PRESS

CAMBRIDGE

LONDON · NEW YORK · MELBOURNE

Published by the Syndics of the Cambridge University Press
The Pitt Building, Trumpington Street, Cambridge CB2 1RP
Bentley House, 200 Euston Road, London NW1 2DB
32 East 57th Street, New York, NY 10022, USA
296 Beaconsfield Parade, Middle Park, Melbourne 3206, Australia

First published 1977

Printed in Great Britain by
W & J Mackay Limited, Chatham

Library of Congress Cataloguing in Publication Data
Fiegehen, Guy.
Poverty and Progress in Britain, 1953–73.
(Occasional papers—the National Institute
of Economic and Social Research; 29)
Includes index.
1. Poor—Great Britain. 2. Cost and standard
of living—Great Britain. I. Lansley, Stewart,
joint author. II. Smith, Anthony Douglas, 1933–
joint author. III. Title. IV. Series: National
Institute of Economic and Social Research.
Occasional papers; 29.
HC260.P6F52 1977   339.4'1   77-2143
ISBN 0 521 21683 4

CONTENTS

TABLES

SYMBOLS IN THE TABLES
.. = not available
n.a. = not applicable
– = nil or negligible

CHARTS

PREFACE

This Occasional Paper is the result of a programme of research designed to cast light on recent trends in the nature and extent of poverty in Britain, using information from the vast body of statistics now collected annually in the Family Expenditure Survey and published by the Department of Employment. The title is evocative of the great work of the late B. Seebohm Rowntree, which inspired many of the themes taken up in this book. We are conscious that our own work is more modest in its aims and scope, but it is offered as a tribute to Rowntree's pioneering work on the 75th anniversary of his first study of poverty in York. We are grateful to the Joseph Rowntree Charitable Trust for permission to reproduce the chart from that study which appears on page 51.

The research has been financed by the Department of Health and Social Security and the Institute is very grateful for the Department's support. Mr J. L. Nicholson, formerly Chief Economic Adviser to the Department and an authority on the analysis of the Family Expenditure Surveys, provided invaluable help in launching the project and remained as a consultant throughout the work. We were also fortunate in having access to Mr S. J. Prais, Senior Research Fellow of the Institute, who made available his own extensive experience in the study of family expenditure, and helped us in the planning of the main lines of the research.

There are many other individuals and organisations who have assisted us in a variety of ways and to whom we are very grateful. The main body of data used for this project, apart from the published *Reports*, was held in confidential form on computer tape by the computing organisation of the Department of Health and Social Security, who, with the consent of the Department of Employment, processed the special tables and statistical calculations. We wish to express particular thanks to the many staff of the two departments, without whose assistance we could not have overcome the difficulties which inevitably arise when obtaining analyses from a data tape originally intended to yield information quite different from our requirements. Mrs Susan Jones of the London School of Economics wrote the program for the special analyses of the 1971 Family Expenditure Survey in chapters 4, 5 and 6, and we also received advice on data preparation and manipulation from the staff of Service in Informatics and Analysis Ltd. The project also benefited from advice on the analysis and interpretation of the

Survey data provided by the Office of Population Census and Surveys, Social Survey Division, who carry out the sampling, field work and coding of the Survey. Mrs Hill, Mrs Watts, Mrs Dolphin, Shirley Lim and Linda Russell of the Institute staff unstintingly undertook the bulk of the statistical analyses. Most of the drafts were typed by Mrs A. Pethig and Angela Manfield. Miss G. I. Little prepared the book for the printer and compiled the index.

The Director and other members of the Institute's staff have guided us through many difficulties and Mrs K. Jones, the Institute Secretary, took a special interest in our work and gave us every possible help and encouragement. Professor P. B. Townsend, of the University of Essex and Professor A. B. Atkinson of University College, London commented on drafts of several chapters but, of course, bear no responsibility for the final text. We are also grateful to Dr K. F. Wallis of the London School of Economics, who developed the formulae for computing confidence intervals used in chapter 7.

The work presented here is very much the result of a team effort. A. D. Smith coordinated the later stages of the project, and was also mainly responsible for chapters 1, 2 and 8, P. S. Lansley concentrated on chapters 3 and 6, and G. C. Fiegehen on chapters 4 and 5. Chapter 7 was contributed by N. C. Garganas, formerly of the Institute, who was a member of the team in the early stages and is now with the Bank of Greece in Athens. Whilst the major areas of responsibility were shared in this way, the final version is very much the result of an inter-change of ideas and of discussions among the team.

G.C.F.

November 1976   P.S.L.

A.D.S.

CHAPTER I

INTRODUCTION

In 1942, after half a century in which considerable attention had been paid to the problem of poverty, the Beveridge Report formulated the first comprehensive official programme for eradicating poverty in this country. Its aim was 'to make want under any circumstances unnecessary'.[1] Until then poverty had been alleviated by a number of separate insurance schemes covering old age, unemployment, sickness and industrial injury, and by the means-tested poor law. But these schemes were not available in all circumstances which might be associated with poverty. In consequence, the principal proposals of the Report were that the coverage should be extended, participation made compulsory, existing schemes coordinated into a system of national insurance and national insurance benefits set at subsistence levels. Beveridge made two further major recommendations: because it was estimated that almost a fifth of 'want' was attributable to income being insufficient for large families, he proposed a system of family allowances and, in an attempt to make the system watertight, he proposed that those who fell 'through the meshes of any insurance' should receive national assistance.

Most of these principles – though not that of setting national insurance benefits at a subsistence level, which Beveridge considered a fundamental element of his plan – were accepted and implemented by the British government in the ensuing decade. In the form of national insurance, supplementary benefits and family allowances they have endured to this day. As a testament to the efficacy with which such a system was thought to eradicate poverty, it was, in its fundamentals, widely adopted in many other developed countries. Indeed there is no doubt that the implementation of this system within the framework of the Welfare State, in conjunction with the achievement of full employment and a period of general prosperity in the postwar years, encouraged the conviction that poverty in this country had all but been eradicated. This attitude was echoed in other countries which had similar social security systems and comparable economic prosperity.[2] But the massive visible poverty of the industrial

This chapter has been prepared mainly by A. D. Smith.

[1] Treasury, *Social Insurance and Allied Services* [Beveridge Report], Cmd 6404, London, HMSO, 1942, p. 9.
[2] See, especially, M. Harrington, *The Other America*, London, Macmillan, 1962; V. Aubert,

revolution and the slumps of the early part of this century had been succeeded by less obtrusive forms of poverty among politically weak groups of society.

During the late 1950s and early 1960s disquieting evidence emerged that poverty had by no means disappeared in the United Kingdom; certain studies revealed that it remained quite widespread among some sections of the population. In particular – and roughly speaking in this order – it was shown that considerable numbers of older people, widows and – even more surprising – families with heads in full-time employment were living below the national assistance standards which society deemed desirable.[1] By the mid-1960s poverty had been 'rediscovered' in this and other developed countries.[2] What factors were responsible for the persistence of poverty in the context of the social security system, the Welfare State and the beneficial economic circumstances of postwar Britain? And why had such poverty remained so long unrecognised?

One answer to the first question is that the supplementary benefit safety net is insufficiently finely woven to catch all those in need. For instance, full-time employment implies ineligibility for supplementary benefits, even though 'there are men working full time in their regular job who earn less than the amount required to keep even a moderate-sized family at the supplementary benefit level'.[3] But more important, there are a large number of eligible recipients who, for a number of reasons, do not take advantage of the safety net.

In part the renewed concern with 'want' reflected generally increased prosperity and the feeling that the standard of living which society guaranteed should be raised accordingly. This led to 'relative' concepts of poverty, by which the extent of poverty is judged not by some absolute historically defined standard of living, but in relation to contemporary standards. By such a moving criterion poverty is obviously more likely to persist, since there will always be certain sections of society that are badly

'Country report: Norway', in OECD Manpower and Social Affairs Directorate, *Low Income Groups and Methods of Dealing with their Problems*, Paris, 1969, p. 17.

[1] D. Bull, 'The rediscovery of family poverty', in D. Bull (ed.), *Family Poverty* (2nd edn), London, Duckworth, 1972. Of these earlier studies, particularly significant landmarks were: P. Townsend, *The Family Life of Old People: an inquiry in East London*, London, Routledge and Kegan Paul, 1957; D. Cole and J. E. G. Utting, *The Economic Circumstances of Old People*, Welwyn, Codicote Press, 1962; B. Abel-Smith and P. Townsend, *The Poor and the Poorest*, London, Bell, 1965; Ministry of Social Security, *Financial and Other Circumstances of Retirement Pensioners*, London, HMSO, 1966, and *Circumstances of Families*, London, HMSO, 1967. See also: Social Science Research Council, *Research on Poverty*, London, Heinemann, 1968 – the point from which this project started – and A. B. Atkinson, *Poverty in Britain and the Reform of Social Security*, Cambridge University Press, 1969.

[2] The Australian Commission of Inquiry into Poverty refers for instance to 'the "rediscovery" of poverty in the 1960s' (Commission of Inquiry into Poverty, *First Main Report: Poverty in Australia*, Canberra, Government Printing Service, 1975, p. viii).

[3] A. B. Atkinson, 'Low pay and the cycle of poverty', in Frank Field (ed.), *Low Pay*, London, Arrow Books, 1973, p. 101.

off in the sense that they receive below-average incomes. Thus renewed interest in poverty stemmed to a considerable extent from a recognition that it is incumbent on society to assist the *relatively* deprived.

Once this view was explicitly adopted there followed a spate of studies, in this country, North America and other industrialised economies, directed at an assessment of the extent of poverty, its nature and causes, and the way in which policy should be modified.[1] And, in view of earlier neglect, it is perhaps not surprising that a major finding of such reports was the comparative lack of knowledge of the extent and nature of poverty. In the mid-1960s Abel-Smith and Townsend pointed out that 'there is very little hard information about changes in the economic condition of the poor',[2] a view repeated a little later by Mencher: 'relatively limited progress has been made in the development of reliable knowledge.'[3] As recently as 1969 it could be said that 'our knowledge of the circumstances of those with low incomes is only very limited'.[4] In other countries, too, it became evident that discussions of poverty were inadequately informed. The Economic Council of Canada 'accepts the statement, which has recently been reiterated in the United States, that it is surprising how little we really know about the nature and extent of poverty'.[5] It was found in Norway that: 'little systematic information is available about the nature and incidence of poverty'.[6] In France too: 'the number of small-income households cannot be calculated strictly from current French statistics and no general survey has yet been conducted into this subject since 1956'.[7] These studies went a long way towards closing the information gap, and today our knowledge of contemporary poverty, in this and other countries, is far less deficient than it was a decade ago. Certainly any residual weaknesses in our understanding of the phenomenon are not serious enough to postpone remedial action.

Nonetheless, our knowledge and understanding of poverty remain incomplete and must be improved to enhance both the evaluation of past policies and the prescription of future anti-poverty measures. It is also clear that, if concern with poverty is to be translated into effective action, it is a problem which needs to be dealt with in a variety of ways. The analysis and alleviation of poverty require multi-disciplinary studies and

---

[1] The recent report by the Australian Commission of Inquiry into Poverty (*Poverty in Australia*) typifies, in terms of its comprehensiveness and methodology, the kind of study which concern with poverty has recently conceived.

[2] Abel-Smith and Townsend, *The Poor and the Poorest*, p. 10.

[3] S. Mencher, 'The problem of measuring poverty', *British Journal of Sociology*, vol. 18, March 1967.

[4] Atkinson, *Poverty in Britain and the Reform of Social Security*, p. 99.

[5] A. Rose, 'Poverty in Canada: an essay review', *Social Service Review*, vol. 43, March 1969, p. 83.

[6] Aubert in OECD, *Low Income Groups*, p. 7.

[7] M. Parodi, 'Country report: France', in OECD, *Low Income Groups*, p. 36.

remedies, embracing sociological, medical and educational, as well as economic, fields. Nevertheless inquiries that are confined to economic aspects can make a useful contribution; this study belongs to that category. It is not our intention to consider all the policy implications of the causes and effects of poverty, still less to specify an anti-poverty programme. But a better understanding of the economic aspects of poverty will be helpful in this wider context.

The present study is the work of several authors and ranges over a number of economic aspects of poverty in the United Kingdom. The precise choice of topics has been shaped to some extent by the important pragmatic consideration of what information is available. The principal source used has been the regular inquiry into the expenditure of a large and representative sample of households conducted by the Department of Employment, known as the Family Expenditure Survey. This Survey, now based on about 7000 households in the United Kingdom, has been undertaken continuously since 1957 and was preceded by the Household Expenditure Enquiry for 1953/4.[1] Though primarily intended to yield weights for the index of retail prices, the information about personal incomes and expenditure is used in compiling the national income accounts and in estimating the incidence of the various forms of taxes and social security benefits. The Survey has also been used before in studies of poverty.

The identification and measurement of poverty poses conceptual and statistical problems of considerable complexity. Much debate has centred around the question whether it is more appropriate to measure poverty in an absolute sense, in relative terms, or by a combination of both in some qualitative way. In chapter 2 an attempt is made to describe and distinguish these approaches, to identify the 'dimensions' of poverty and to establish a framework in which can be set the methods of analysing poverty employed in this study. Thus it is possible to select a standard – for example the supplementary benefit scales – and to measure poverty in terms of the numbers with incomes below that standard. It is also possible to use a relative standard, such as a certain proportion of median earnings. A combination of these two measures might also be used. A completely different approach is to identify poverty in terms of absolute (or relative) consumption (for example number of calories or other nutrients consumed).

None of these standards is ideal. Family income without adjustment does not allow for different family needs or commitments, or for the possibilities that some families may have other resources, and that some may spend their income more efficiently than others. It is necessary to make assumptions which may not be fulfilled about the way people spend their income. The selection of any one standard involves an arbitrary

---

[1] Ministry of Labour, *Household Expenditure 1953–54. Report of an enquiry*, London, HMSO, 1957 (subsequently referred to as the 1953/4 Survey).

judgement. With the behaviouristic approach it is also necessary to take for granted current customs and expenditure habits.

This study therefore makes use of different standards depending on the context, various adjustments and refinements being made to the data because of their recognised limitations. Chapter 3 employs both absolute and relative concepts to portray the historical development of the numbers in poverty and living standards between 1953 and 1973. There follow four chapters in which various aspects of poverty are examined in detail, using special tabulations of the 1971 Family Expenditure Survey made available by the Department of Health and Social Security.

In chapter 4, the numbers in poverty in 1971 are estimated by comparing household incomes with the supplementary benefit scales. As well as establishing, on this basis, the extent of poverty in 1971, the chapter attempts to quantify the effects on the resulting estimates of certain alternative assumptions. In particular, it shows the effect on the estimates of the unit of measurement – household or tax unit – and of the measure of economic resources – income or total expenditure.

The *causes* of poverty are not well understood. This deficiency cannot be entirely explained by lack of relevant data, or lack of techniques for analysing them – though both factors are partly to blame. The difficulty of separating proximate causes of poverty (for example, unemployment) from more fundamental roots, such as lack of skills or of educational facilities, is doubtless part of the problem. But possibly more important is the fact that society has increasingly chosen to alleviate the symptoms of poverty – by attempting to assure a minimum weekly income below which living standards should not fall – rather than to treat its causes. Yet it is a matter of considerable interest to determine both the extent to which households with certain characteristics are in danger of being in poverty, and the degree to which these characteristics are responsible for their poverty. Chapter 5 sets out to examine the characteristics of the poor in 1971, and in view of the close association that is thought to exist between poverty and the life-cycle this subject is accorded a separate section.

Because society has chosen to treat poverty by attempts to alleviate through the medium of supplementary benefits a primary symptom – low family income – it might be supposed that the *effects* of poverty have attracted more attention than its causes. In fact, some ways in which poverty manifests itself have received little consideration. One which provided an initial impetus for this study is the expenditure behaviour of the poor. It is possible that households in poverty have expenditure and consumption patterns that differ significantly from those of the rest of the population, but little is known about the nature of these differences. It is important in regard to the policy of providing a minimum income to know how far expenditure behaviour in poor families will ensure the living standards for which the policy was designed, or whether Rowntree's concept of 'secondary poverty', where income would be sufficient but for the fact that expenditure is not efficiently allocated, is still relevant in the 1970s.[1] Chapter 6 goes into these questions and, because of the importance of the relationship between housing and poverty, some aspects of housing are also examined there.

A key element in most attempts to measure poverty is the assessment of the relative needs of families of different size and composition. The 1971 Family Expenditure Survey can be used to yield estimates of equivalence scales – the comparative requirements of different kinds of individual for various goods and services; alternative methods for deriving such scales are considered and applied in chapter 7.

Although this volume is intended to present the results of an essentially fact-finding exercise, it would be wrong to neglect any possible implications for anti-poverty policy; this task and the identification of further research needs are attempted in chapter 8.

[1] B. S. Rowntree, *Poverty: a study of town life* (3rd edn), London, Macmillan, 1902.

CHAPTER 2

CONCEPTS OF POVERTY

INTRODUCTION

Before proceeding to a statistical analysis of trends in poverty, the reader may find it helpful to have a general explanation of the different measures of poverty we shall use and the way they are related. We consider three basic concepts of poverty – absolute, relative and behaviouristic.

Although absolute and relative poverty are significantly different, both can be summarised in terms of two dimensions – the proportion in poverty and comparative levels of living. Income distributions can be drawn in a number of different ways. In chart 2.1 incomes of size $£y$ are shown on the vertical axis and the number of units with income less than $£y$ on the horizontal axis. With an arbitrary poverty standard a_p, the numbers below it are expressed as b_p. The proportion in poverty is then $b_p/2b_m$ (where b_m is half the total population), and the comparative living level of the poor may be measured as a_p/a_m (where a_m is the median income).

At any one time, when the size and distribution of incomes are constant, the proportion in poverty and the comparative living level of the poor are not independently determined. If, for instance, a more rigorous view was taken of poverty in the sense that a smaller proportion of the population was regarded as poor, then automatically the *intensity* of this poverty in terms of the comparative living level would rise. In other words, the lower the value of $b_p/2b_m$ the greater the disparity between a_p and a_m.

This 'trade-off' between the proportion in poverty and the comparative living level does not necessarily apply when incomes or the income distribution change over time. Then it is feasible for both the proportion in poverty and the comparative living level to worsen or improve simultaneously. The change from the income distribution Y to Y' in chart 2.1 illustrates this case – a fall in the proportion in poverty and a narrowing of the gap between living levels.

These two dimensions provide a framework in which the basic features of the absolute and relative measures of poverty can be compared; in addition they have an important operational role. For it is possible, and in fact common practice, for society to make a value judgement about the definition of poverty using one of the measures, and then to regard the other as the objective to which policy should be directed. Thus, it is possible to define poverty as those in the bottom 10 per cent (by income) of

This chapter has been prepared mainly by A. D. Smith.

the population, and then to use the associated difference in living levels of poor and non-poor as the criterion of policy. It is more common, however, first to stipulate a living level – say supplementary benefit scales – then to measure the poverty requiring treatment in terms of the associated proportion in poverty.

Chart 2.1. *The dimensions of poverty*

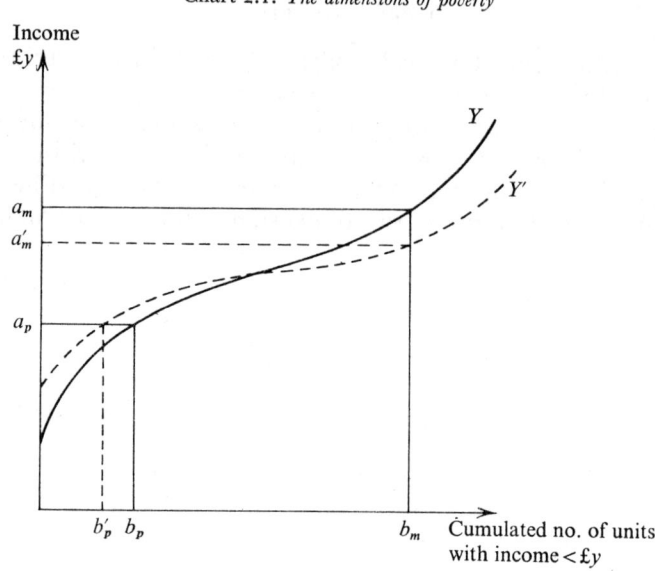

POVERTY AND THE DISTRIBUTION OF INCOMES

Before examining further these alternative concepts, we consider the extent to which the whole size-distribution of incomes needs to be known for the purpose of analysing poverty. It is important to distinguish the measurement and study of poverty from the analysis of income distributions, but to remember the relevance of the latter to the former. A common expression of the relationship between the two takes the form that, with a given average living standard in the community, there will be less poverty the less unequal the distribution of incomes. It is also widely accepted that (barring a fall in average living standards) a trend towards a less unequal income distribution implies a decrease in poverty.

It is not the purpose of this study to measure the whole distribution of incomes in the United Kingdom, nor to relate its development over time to measures of poverty. It is nevertheless worth giving a specification of the relationship between income distributions and poverty.

Clearly a detailed specification of the distribution of incomes on which could be based the kind of curve portrayed in chart 2.1 would enable the two dimensions of poverty to be identified and measured. Moreover, in the postwar years there have been a series of attempts to measure the distribution of incomes,[1] from which it might appear that much information about poverty could be directly derived. In fact, there are several reasons why they are of limited use in the measurement of poverty. In the first place, it is unfortunate that statistical sources which are best suited to providing data about most of the distribution of incomes are least appropriate for specifying that part which covers the incomes of the poor; the major source is tax returns, which are more reliable for the better-off sections of the community who pay income tax than for those who merely have to file returns.[2]

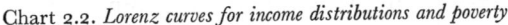

Chart 2.2. *Lorenz curves for income distributions and poverty*

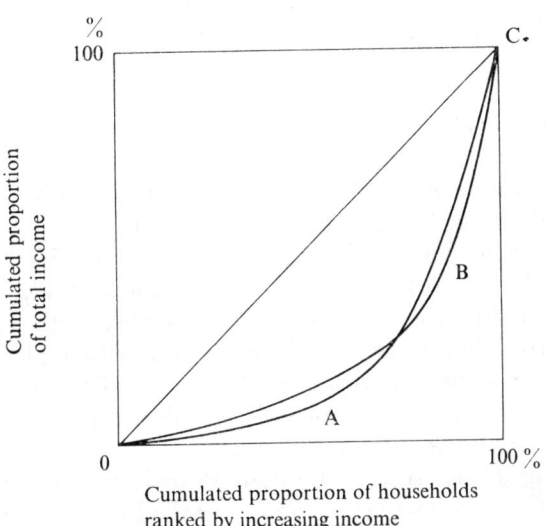

Cumulated proportion of households
ranked by increasing income

Secondly, the results of many of these studies are presented in the form of summary indicators, in which changes are a poor guide to the extent of poverty. For instance, income distributions may be displayed in the form of a Lorenz curve as in chart 2.2, where the inequality of the distribution is measured in terms of the associated Gini coefficient.[3] An unchanged Gini

1 For a brief survey of these studies and a conspectus of their results, see P. Roberti, 'Did the U.K. trend towards equality really come to an end by 1957?', *International Journal of Social Economics*, vol. 2, no. 1, 1975, p. 52.

2 This weakness is found in all countries. In the United Kingdom, attention has been drawn to this problem by R. M. Titmuss in *Income Distribution and Social Change*, London, Allen & Unwin, 1962.

3 The Lorenz curve shows what percentage of the total of all incomes is received by the lowest x per cent of households for all possible values of x. If all persons have the same income (x per cent of households always have x per cent of total income whatever the value of x) then

coefficient, implying that the distribution of incomes taken as a whole is unaltered, does not necessarily imply that poverty is unchanged. In chart 2.2 the Gini coefficient of concentration of income is identical for the two Lorenz curves, but clearly in situation B – where there is comparatively greater equality at lower income levels and greater inequality at higher income levels – poor households enjoy higher incomes than in situation A where the reverse obtains. Such situations are not mere theoretical possibilities. Results produced by Soltow suggest that between 1801–3 and 1867 there were more significant changes towards greater equality in the lower income ranges of the British population than in the income distribution as a whole.[1] But even if a consistent picture does emerge in all parts of the distribution – for example, the generally accepted tendency for incomes in the United Kingdom, both before and after direct tax, to become more equal in the postwar period up to the late 1950s[2] – the full impact of changes in the income distribution can only be learnt from a detailed inspection of the fortunes of component groups in the population.

A third limitation on the usefulness for the analysis of poverty of studies of the full spectrum of incomes is that generally they fail to take account of variations in the needs of families as shaped by contrasts in family size and composition; allowance for such factors is essential.[3]

Analyses of the income distribution nevertheless provide some information which is relevant to poverty. Chart 2.1 suggests that, as long as the distribution at the lower end of the scale is described with some precision, both the proportion in poverty and the comparative living level of the poor can be measured without knowledge of the rest of the distribution. To know the proportion in poverty the only additional information needed is the total number of units in the population (households or individuals); in comparing living levels, average (household or individual) income could be used rather than the median income. Detailed knowledge of the whole income distribution is, however, needed to identify the sections of society from which resources might be transferred to the poor; also to compare the results of using different measures of poverty.

the Lorenz curve is the straight line OC in chart 2.2. If income is unequally distributed a curve such as OAC or OBC results.

[1] L. Soltow, 'Long-run changes in British income inequality', *Economic History Review*, vol. 21 (2nd series), April 1968, p. 17.

[2] See R. J. Nicholson, 'The distribution of personal income', *Lloyds Bank Review*, no. 83, January 1967, p. 11; T. Stark, *The Distribution of Personal Income in the United Kingdom 1949–1963*, Cambridge University Press, 1972; Royal Commission on the Distribution of Income and Wealth, *Report No. 1: initial report on the standing reference*, Cmnd 6171, London, HMSO, 1975.

[3] In J. L. Nicholson, 'The distribution and redistribution of income in the United Kingdom', in D. Wedderburn (ed.), *Poverty, Inequality and Class Structure*, Cambridge University Press, 1974, this problem is avoided by the provision of separate estimates for families of different sizes and types.

MEASURING POVERTY BY ABSOLUTE LIVING STANDARDS

'Absolute poverty is often distinguished from relative poverty as emphasising economic insufficiency [rather than] economic inequality as the primary indicator of poverty';[1] or as 'the poverty of insufficiency rather than...the poverty of inequality'.[2] Even if this is an over-simplification it reflects the objective in measuring poverty by absolute standards: the prescription of a minimum standard to be compared with household incomes so as to identify those below the standard.

Chart 2.3. *Absolute and relative poverty*

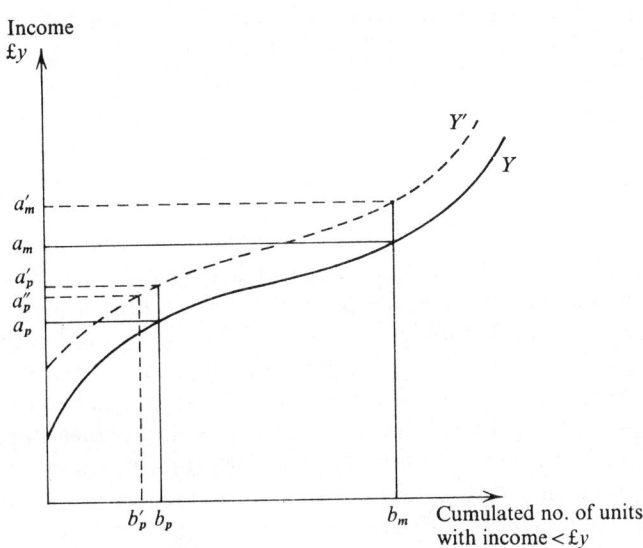

In terms of the dimensions of poverty already identified in chart 2.1, the use of an absolute standard comprises two basic steps illustrated in chart 2.3: the selection of the absolute poverty standard a_p, and its application to the income distribution in order to identify the numbers in poverty b_p, which may then be related to the size of the total population $2b_m$ to measure the proportion in poverty. And the comparative living level of the poor may be measured by the relationship between the absolute standard a_p and the median income a_m. This method was used in Rowntree's 1899 survey of working class households in York,[3] and during the early part of this century several other attempts were made to measure poverty by this means.[4]

---

1 Mencher, 'The problem of measuring poverty'.
2 O. Ornati, *Poverty Amid Affluence*, New York, Twentieth Century Fund, 1966, p. 2.
3 Rowntree, *Poverty*.   4 See appendix II.

One problem common to all studies of poverty is how to make allowance for variations in family needs, although this can be overcome to some extent by using income equivalence scales, which relate, for instance, the consumption needs of a child to those of a 'standard' adult. It is then possible to adjust the minimum standard – or any other – to take account of differences in family size and composition and the consequent family income requirements. Different methods yield different values for these scales, but not so different that they invalidate the use of the refinement.[1]

There are, however, other drawbacks of the absolute approach which cannot be overcome so easily. In the first place family income may not be a satisfactory indicator of living standards and for some time it has been accepted that 'net economic resources', embracing especially the capital situation of households, more faithfully reflect potential living standards.[2]

Another difficulty is the need to make assumptions about consumers' behaviour which may not be realistic. Subsistence budgets which vary for different individuals ensure the specified minimum living standards only if poor households spend their income in the manner prescribed. Such behaviour requires, first, a greater knowledge than most consumers have of the range of qualities of goods available; secondly, an improbable degree of skill in the exercise of choice; thirdly, a willingness on the part of poor households to sacrifice non-essential and luxury items in favour of the prescribed necessities. It follows that the number designated as poor by the strict application of minimum living standards underestimates actual poverty to the extent that these assumptions are unrealistic. As Townsend points out, 'to establish a minimum income standard is meaningless unless we also show that there are some families with that income who do in fact secure a defined level of nutrition. This fundamental criticism could be made of nearly all studies of poverty.'[3] It is a problem of which Rowntree was fully aware. He called 'secondary poverty' situations where families receive income that is sufficient 'were it not that some portion of it is absorbed by other expenditure, either useful or wasteful'.[4] In view of the importance of this qualification to accepted measures of poverty it is surprising that so little has been done to assess its significance.

The absolute approach also involves the basic difficulty of selecting the minimum living standard. Most such standards aim to be 'objective' and are based as far as possible on minimum requirements valued at current prices.[5] Even in the case of food, however, differences in minimum diets prescribed by various nutritional experts reveal that such standards can-

---

[1] See chapter 7.

[2] See Titmuss, *Income Distribution and Social Change*. The adoption of total family expenditure in the place of income may go some way towards solving this problem (see chapter 4).

[3] P. Townsend, 'The meaning of poverty', *British Journal of Sociology*, vol. 13, September 1962, p. 210.   [4] Rowntree, *Poverty*, p. 86.

[5] See the British examples referred to in appendix II.

not be wholly objective. Standards for other categories of expenditure are even more arbitrary; frequently the extension from a standard for food to cover the whole budget is carried out in a very rough and ready fashion. In the United States the poverty index devised by the Social Security Administration was simply the cost of a low-budget nutritious diet for households of various sizes, 'multiplied by three to reflect the fact that food typically represents one-third of the expenses of a low-income family'.[1] Sometimes those items which cannot be prescribed in the standard on a 'scientific' basis are estimated from observed consumer behaviour. So, for instance, while Beveridge's standard for food was based on nutrient standards prescribed by the League of Nations, his standard for other items was derived from the expenditure behaviour of working class households as revealed in the 1937/8 Family Budget Survey.[2] As Ornati points out, such a procedure introduces circularity, for 'income level largely determines choice; choice determines alleged needs'.[3]

Partly in acknowledgement of these arbitrary procedures and partly as a matter of expediency, the standards which emerge are rarely applied without further adjustment. The national assistance scales introduced in the United Kingdom in 1948, though founded on the minimum standard calculated by Beveridge, were set above it for single adults and couples, but below it where there were dependent children.[4] The room which exists for manoeuvre when establishing such scales is so wide that they can easily be made comparatively strict or comparatively generous. In their use of national assistance scales to measure the numbers in poverty according to State standards, Abel-Smith and Townsend used not only the scales *per se*, but also the scales plus an arbitrary 40 per cent.[5]

An absolute standard is open to criticism not only on the mechanics of its application but also in its practical relevance. With an absolute concept, poverty in the long term is gradually eradicated by economic growth. A principal finding of chapter 3 is that the proportion in absolute poverty in the United Kingdom had by 1973 contracted to only a tenth of what it had been twenty years earlier. However there is now a widespread feeling that poverty should be judged in whole or in part in the light of contemporary standards.

With the help of a constant standard one can assess how far economic growth and anti-poverty policy have been effective in eradicating that

[1] 'Poverty amid plenty: the American paradox' [Report of the US President's Commission on Income Maintenance Programs], in J. L. Roach and J. K. Roach (eds.), *Poverty*, Harmondsworth, Penguin Books, 1972.
[2] Ministry of Labour and National Service, 'Weekly expenditure of working-class households in 1937–38' (duplicated), 1949. [3] Ornati, *Poverty Amid Affluence*, p. 13.
[4] Appendix II.
[5] Abel-Smith and Townsend, *The Poor and the Poorest*. To some extent this takes account of the 'disregards' which are a feature of the British system and all additional payments made in practice.

poverty which some years ago was regarded as undesirable. As an *ex post* test of the success of past anti-poverty measures, absolute poverty will necessarily exert some influence on contemporary efforts. Moreover, if there are households which have an income below the minimum standard of twenty years ago, it must surely have important implications for current policy.

RELATIVE POVERTY

It is possible to distinguish two concepts of relative poverty, also shown by chart 2.3. If the proportion in poverty $b_p/2b_m$ is arbitrarily selected – say the lowest 5, 10, 20 or 30 per cent of the population – an associated comparative living level of the poor a_p/a_m can then be measured. If the proportion in poverty is held constant over time, then changes in relative poverty as measured by changes in comparative living levels – to a_p'/a_m', for example – can also be traced over time. The alternative approach is the obverse: comparative living levels a_p/a_m are stipulated *a priori* and the associated proportion in poverty $b_p/2b_m$ is observed. In this case, with comparative living levels held constant over time at $a_p/a_m = a_p''/a_m'$, developments in relative poverty, as measured by changes in the proportion in poverty – to $b_p'/2b_m$, for example – can be described. This relative approach has been used in this country by, for instance, Stark.[1] It has also been used in Japan, where it was decided 'to define the level of low income as a given fraction, one-half or one-third, of the average income in any year and…observe changes over years in the proportion of households with income at or below that level'.[2]

There is an interesting distinction between these two variants; they are in effect two aspects of a single phenomenon and, if they are measured in the same region of the income distribution, a change in the income distribution which narrows the gap between living levels of the poor and the non-poor may be associated with a fall in the proportion in poverty and vice versa. This does not imply, however, that specified changes in the comparative living level and the proportion in poverty are equally satisfactory. For if poverty is defined as a fixed percentage of the income distribution then indeed 'the poor are always with us'. If, however, poverty is identified with an income below a given percentage of the average, then it may be eradicated by appropriate policy. Thus only one of these two concepts could constitute a long-term objective for anti-poverty measures.

Some of the problems that arise with the concept of absolute poverty apply equally to the relative approach: particularly the need to make

[1] Stark, *The Distribution of Personal Income in the United Kingdom 1949–1963*.
[2] K. Taira 'Country report: Japan', in OECD, *Low Income Groups*, pp. 143 and 144.

allowances for different needs in families of different composition, the identification of living levels with income and the need to make somewhat unrealistic assumptions about consumers' behaviour. An element of arbitrariness is also involved, for a single dividing line is often chosen for purposes of analysis, although the existence of other possible dividing lines is unlikely to be overlooked. The choice of the bottom 5, 10, 20 or 30 per cent of the population, or some other fraction of mean or median, has been described as 'a poor statistical substitute for an appropriate description of poverty'.[1]

Either changes in comparative living levels or changes in the proportion in poverty can be estimated over time if the other variable is held constant. But such comparisons cannot reveal, for instance, whether there are today any households with living standards below the minimum considered acceptable twenty years ago. However, employed in conjunction with concepts of absolute poverty, as in chapter 3, relative measures can be used to consider whether the decline in absolute poverty is attributable primarily to economic growth or to income redistribution.

THE CONVENTIONAL METHOD: A COMBINATION OF ABSOLUTE AND RELATIVE

Since both the absolute and relative approaches have advantages and disadvantages, it is natural that attempts to measure poverty have sought, implicitly if not explicitly, to combine elements of the two approaches. On occasion positive attempts have been made to combine them,[2] but the mixed approach is more often adopted in an *ad hoc* fashion.

The conventional approach involves the selection of a poverty standard, which is then applied to the income distribution to yield an estimate of the proportion in poverty. Since the first Rowntree standard of 1899 there has been a tendency to raise the minimum standard as general living standards improve. The standard used by Rowntree for measuring the numbers in poverty in York in 1936 was more generous than that used in 1899, in terms both of the coverage of items and of the quantities allowed; Rowntree's 1950 standard was more generous still.[3] The Rowntree 1936 standard greatly influenced the standards proposed in the Beveridge Plan, which in turn formed the basis of the postwar British national assistance

---

[1] Rose, 'Poverty in Canada'.

[2] In the United States, Morgan devised a 'welfare ratio' with some of the advantages of both absolute and relative approaches. Households are ranked by the ratio of income to a standard budget, and those in poverty are delimited by the application of an arbitrarily chosen relative cut-off point. See J. N. Morgan, M. H. David, W. J. Cohen and H. E. Brazer, *Income and Welfare in the United States*, New York, McGraw-Hill, 1962 (referred to in Mencher, 'The problem of measuring poverty').

[3] See appendix II; also Atkinson, *Poverty in Britain and the Reform of Social Security*, p. 15.

and supplementary benefit scales. These scales have been continually raised when valued in constant prices,[1] and this has applied also in a large number of developed countries. The fact that the conventional standard is raised periodically in an unsystematic fashion means that any attempt to trace past changes in poverty by that method is faced with separating the influence of such factors as unemployment and age structure from that of alterations in the standard. In Ornati's words such an exercise 'tells us more about changing standards than about those judged to be poor'.[2]

In the United Kingdom the national assistance scales, later renamed the supplementary benefit scales, form the basis of most estimates of the proportion in poverty.[3] Similarly, the income standards of the Federal Social Assistance Law have been used to measure the proportion in poverty in West Germany. In France the statutory minimum wage has been used.[4] Whilst the weakness of the conventional concept is that it may use standards which change over time, its strength is that they are the standards officially regarded as the minimum which society regards as acceptable. As Atkinson writes, 'in Britain, the definition has conventionally been based on the standards of eligibility for National Assistance/Supplementary Benefits – *or the minimum standard of living that the Government considers necessary at a particular time*'.[5] It is for this reason that we have chosen this standard as the best measure for estimating the numbers and proportion in poverty in 1971 and applied it with some refinements in chapter 4.

Finally, it is relevant to ask why, if the standards applied to measure poverty are those which government action is, in principle, designed to sustain, the conventional approach reveals any poverty whatever. There are several reasons why the income of some households in Britain falls below the level prescribed.

First, not all poor households are eligible for supplementary benefits. Those in full-time employment are not eligible – even if their earnings are insufficient to maintain the family at the supplementary benefit level – nor are young people staying on at school, nor are people able to work but not signing on; and, where employment is available, benefit is restricted to four weeks for single people without dependants who are out of work and not sick. Secondly, until 1975, where a claimant was unemployed his total income from supplementary benefits and other sources was not allowed to exceed his previous take-home earnings (the 'wage stop'); certain families

[1] Appendix table II.2.   [2] Ornati, *Poverty Amid Affluence*, p. 31.

[3] See Abel-Smith and Townsend, *The Poor and the Poorest*; I. Gough and T. Stark, 'Low incomes in the United Kingdom, 1954, 1959 and 1963', *Manchester School of Economic and Social Studies*, vol. 36, June 1968; Atkinson, *Poverty in Britain and the Reform of Social Security*.

[4] Otto Blume, 'The poverty of old people in urban and rural areas', in P. Townsend (ed.), *The Concept of Poverty*, London, Heinemann, 1970; Parodi in OECD, *Low Income Groups*, p. 35 *et seq.*

[5] A. B. Atkinson, 'Poverty and income inequality in Britain' in Wedderburn (ed.), *Poverty, Inequality and Class Structure*, p. 48 (our italics).

receiving supplementary benefits thus had incomes below the normal supplementary benefit level. Thirdly, whether through ignorance or choice, some who are eligible for supplementary benefits do not apply for them.

BEHAVIOURISTIC APPROACHES

The development of behaviouristic approaches to the identification of poverty and its measurement has attracted some interest in recent years,[1] yet behaviouristic concepts are not entirely novel and in one respect they can be traced back to the earliest attempts to assess the extent of poverty. The first studies of household budgets revealed that the poor have a distinctive expenditure pattern and devote a significantly higher proportion of their income to the consumption of food – a phenomenon which has become known as Engel's Law. In turn, this law has been used not merely to describe the expenditure behaviour of different income groups, but also on occasion as a means of identifying those in poverty. In Canada, for instance, 'low income families. . . were defined as those using 70 per cent or more of their incomes for food, clothing and shelter'.[2]

Contemporary attempts to revive the behaviouristic approach display two principal features: they emphasise the relative aspect of poverty and they extend beyond a preoccupation with income to embrace other indicators of deprivation. Thus Townsend, a principal exponent of this approach, has emphasised, on the one hand, that 'poverty can be defined objectively and applied consistently only in terms of the concept of relative deprivation' and, on the other, that individuals are in poverty 'when they lack the resources to obtain the type of diets, participate in the activities and have the living conditions and amenities which are customary...in the societies to which they belong'.[3]

In part, dissatisfaction with the role played hitherto by income in identifying poverty reflects unease at the implied neglect of other economic resources – capital assets, fringe benefits, public social services, income in kind, etc. – which affect living standards, but this consideration has also influenced more conventional concepts of poverty. More pertinently it reflects concern that relative deprivation is signified as much by relative participation in common 'activities and customs' as by income levels. With

[1] P. Townsend, 'Poverty as relative deprivation: resources and style of living' in Wedderburn (ed.), *Poverty, Inequality and Class Structure.*

[2] Rose, 'Poverty in Canada', pp. 74–84.

[3] Townsend, 'Poverty as relative deprivation', p. 15.

In another paper Townsend writes in the same vein: 'the view taken in this chapter is that needs which are unmet can be defined satisfactorily only in terms relative to the society in which they are found or expressed'; and 'that section of the population whose resources are so depressed from the mean as to be deprived of enjoying the benefits and participating in the activities which are customary in that society can be said to be in poverty.' (Townsend (ed.), *The Concept of Poverty*, pp. 2 and 19.)

this in mind, Townsend has experimented with certain indices of deprivation. He has selected a series of indicators, such as holidays away from home, possession of a refrigerator, frequency of meat for meals, and determined the proportions of the population participating in and being denied each facility or activity. The approach is still experimental and many problems need to be solved before it can justify a position alongside the other concepts considered in this chapter. In the first place, tastes vary: some people are vegetarian or abstemious in other ways and by no means in poverty. Clearly, further consideration needs to be given to precisely which of these behaviouristic indicators can be adopted without a risk of producing misleading results. Secondly, a series of indicators rather than a single poverty criterion may yield ambiguous answers. In practice, certain households will be deprived on the basis of some indicators but not others. Will it then be necessary to define a series of populations in poverty, or can some kind of weighting system be attached to the indicators? Only time and further analysis will show whether 'such indices provide the means of exploring whether or not there is a marked threshold of resources below which deprivation becomes marked'.[1]

In chapter 6 of this study a modest attempt is made to contribute to the development of this concept. The chapter contains comparisons over time and in 1971 of expenditure patterns of the poor and the non-poor. In part the aim is to help establish whether or not contrasts in expenditure behaviour can or cannot be used as a means of identifying and gauging poverty. In part, however, the analysis is intended to convey a more graphic picture of the nature and effects of poverty than do the proportions in poverty and the comparisons of overall standards of living.

[1] Townsend, 'Poverty as relative deprivation', p. 36.

CHAPTER 3

POSTWAR CHANGES IN THE EXTENT OF POVERTY

INTRODUCTION

Earlier in this century most studies of poverty were focused on the prescription of minimum living standards.[1] In some studies these standards were used as a basis for calculating the numbers in poverty, a practice continued in the postwar period, when national assistance and supplementary benefit scales have been used as poverty standards.[2] Clearly, estimates of the numbers in poverty based on contemporary levels help to evaluate policies aimed at preventing the living standards of individuals from falling below the minimum set by governments. But, from a historical point of view, changes in the proportions in poverty revealed by this method may tell us as much about alterations in standards as about numbers in poverty.

Other ways of estimating the extent of poverty have been neglected, although they have advantages in historical comparisons. In the prewar period especially, little attention was devoted to the relative living standards of the poor – their income levels compared with the average for the community as a whole. In the postwar period this deficiency has to some extent been remedied.[3] However, these studies are primarily concerned with overall developments in the income distribution, and do not focus, as we seek to do, on the comparative incomes of the poor. Also, for the most part, they do not allow for variations in the size and composition of households, a factor of great importance in measuring poverty.[4] In

This chapter has been prepared mainly by P. S. Lansley.

[1] For a survey of these standards see appendix II.

[2] In particular, Abel-Smith and Townsend made such estimates for 1953/4 and 1960 in *The Poor and the Poorest*; Gough and Stark for 1963 in 'Low incomes in the United Kingdom'; Atkinson for 1967 in *Poverty in Britain and the Reform of Social Security*; see also chapter 4 below.

[3] D. Seers, *The Levelling of Incomes since 1935*, Oxford, Blackwell, 1951; F. W. Paish, 'The real incidence of personal taxation', *Lloyds Bank Review*, no. 43, January 1957; H. F. Lydall, 'The long term trend in the size distribution of income', *Journal of the Royal Statistical Society* (series A), vol. 122, part 1, 1959; J. A. Brittain, 'Some neglected features of Britain's income leveling', *American Economic Association Papers and Proceedings*, vol. 50, May 1960; Titmuss, *Income Distribution and Social Change*; Nicholson, 'The distribution of personal income'; P. J. D. Wiles and S. Markowski, 'Income distribution under communism and capitalism', *Soviet Studies*, vol. 22, January and April 1971; Stark, *The Distribution of Personal Incomes in the United Kingdom, 1949–1963*. For a brief survey of these studies see Roberti, 'Did the U.K. trend towards equality really come to an end by 1957?'.

[4] But income distributions were calculated *per capita* using Inland Revenue data by A. R. Prest and T. Stark in 'Some aspects of income distribution in the U.K. since World War II' (paper read 8 March 1967), Manchester Statistical Society, 1967, and by Stark in *The Distribution of Personal Incomes in the United Kingdom, 1949–1963*. Wiles and Markowski, using the Family

contrast, virtually no attention has been devoted to changes in poverty as assessed by absolute standards – either absolute living levels of the poor, or the numbers in poverty on the basis of a poverty standard held constant over time.

An attempt is therefore made in this chapter to trace over the past two decades four facets of changes in poverty: the absolute living levels of those in poverty, the proportion in poverty measured by a constant absolute poverty level, comparative income levels of the poor and the proportion in poverty as suggested by relative standards.

Before coming to this analysis, we consider briefly the limitations of the data and describe the refinements made to arrive at the series used. From the Household Expenditure Survey of 1953/4 and the Family Expenditure Survey, which has been undertaken continuously since 1957, there is available a body of data stretching over twenty years or so. Though the definitions and methods of successive Surveys are not entirely consistent, the interpretation of the results is not greatly circumscribed. For the most part developments have been traced between 1953/4 and 1963 (as a reflection of the position in the early 1960s), 1967 (when the number of households in the sample was doubled), 1971 (a year subject to more detailed analysis in other chapters) and 1973 (the latest available Survey when this research was undertaken).

HOUSEHOLD AND INDIVIDUAL INCOMES

The extent to which such matters as inaccuracies in the basic data, sampling errors, choice of units and of income or expenditure concepts associated with the Family Expenditure Surveys might introduce bias into our measures is considered in chapter 4 and appendix I. To some extent the problems of statistical interpretation are less significant in historical comparisons than when measuring poverty at any one time, since the biases which they introduce are often systematic through time, but this is not true of all features of the Surveys.

In order to trace the extent of poverty over time it is not necessary to specify the full income distribution. All that is required is knowledge of the poorer 'tail' of the distribution, together with – in the context of an assessment of comparative living levels – average income for all households; the analysis of income inequality is for the most part separate and distinct from the analysis of poverty. However, the *Family Expenditure Survey Reports* are published in such a form that to specify the full income distribution in each year proves to be a convenient way of tracing poverty over time.

Expenditure Survey, made allowance for the size of family but not its composition in 'Income distribution under communism and capitalism'.

Distributions derived from the published tables of the Family Expenditure Surveys reflect in part the methods used in the collection and analysis of the data, and two of the definitions used are of particular relevance in the case of low incomes. First, being based on a sample of private households, the Surveys do not cover individuals living in institutions, so that no estimate of their poverty can be made using this source. Perhaps more important, it is necessary to assume that all the members of a household enjoy an appropriate share of the total household income; no allowance can be made for the cases which must arise where someone with little or no income of his own does not benefit from the income of the rest of his household.[1] Secondly, the use since 1960 of 'normal' rather than current income in the published tables overstates the income actually received by most individuals who have been out of work for less than thirteen weeks, even though it appears that the households involved are able to maintain their expenditure at or near to the level suggested by their 'normal' income.

Some groups amongst the poor are under-represented in the Family Expenditure Surveys; others are over-represented. In appendix I we show that correcting for some of such biases does not change appreciably the extent of poverty found; it is also shown (in chapter 4) that at least some ostensibly poor households understate their incomes. Given the doubts that concern this area, the balance of the argument would seem to be that for any one year the Family Expenditure Survey gives a reasonably reliable picture of low income amongst households. We must also consider, however, whether changes in the Surveys over time might distort our findings.

Leaving aside the 1953/4 Survey, which had a somewhat lower response rate of 67 per cent, there appears to have been a small but distinct deterioration in the response rate from 71 per cent in 1963 and 1967 to 70 per cent and 68 per cent in 1971 and 1973 respectively. But, against this, the doubling of the sample in 1967 and gradual improvements over time, especially as a result of more experience, should have been conducive to an improvement in the accuracy and representativeness of the results. Certainly income data from the 1953/4 Survey were considered somewhat inaccurate.[2] In addition, that Survey is known to have been not entirely representative of the population in general and of poorer groups in particular.[3] Any subsequent improvement in representativeness and in the coverage of the tails of the distribution would have itself contributed to an apparently wider range of relative living levels. It is also known that subsidiary sources of income are better covered in the later years, but we

[1] See chapter 4.
[2] Ministry of Labour, *Household Expenditure 1953–54*, p. 15, para. 73.
[3] There was inadequate coverage of elderly persons and of single-person households (ibid., p. 12).

do not know whether such income is likely to be enjoyed by some income groups more than others.

On the other hand, in 1953/4 households were classified on the basis of 'last week's' income. From 1960 onwards, questions have been posed about, and households classified on the basis of, their gross 'normal' income, as well as any wage or salary last received. Since normal income tends to be distributed more narrowly than immediate income, a comparison of the results of earlier Surveys with those of later ones might suggest on this account a fall in the proportion in poverty and a narrowing of the dispersion of incomes. Also in 1973 the definition of a child was changed from 'under 16' to 'under 18 and unmarried' and this may have distorted the comparisons with earlier years.[1]

In principle, three adjustments should be made to the distributions derived from the Family Expenditure Surveys before they are used for estimating changes in poverty over time. They should first be converted to an equivalent adult basis; secondly they should relate to individuals; thirdly they should be based on net rather than gross income. These adjustments can only be made approximately if they are based on the published material. The published tables make no attempt to do so: there is no table which shows income distributions on a *per capita* basis (which would allow for variations in family size), let alone on an equivalent adult or equivalent household basis (which would also allow for differences in the needs of children and additional adults).[2] The published data which most nearly approach our requirements are the tables showing households classified both by income and by household type (for example two adults and two children). From these it is possible to derive distributions in which households are grouped on the basis of income per equivalent adult couple. The method used, which is described more fully in appendix III, consists briefly of the following steps. For households of each type grouped in a given income range, income is recalculated using an income equivalence scale to give the income per equivalent adult couple. Frequency distributions in terms of equivalent income can then be derived for each household type and from these a composite distribution for all family types is finally obtained.[3]

---

[1] There has also been a series of less significant changes. For instance, in the 1953/4 Survey detailed expenditure records were kept for 21 days rather than 14 as in the subsequent Family Expenditure Surveys. The estimate of imputed weekly income from owner-occupation has been derived from the net rateable value of dwellings from 1957 onwards, but was based on gross valuation for income tax purposes under Schedule A in 1953/4.

[2] This is probably because there has been official reluctance to use particular equivalence scales for this purpose, and it was not considered adequate to allow for family size alone (see Ministry of Labour, *Household Expenditure 1953–54*, p. 21, para. 94).

[3] All results in this chapter are based on data contained in the published *Family Expenditure Survey Reports*. We had access to special tabulations of the original ungrouped data for one year – 1971 – and appendix III, which compares results from the published grouped data and the original ungrouped data, shows that the patterns obtained are very similar.

The final outcome of this procedure depends on the particular income equivalence scale used. Such scales are considered in greater detail in chapter 7, which suggests that different methods of estimation yield reasonably consistent scales. In the present exercise, taking an adult couple as unity, a scale of 0.21 has been assumed for a child and scales of 0.60 and 0.40 respectively for single adults living alone and additional adults (beyond the original couple).

TABLE 3.1.   *Unadjusted and equivalent gross household incomes, 1953/4 to 1973*

	1953/4	1963[a]	1967	1971	1973	
	(£s per week)	(£s per week)	(£s per week)	(£s per week)	(£s per week)	(Index, 1953=100)
Households			*Unadjusted incomes*			
5th percentile	2·80[b]	5·05	6·90	7·85[b]	10·55	377
10th percentile	4·30	6·80	9·20	10·64	13.09	304
25th percentile	7·70	12·25	16·60	20·00	25·21	327
50th percentile	11·00	19·30	25·10	34·89	44·89	408
75th percentile	15·40	27·50	35·80	49·63	63·82	414
90th percentile	20·80	37·80	48·00	67·62	87·29	420
Households			*Equivalent incomes*			
5th percentile	3·60	6·10	8·55	11·45	14·50	403
10th percentile	4·40	7·60	10·15	13·25	17·20	391
25th percentile	6·10	10·50	14·05	18·50	24·05	394
50th percentile	8·30	15·25	20·15	27·80	36·75	443
75th percentile	11·30	21·90	28·75	39·50	52·50	464
90th percentile	15·00	29·00	37·90	54·00	71·00	473
Individuals			*Equivalent incomes*			
5th percentile	3·90	6·50	8·70	11·80	15·50	397
10th percentile	4·65	7·95	10·45	14·10	18·65	401
25th percentile	6·15	10·75	14·20	19·60	25·60	416
50th percentile	8·20	15·10	19·70	27·65	37·00	451
75th percentile	10·90	21·05	27·50	38·00	51·00	468
90th percentile	14·35	27·90	35·80	51·10	68·00	474

Sources: Ministry of Labour, *Household Expenditure 1953–54*; Department of Employment, *Family Expenditure Survey Reports* (various years); NIESR estimates.

[a]Based on small sample.
[b]Extrapolated values.

The values of the 5th, 10th, 25th, 50th, 75th and 90th percentiles of the unadjusted and equivalent household income distributions are compared in table 3.1.[1] The difference between the unadjusted and adjusted distributions depends on the association between income and household size, which is shown by the unbroken line in chart 3.1. Average household size

[1] These were obtained by interpolation from distributions plotted on log-probability paper. While a few values were obtained by extrapolation, an independent check using unpublished data (see appendix III) showed that this does not introduce serious errors.

rises steadily throughout the income range and is about three times higher in the 90th than in the 5th percentile, so that adjustment simply to a *per capita* basis would narrow the dispersion of household incomes. Adjustment to an equivalent adult basis has the advantage of allowing for the differing needs of adults who do and do not share households, and of children.

Chart 3.1. *Household size and income, 1971*

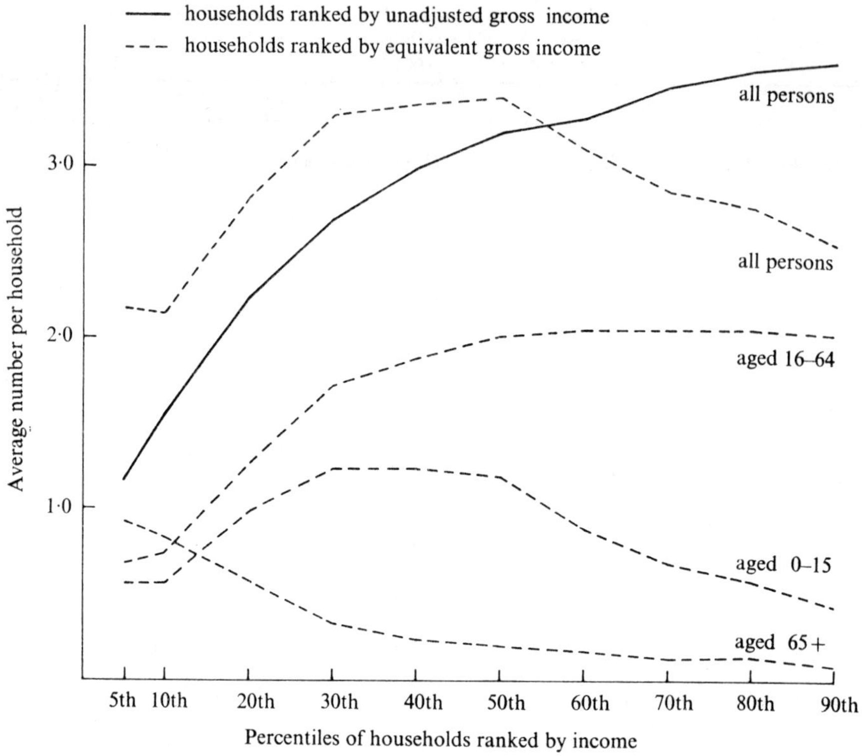

Sources: Department of Employment, *Family Expenditure Survey Report for 1971*, table 43; special tabulations of the 1971 Family Expenditure Survey.

The extent to which the equivalence scales specified above narrow the dispersion of income in each year can be seen in table 3.1. In 1971, for example, unadjusted household income ranged from £7·85 per week for the lowest 5th percentile to £67·62 for the highest decile; for equivalent income the range was appreciably narrower – from £11·45 to £54·00. As a proportion of the median, unadjusted household income ranged from 22·5 to 193·8 per cent, and income per equivalent couple from 41·2 to 194·2 per cent; the adjustment to equivalent income has a greater impact in the lower half of the distribution because household size rises particularly sharply with income over the lower half of the range.[1]

It is more meaningful, and perhaps more democratic, to consider the proportion of individuals in poverty rather than the proportion of households. The differences between the distributions of income per person and per household depend on the relationship between household composition and equivalent income, also shown in chart 3.1. Average household size is at its greatest in the middle ranges of equivalent income, so that we expect some further narrowing of the distribution about the median when considering individuals. Table 3.1 confirms this, though the effect is appreciably less than in the transition from unadjusted to equivalent household incomes. Essentially this reflects the fact that on average poor households are smaller than other households, so that there is a smaller proportion of individuals than of households in poverty.

TABLE 3.2.   *Equivalent net household incomes, 1953/4 to 1971*

	Individuals		
	5th percentile	Median	5th percentile/ median
	(£s per week)		(%)
1953/4	3·83	7·84	49
1967	8·55	17·52	49
1971	11·43	23·56	49

Source: Appendix table III.3.

The above results all relate to gross incomes: the basic Survey data include cash benefits from the State, but are not net of direct taxation. Special estimates of net income were made for 1953/4, 1967 and 1971 as described in appendix III, and are shown in table 3.2 for the 5th and 50th quantiles of individuals. The apparent differential between low and median incomes is again narrowed – in fact the poorest 5 per cent of the population is seen to have an unchanged proportion (49 per cent) of the net income of the median household throughout the period.

CHANGES IN ABSOLUTE POVERTY

In table 3.3 an attempt is made to ascertain by how much real incomes of the poor – defined for this purpose as the 5th and 10th percentiles in the income distribution – have increased in the period from 1953/4 to 1973. This table is derived from data in tables 3.1 and 3.2 converted to constant 1971 prices by means of the retail price index. Real improvements in the

[1] G. C. Fiegehen and P. S. Lansley, 'The measurement of poverty: a note on household size and income units', *Journal of the Royal Statistical Society* (series A), vol. 139, part 4, 1976.

incomes of the poor may be overstated for the period 1953/4 to 1971 by about
1 or 2 per cent, and by about 2–4 per cent for the period 1953/4 to 1973, because the retail price index underestimates their cost of living increases. The
cost of living has risen somewhat faster for this group than for better-off
households, because the prices of necessities, such as housing and light and
fuel, which attract a high proportion of poor households' expenditure, have
risen relatively rapidly over the last two decades (this question is examined
more closely in chapter 6).[1]

TABLE 3.3.   *Real household incomes* of the poor, 1953/4 to 1973*

	1953/4	1963	1967	1971	1973	Increase 1953/4–71 (%)	Increase 1953/4–73 (%)
	(£s at 1971 prices)						
Households			*Unadjusted gross incomes*				
5th percentile	5·48	7·48	8·87	7·85	9·02	43	65
10th percentile	8·41	10·08	11·82	10·64	11·19	27	33
Households			*Equivalent gross incomes*				
5th percentile	7·04	9·04	10·99	11·45	12·40	63	76
10th percentile	8·61	11·26	13·04	13·25	14·71	54	71
Individuals			*Equivalent gross incomes*				
5th percentile	7·63	9·63	11·18	11·80	13·25	55	74
10th percentile	9·10	11·78	13·43	14·10	15·95	55	75
Individuals			*Equivalent net incomes*				
5th percentile	7·49	..	10·99	11·43	..	53	..
10th percentile	8·88	..	12·98	13·51	..	52	..

Sources: Tables 3.1 and 3.2; appendix III.
*Deflated by the retail price index.

On the basis of unadjusted income, real incomes of the 5th percentile
increased by 43 per cent between 1953/4 and 1971, and of the 10th percentile by no more than 27 per cent. The effect of changing to equivalent
net income for individuals is to alter this picture substantially: on this
basis real living standards of both the 5th and the 10th percentiles increased by about 50–55 per cent. Over the slightly longer period 1953/4 to
1973 the rise was probably nearer 75 per cent (2–4 per cent less if we make
allowance for the bias in the price index). Such improvements in the real
incomes of the poor may reflect general improvements in living standards

[1] There is a similar divergence between the official indices of retail prices for pensioner households and for all households for the period 1962–75 (CSO, *Social Trends*, no. 6, 1975, p. 124),
though most of the divergence arose after 1971. On the other hand, because of the constant
introduction of new varieties and qualities, there is a general presumption that price indices
understate the real improvement in living standards. It is difficult to form an objective view of
the size of this element, but J. L. Nicholson ('The measurement of quality changes', *Economic
Journal*, vol. 77, September 1967, p. 512) suggests that it is significant.

as a consequence of economic growth, or a redistribution of incomes in favour of the lower income groups, or a combination of both. These possibilities are considered below.

TABLE 3.4. *The proportion in poverty measured by absolute standards, 1953/4 to 1973*

	1953/4 national assistance scale				1971 supplementary benefits scale			
	Poverty standard[a]	House-holds[b]	Individuals		Poverty standard[a]	House-holds[b]	Individuals	
	(£s per wk)	(%)	(%)	(millions)	(£s per wk)	(%)	(%)	(millions)
1953/4	3·84	6·5	4·8	2·4	5·83	22·5	21·0	10·6
1963	5·07	2·5[c]	1·4[c]	0·8	7·69	10·5	9·4	5·0
1967	5·86	0·9[c]	0·9[c]	0·5	8·87	6·0	5·5	3·0
1971	7·51	0·5[c]	0·5[c]	0·3	11·40	4·9	4·2	2·3
1973	8·78	0·3[c]	0·2[c]	0·1	13·83	3·5	2·3	1·3

Sources: Department of Health and Social Security, *Social Security Statistics 1974*, London, HMSO, 1975, table 34.01, p. 144; NIESR estimates.

[a]Basic scale rates for a married couple, plus 30 per cent for rent and other discretionary additions. Long-term addition introduced in 1966 excluded from 1971 scale. A weighted average used where scales changed during a year. All converted to current prices of other years by means of the retail price index.

[b]Estimates derived by applying the poverty standard to the composite income distributions (see appendix III).

[c]Approximations based on extrapolated values.

Changes in the proportion and numbers in poverty using an absolute poverty standard are shown in table 3.4: the proportion in poverty has declined sharply over the two decades when measured by national assistance or supplementary benefit scales held constant in real terms. The estimates were derived by applying supplementary benefit standards for a married couple to the composite distributions of equivalent gross income.[1] In real terms the benefit scales have risen substantially: the 1953/4 assistance would have been worth no more than £7·51 in 1971, compared with the benefit then current of £11·40. As a result, the proportion in poverty measured by the 1971 scale is much larger in each year than that measured by the lower (1953/4) scale. By 1971 standards the proportion in poverty in 1973 was less than a fortieth of the population, while on the same standard over a fifth would have been regarded as poor in 1953/4; using the 1953/4 standard suggests that about 5 per cent of the population was poor in that year, compared with an estimate of only 0·2 per cent in

1 The estimates involve a number of approximations which are considered further in chapter 4. For all the years except 1953/4 supplementary benefit rates were raised during the year. The procedure of using a weighted average of the rates as the poverty line has the effect of ignoring the change in the incomes of benefit-receiving households. Chapter 4 shows that such households are preponderant in the lowest decile, and that the use of a weighted average rather than the scales in force at the time the households participated in the Survey artificially raised the proportion in poverty by about 1½ percentage points in 1971. This cannot substantially change the trend from 1953/4 to 1973.

1973.[1] By this type of criterion it thus appears that poverty has declined in these decades to a tenth, or even a twentieth, of its original level. This reflects great economic progress, but perhaps also demonstrates the element of artificiality in applying so far away from the time when they were implemented standards which do not allow for changes in social habits.

CHANGES IN RELATIVE POVERTY

We have seen that the real incomes of those in poverty have risen appreciably over the last twenty years or so. Has this been wholly or in part attributable to a transfer of real income from other sections of society, or have other factors been responsible? An examination of changes in comparative incomes helps to answer this question.

TABLE 3.5.   *Comparative household incomes of the poor, 1953/4 to 1973 (Percentages of median incomes)*

	1953/4	1963[a]	1967	1971	1973
Households	*Unadjusted gross incomes*				
5th percentile	25·5[b]	26·2	27·5	22·5[b]	23·5
10th percentile	39·1	35·2	36·7	30·5	29·2
Households	*Equivalent gross incomes*				
5th percentile	43·3	40·0	42·4	41·0	39·5
10th percentile	53·0	49·8	50·4	47·7	46·8
Individuals	*Equivalent gross incomes*				
5th percentile	47·6	43·0	44·2	42·7	41.9
10th percentile	56·7	52·6	53·0	51·0	50·4
Individuals	*Equivalent net incomes*				
5th percentile	48·8	..	48·8	48·5	..
10th percentile	57·9	..	57·7	57·4	..

Sources: Tables 3.1 and 3.2; appendix III.

[a]Based on small sample.
[b]Extrapolated values.

In table 3.5 incomes of the 5th and 10th percentiles are expressed as a percentage of median income, using a number of alternative measures. The effect of each adjustment to the recorded data is to narrow the differentials between low and median incomes for all years. The total effect of the adjustments in 1971, for example, is to raise the income of the lowest 5th percentile from 22·5 to 48·5 per cent of the median value.

The original data show a deterioration over time in relative incomes of

---

[1] These proportions are unlikely to be affected much by a change in the basis of measurement from gross to net income. This is largely confirmed by a comparison of these results with estimates derived from a series of net income distributions based on unpublished Central Statistical Office data.

the poor: on this basis, the income of the 10th percentile was 39 per cent of the median in 1953/4, but little more than 29 per cent in 1973. The trend towards smaller households caused by young adults leaving home earlier and by increasing longevity will have contributed to this effect.[1] Adjustment to equivalent gross income and to individuals changes the picture marginally; it is substantially modified only when allowance is made for direct tax payments and national insurance contributions. When measured by equivalent net income, the relative living standards of the poor appear to have remained approximately constant between 1953/4 and 1971, at about 49 per cent of the median for the 5th percentile and about 58 per cent for the 10th percentile. This reflects the much sharper rise between 1953/4 and 1971 in the direct tax burden of median households (4·3 per cent of gross income to 14·8 per cent) than of poor households (1·8 to 3·2 per cent).[2]

In view of the qualifications to the data noted earlier, it is perhaps best to conclude that the evidence points to neither a significant deterioration nor an improvement in the relative incomes of the poor over this period. This has the important implication that, if the substantial rise of about 75 per cent recorded in the real incomes of the poor over the last two decades is not attributable to any appreciable change in their relative standards, it must reflect participation in a general improvement in living standards.

TABLE 3.6. *The population in relative poverty, 1953/4 to 1973*

	Poverty standard[a]	Households[b]	Individuals[b]	
	(£s per week)	(%)	(%)	(millions)
1953/4	3·84	6·5	4·8	2·4
1963	6·63	6·8	5·5	3·0
1967	8·78	5·8	5·3	2·9
1971	11·40	4·9	4·2	2·3
1973	14·17	4·3	3·0	1·7

Source: NIESR estimates.

[a] Current national assistance or supplementary benefit scales for a married couple, plus 30 per cent for rent and other discretionary additions. Statutory long-term addition introduced in 1966 excluded. A weighted average used where scales changed during the year.
[b] Estimates derived by applying the poverty standard to the composite gross income distributions (see appendix III).

Finally, in table 3.6 changes in the numbers in poverty are estimated by relative criteria; a standard of current national assistance or supplementary benefits plus 30 per cent is applied to the gross income distribution,

---

[1] See CSO, 'The effect of changes in household composition on the distribution of income 1961–73' by M. Semple, *Economic Trends*, no. 266, December 1975, p. 99, for an analysis of what the distribution might have been if the population structure had not changed over the period.
[2] See appendix table III.3.

producing in effect the proportions measured by the conventional method-ology.[1] As such these results are unsuitable for tracing changes in poverty over time, since the changes revealed may owe as much to modifications of the standards as they do to developments in the nature and extent of poverty. Indeed, since the value of the scales as a proportion of estimated median gross income fell from 46·3 per cent in 1953/4 to 38·6 per cent in 1973, the fall in the proportion in poverty from 4·8 to 3·0 per cent may only reflect the fall in the ratio between supplementary benefit scales and median gross income.[2]

CONCLUSIONS

We have been concerned in this chapter with establishing a record of changes in the extent of poverty over the last twenty years. In order to give a fairly complete picture we have considered both absolute and relative concepts of poverty, and in both cases changes in incomes and in propor-tions in poverty were estimated.

In the course of refining the basic data, it was established how very im-portant it is for an accurate assessment of poverty in an individual year to allow for household size and composition. When this adjustment is made by converting data on household units to individuals, also making some

---

[1] The figures of 6·5 per cent of households and 4·8 per cent of individuals below the national assistance level in 1953/4 shown in table 3.6 compare with figures of 2·1 per cent and 1·2 per cent respectively in Abel-Smith and Townsend, *The Poor and the Poorest*. There are three main reasons for the difference. First, we have applied a single poverty line – that for married couples – to the estimated composite distribution of income per equivalent couple, while Abel-Smith and Townsend applied the appropriate national assistance scale separately to each type of household. The consequent discrepancies are likely to be small, since the equivalence scales implicit in the national assistance scales are similar to those adopted in this study for deriving the composite income distribution. Secondly, the poverty line used here comprises the national assistance scale plus 30 per cent, while Abel-Smith and Townsend, having access to the actual returns for 1953/4, used the national assistance scale plus actual housing costs; our poverty line is likely to be slightly higher as a result. Thirdly, Abel-Smith and Townsend's estimates were based on expenditure widely defined to include mortgage payments, life assurance and other forms of saving, but excluding income tax and national insurance contributions; ours are based on gross income.

The figures of 5·8 per cent of households and 5·3 per cent of individuals given for 1967 in table 3.6 compare with 4·9 per cent and 3·5 per cent respectively in Atkinson's *Poverty in Britain and the Reform of Social Security*. The main reason for the difference is that Atkinson used a lower poverty line based on the supplementary benefit scales effective between January and October 1967 (rather than a weighted average of the scales applicable during the year), and basic scales for each type of household plus an estimated sum for rent, which in the majority of cases was less than the 30 per cent addition adopted here. Other differences between the methods used in this chapter and by Atkinson are less important.

[2] Ideally estimates of relative poverty should be based on net income data, using a poverty line determined systematically in each year in relation to changes in average or median net income. Although we have not been able to make such estimates, our earlier finding – that the distribution of net income has remained approximately constant over the period – implies that such a poverty line would show no significant changes in the extent of relative poverty since the Second World War.

allowance for direct tax payments, the income of the lowest decile in 1971 rises from some 30 per cent to 57 per cent of median income.

The dispersion of gross income, unadjusted and adjusted, widened over the period, but adjustment for direct tax payments negated this apparent deterioration in the comparative living level of the poor. We conclude that the extent of *relative* poverty has probably changed little over the past twenty years. This implies that the substantial decline recorded in absolute poverty is attributable more to the general improvement in living standards than to a rise in the relative living standards of the poor, though it should be remembered that the group with the highest poverty risk – the elderly – has grown as a proportion of the population. For this group with incomes strongly determined by State pensions to maintain their relative position, the government has had to redistribute more from the working population.

As expected, there has been a substantial fall in absolute poverty. Real incomes of the poor increased by about 60–70 per cent over the past twenty years and, more significantly still, when measured by a (1971) living standard held constant over time, the proportion of individuals in poverty thus defined fell from about a fifth of the population in 1953 to about a fortieth in 1973. The estimates show that approximately $2\frac{1}{2}$ million people were below the 1971 supplementary benefit standard in 1971. However, while suitable for historical analysis, such figures for any one year should be treated with caution in view of the biases and inconsistencies to which we have already referred. For a more precise and detailed count of the numbers in poverty in a recent year we turn to the next chapter.

CHAPTER 4

COUNTING THE POOR ON ALTERNATIVE DEFINITIONS

INTRODUCTION

In spite of the decline in poverty in absolute terms over the past twenty years revealed in the last chapter, it is apparent that on the basis of contemporary standards there was a large number in poverty in 1971. In an attempt to reach more precise estimates than were possible in the historical survey, we now turn to a detailed analysis of those in poverty in 1971, defined on the basis of the supplementary benefit scales applicable in that year.

The supplementary benefit scheme sets a scale of weekly income sufficient to cater for minimum needs, to which each family without a full-time working member is entitled. The rates depend on the number of persons in the family, their ages, the rent of their accommodation and certain special needs. In principle, application of these scales to what is known of the income distribution should yield an unambiguous estimate of the numbers enduring poverty so defined. In practice such an estimate cannot be obtained: results vary from one time to another as a consequence of changes both in incomes and in supplementary benefit scales; also the extent of poverty depends on the precise manner in which this approach is applied to the statistics.

There are a number of choices when assessing incomes in relation to supplementary benefit scales (and, indeed, to any other poverty cut-off line). In the first place, alternative sources of data are usually available and results vary according to which is used. Two sources in the United Kingdom contain particularly relevant information about families' economic resources and the characteristics on which needs can be assessed: the Family Expenditure Survey, and Inland Revenue data derived from tax returns and published annually in the *Survey of Personal Incomes*. The principal advantage of the Inland Revenue source in the present context is that it gives annual incomes, whereas incomes from the Family Expenditure Survey are for shorter periods. However, information from tax returns is unsuitable for a study of poverty because it relates to the tax paying population and the poor are unlikely to feature in it to any great extent.[1] We have therefore used the Family Expenditure Survey as our source.

This chapter has been prepared mainly by G. C. Fiegehen.

[1] Information derived from tax returns and published in Inland Revenue, *Survey of Personal Incomes*, London, HMSO (annual), may be supplemented by other data in such a way that it

The estimated numbers in poverty also depend on the precise measure used of a household's economic resources (income or total expenditure), the unit of measurement (household or tax unit) and the period over which the assessment is made. Each of these facets is discussed in this chapter, so that, in addition to measuring numbers in poverty in 1971 by the conventional method, we can attempt to quantify the effect on such an estimate of variations in certain key assumptions.

A FIRST COUNT

Table 4.1 gives our estimates of the proportions of households and individuals living in households where net incomes fell below the supplementary benefit scale in 1971; on this criterion 7·1 per cent of households were in poverty. In terms of individuals the proportion in poverty was considerably lower, at 4·9 per cent of the total or about 2½ million people, since poor households are on average smaller than other households.

TABLE 4.1. *The proportion in poverty, 1971*

	Households	Individuals	
	(%)	(%)	(millions)
Income below poverty line[a]	7·1	4·9	2·6
Income above poverty line	92·9	95·1	51·3
Total	100·0	100·0	53·9[b]

Sources: Special tabulations of the 1971 Family Expenditure Survey; CSO *Annual Abstract of Statistics 1975*, London, HMSO, 1975.

[a] Households with net normal income below supplementary benefit levels operating at the date of interview.

[b] United Kingdom mid-year population adjusted to exclude those not in private households.

Whilst, in principle, the application of supplementary benefit scales to household incomes for measuring the extent of poverty is a straightforward procedure, in practice it involves a number of technicalities which are described in detail in appendix IV. It is necessary to draw attention here to only one or two of the more salient features of the method.

In effect, the income, inclusive of any supplementary benefits, recorded for each household in the 1971 Family Expenditure Survey was compared with the assessment which would have been made by the Supplementary Benefits Commission to determine whether the household's income was above or below supplementary benefit rates. Given the nature of the

relates to the whole population (CSO, 'Distribution of income statistics for the United Kingdom, 1972/73: sources and methods' by D. Ramprakash in *Economic Trends*, no. 262, August 1975). Stark has demonstrated how such data can be made to yield poverty estimates (*The Distribution of Personal Income in the United Kingdom 1949–1963*). Even so, the Family Expenditure Survey provides data on a number of economic and social characteristics that the *Survey of Personal Incomes* does not, and is more suited to an analysis of poverty.

supplementary benefit system and the fact that entitlement varies according to the status of the applicant (single householder, husband and wife, non-householder), whether a pensioner or not, and the number and age of any dependent children, it follows that measuring poverty in this way takes account of household size and composition as well as income. However, our procedure did not allow all the supplementary benefit rules to be taken into account. For instance, it was necessary to ignore 'discretionary' payments to which a family might be entitled, and certain approximations were adopted because the supplementary benefit scales were applied to households rather than the tax (or family) units to which they relate.

These estimates are somewhat higher than the proportions in poverty in 1971 calculated in chapter 3 for purposes of historical comparison. There is also a larger differential between the proportions of households and of individuals in poverty. The discrepancies are due to deriving the estimates in chapter 3 from grouped data as published in the *Family Expenditure Survey Reports*, and the present estimates from special tabulations of ungrouped data from the 1971 Family Expenditure Survey. They can be traced principally to the following factors: different methods of dealing with the change in supplementary benefit rates in September 1971 (the scales in operation when the household was interviewed are used here – an average of the scales throughout the year in chapter 3); the inability to allocate the 'long-term addition' to retired persons in chapter 3; the use of net income here and gross income in chapter 3; the use here of the equivalence scales implied in the supplementary benefit rates, rather than those employed in chapter 3; the use of actual rents here, instead of an addition of 30 per cent of supplementary benefit rates as a 'rent allowance' in chapter 3.

Using the actual supplementary benefit rates in operation when each household is surveyed rather than average rates causes a fall in the estimated proportion in poverty (due to the particular distribution of supplementary benefit recipients about their calculated entitlement – see appendix IV). Had the same (less satisfactory) approach been used here as in chapter 3, the proportion of households in poverty would have been higher still – 8·5 and not 7·1 per cent. The next two factors, however, explain much of the difference between this 8.5 per cent and the estimate of 4·9 per cent in chapter 3: the needs of retired people are set higher in this chapter than in chapter 3; also household income is reduced in this chapter by income tax and national insurance contributions. The net effect of the last two factors listed above is more difficult to judge; they certainly alter the composition of households found to be poor and help to explain why the average size of poor households in chapter 3 is higher than in this chapter, since the addition of 30 per cent for housing costs tends to overcompensate larger households.

Some individuals and households receiving supplementary benefits in 1971 are included in the poor group in table 4.1; the rest, of course, are in the non-poor group. The reasons why households with members receiving supplementary benefits have incomes below the supplementary benefit scales are discussed in appendix IV. Some of these households were affected by such regulations as the 'wage stop', although they account for only a small proportion.[1] In most cases, their inclusion is due to changes in family circumstances since the last calculation of the entitlement or to misreporting of income or an inappropriate calculation of needs. In a small number of households containing more than one tax unit, one unit may be receiving supplementary benefits whilst the others have failed to claim or do not qualify through being in work. Whatever the reasons, we feel that households receiving supplementary benefits should not be excluded from those in poverty as appears to be the practice in the official estimates.[2] The main components of the current needs of these households have been estimated accurately, whilst some parts of their entitlement have been excluded; it would seem unfair therefore to exclude them *a priori*. The accuracy of the income information in general is discussed later in this chapter.

TABLE 4.2. *Poor and non-poor households receiving supplementary benefits, 1971* (*Percentages*)

	Receiving benefits	Not receiving benefits	Total
Income below poverty line	2·7	4·4	7·1
Income above poverty line	9·9	83·0	92·9
Total	12·6	87·4	100·0

Source: Special tabulations of the 1971 Family Expenditure Survey.

Note: See note *a* to table 4.1.

The numerical importance of those receiving supplementary benefits in both the poor and non-poor groups is shown in table 4.2, which indicates that nearly 40 per cent of poor households received some benefits, and that more than three-quarters of those receiving benefits were above our poverty line. Not surprisingly, poor households which received some supplementary benefits were better off than those which did not. Only 3 per cent of poor households receiving supplementary benefits had an income lower than 90 per cent of the poverty level, whereas as many as 55 per cent of poor households without benefits were in that category.[3]

[1] The wage stop no longer exists.
[2] See, for example, CSO, *Social Trends*, no. 6, 1975, table 5.31, p. 116.
[3] Further discussion of these points can be found in chapter 5 (pp. 67–9) and appendix IV (pp. 150–2), especially table IV.2.

LOW INCOME OR LOW EXPENDITURE

In the previous section the extent of poverty was measured by a comparison between net normal household income and a poverty level based on supplementary benefit scales. Table 4.3 shows the total expenditure levels recorded for these categories of household. It emerges that rather more households, 9·4 per cent of the total, are designated as poor on the basis of total expenditure, than the 7·1 per cent on the basis of income. The size of the disparity between the two percentages must raise doubts about the consistency of the results, especially since no more than 2·9 per cent of households would be regarded as poor on the basis of a dual criterion – low income *and* low expenditure. In short, those in poverty may be quite a different group depending on whether they are defined by income or by expenditure – many households have incomes above the poverty level, but total expenditure below, and vice versa – and it is clearly important to consider the relative suitability of income and expenditure as criteria for measuring poverty.

TABLE 4.3.   *Households in poverty as determined by income or expenditure, 1971 (Percentages)*

	Income below poverty line	Income above poverty line	Total
Expenditure below poverty line	2·9	6·5	9·4
Expenditure above poverty line	4·2	86·4	90·6
Total	7·1	92·9	100·0

Source: As table 4.2.

Note: See note *a* to table 4.1.

One reason for estimating poverty by means of total expenditure is that it may tell us something about a household's behaviour which income cannot; it may be a better guide to the actual standard of living of a household. In particular, total expenditure might seem to be a better approximation than income to actual consumption of goods and services, even though the relationship may be disturbed by changes in household stocks of goods and by the consumption of free goods and services. A second reason for considering the extent of poverty as suggested by total household expenditure is that these data may be statistically more reliable than information about incomes. After all, collection of expenditure data, not incomes, is the main objective of the Family Expenditure Surveys.

Comparing income and expenditure

A useful starting point for exploring the relative merits of household income and total expenditure as poverty criteria is a comparison of total household expenditure and incomes over the income range. Such a comparison is presented for 1973 in table 4.4, the first three columns of which show households grouped on the basis of their income, together with the average income and average total expenditure for each range. In the penultimate column the difference between total expenditure and income is expressed as a percentage of average income for each range.[1] These columns would appear to confirm commonsense expectations: that in the upper income range there is an excess of income over expenditure, presumably reflecting savings, and that poorer households apparently succeed to some extent in maintaining living standards by dis-saving. If the analysis were left at this point, there would seem to be a conceptual preference for delineating poverty on the basis of expenditure rather than income.

TABLE 4.4. *Household incomes, expenditure and payments, 1973*

Gross 'normal' income	Average income	Average expenditure	Other payments[a]	Total payments	Excess expenditure[b]	Excess payments[c]
		(£s per week)			(%)	(%)
0–9·99	8·87	10·21	0·28	10·49	+15	+18
10–14·99	12·25	13·45	0·57	14·02	+10	+14
15–19·99	17·27	18·57	2·50	21·07	+8	+22
20–24·99	22·48	23·45	2·58	26·03	+4	+16
25–29·99	27·53	27·30	4·26	31·56	−1	+15
30–34·99	32·61	31·34	6·34	37·68	−4	+16
35–39·99	37·61	33·83	8·39	42·22	−10	+12
40–44·99	42·43	37·14	10·34	47·48	−13	+12
45–49·99	47·63	40·02	11·69	51·71	−16	+9
50–59·99	54·82	44·36	17·76	62·12	−19	+13
60–69·99	64·58	48·71	18·63	67·34	−25	+4
70–79·99	74·73	56·80	26·06	82·86	−24	+11
80–99·99	88·55	63·33	28·53	91·86	−29	+4
100+	138·57	87·88	52·04	139·92	−37	+1
All households	49·41	39·43	14·21	53·64	−20	+9

Source: Department of Employment, *Family Expenditure Survey Report for 1973*, table 1 and appendix 6, table A.

a For example, income tax, mortgage payments, life insurance premiums, etc.
b Excess of expenditure over income as a percentage of income.
c Excess of total payments over income as a percentage of income.

However, further examination reveals that this picture is misleading and that the explanation of observed differences between household incomes and expenditure is quite complex. In theory, if the information in

[1] 1973 rather than 1971 was chosen, as the Family Expenditure Survey for that year contained an appendix analysing the relationship between household expenditure and income. The first three columns of table 4.4 are taken from that source.

the Survey on other payments is added to total expenditure, one would expect a full reconciliation with household income data. These payments comprise: income tax (less refunds) and national insurance contributions;[1] mortgage and other payments for the purchase or alteration of dwellings; life assurance and contributions to pension funds; sickness and accident insurance, subscriptions to sick clubs and friendly societies; contributions to Christmas, savings and holiday clubs; savings and investments; betting stakes less winnings. Taken together, the average value of these items was £14·21 per household per week in 1973 – more than a third of the value of 'total expenditure', and over a quarter of average household income. More to the point, when this sum is added to average total weekly expenditure of £39·43, the resulting total payments by the average family, £53·64, are 8·6 per cent greater than average household income. The implication is that the disparities between income and total expenditure reflect not only, or even mainly, the saving and dis-saving propensities of the various income groups, but also statistical or definitional discrepancies in the income and expenditure series as collected by the Family Expenditure Surveys. Moreover, the final column of table 4.4. suggests that such a discrepancy is a feature of every income group, though it is most pronounced in the lower income ranges.

Significant discrepancies can arise between income and expenditure data for several reasons. In the first place, whilst the Family Expenditure Survey seeks to record every payment by the household, certain important data on receipts are excluded: 'information on changes in financial and other assets is not collected, and income, as measured in the survey, excludes withdrawals of savings, receipts from maturing insurance policies, from repayment of loans, legacies, lump sum gratuities and other gains and windfalls.'[2] Though not all such items might be regarded as 'income' in the economic sense, they constitute financial resources that can be used to meet expenditure. Another deficiency is that for certain sources of income completely up-to-date information cannot be collected. In particular, income from investments, self-employment and certain other sources – accounting in all for about 15 per cent of total income recorded in the Survey – is not current, but relates to a previous twelve-month period. In periods of rising prices, therefore, expenditure – recorded on an essentially current basis – will tend to exceed income for this reason alone.

Whilst there are reasons to expect that households may be reluctant, or unable, to divulge details about all their income – especially investment income and income from self-employment – there may also be a tendency

[1] In the published *Family Expenditure Survey Reports* income is defined as gross income, that is before deduction of income taxes and national insurance contributions.

[2] Department of Employment, *Family Expenditure Survey Report for 1973*, London, HMSO, 1974, p. 147.

to exaggerate actual expenditure – to write into their records purchases not actually made in the period of the Survey, but which households feel would give a more representative picture of their expenditure or, indeed, a more socially acceptable one. However, the opportunities for misrecording expenditure do not lie in one direction only. As items of income may be forgotten, so too can individual purchases. Moreover, the estimates of purchases of alcoholic drink and tobacco recorded in the Family Expenditure Surveys are substantially below those based on Customs and Excise sources. There has been considerable debate about the net effect of these under- and over-recordings of expenditure.[1]

There is no simple way for the analyst of the Family Expenditure Surveys to determine the extent to which the discrepancy between household payments and recorded income is due to the omission of certain items, to the fact that certain forms of income are recorded retrospectively, or to misreporting. And it is only after allowances are made for such features that we can be certain which low income households are maintaining living standards by dis-saving. In theory it is possible to solve the problem by asking each household for a complete statement of its finances before and after the diary-keeping period. Unfortunately, the addition of further, more searching questions to an already formidable list would probably discourage participation in the Survey.

Does this imply that table 4.3 can be interpreted only in one of two ways: either only 2·9 per cent of households, those with both income and expenditure below supplementary benefit levels, are poor; or as much as 13·6 per cent (2·9 plus 4·2 plus 6·5 per cent) should be regarded as poor on the basis that neither income nor expenditure should be allowed to fall below supplementary benefit level? Neither option is very attractive. In the case of the narrow dual criterion, it would be unreasonable to exclude from the poor households where expenditure only marginally exceeds the supplementary benefit level. It might be equally misleading to class as poor households whose income takes them out of poverty, but whose expenditure in the given period was rather low (perhaps because of illness or a holiday).

The variability of household expenditure

A further attempt, based on households cross-classified by income and expenditure, was therefore made to determine which of the income or expenditure criteria is to be preferred for our purpose. When the sample of households is cross-classified by equivalent net normal income and by equivalent total expenditure there emerge considerable discrepancies

---

[1] See, for example, S. J. Prais, 'Some problems in the measurement of price changes with special reference to the cost of living', *Journal of the Royal Statistical Society* (series A), vol. 121, part 3, 1958; also Government Social Survey, *Family Expenditure Survey. Handbook on the sample, fieldwork and coding procedures* by W. F. F. Kemsley, London, HMSO, 1969.

between total expenditure and income at all levels.[1] We have examined the pattern of these variations: the 10th, 25th, 50th, 75th and 90th percentile values of expenditure within each income range, and the corresponding percentile values of income within each total expenditure range. The results plotted in charts 4.1 and 4.2 show how variable total expenditure is at a given income level, and similarly how, at a given level of expenditure, there is a wide range of incomes.

Chart 4.1. *Percentiles of equivalent total expenditure for ranges of equivalent net income, 1971*

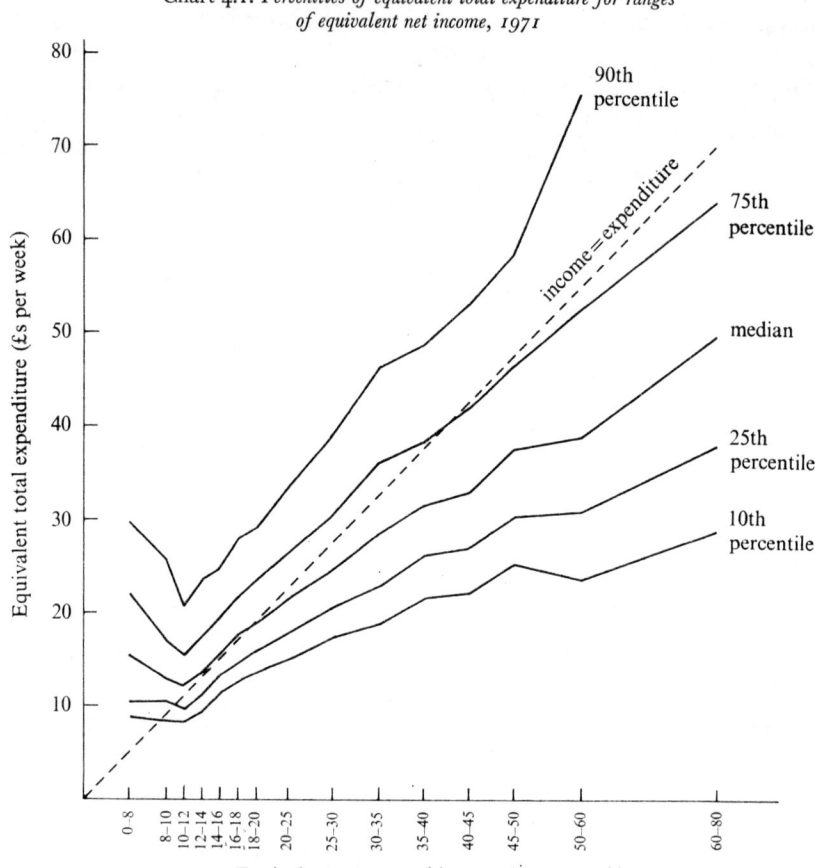

Equivalent net normal income (£s per week)

Source: Special tabulations of the 1971 Family Expenditure Survey

Note: Left-hand point on each curve based on 41 households with equivalent incomes less than £8 per week, and subject to large sampling error.

[1] Equivalent in the sense that both are adjusted to a common basis (per equivalent couple): a two-adult household being equal to unity, one adult to 0·60, additional adults to 0·40, children up to four years to 0·14, children five to ten years to 0·21 and children eleven or over to 0·30. The adjustment facilitates identification of households in poverty, but does not, of course, affect the relationship between income and total expenditure for each household.

Chart 4.2. *Percentiles of equivalent net income for ranges of equivalent total expenditure, 1971*

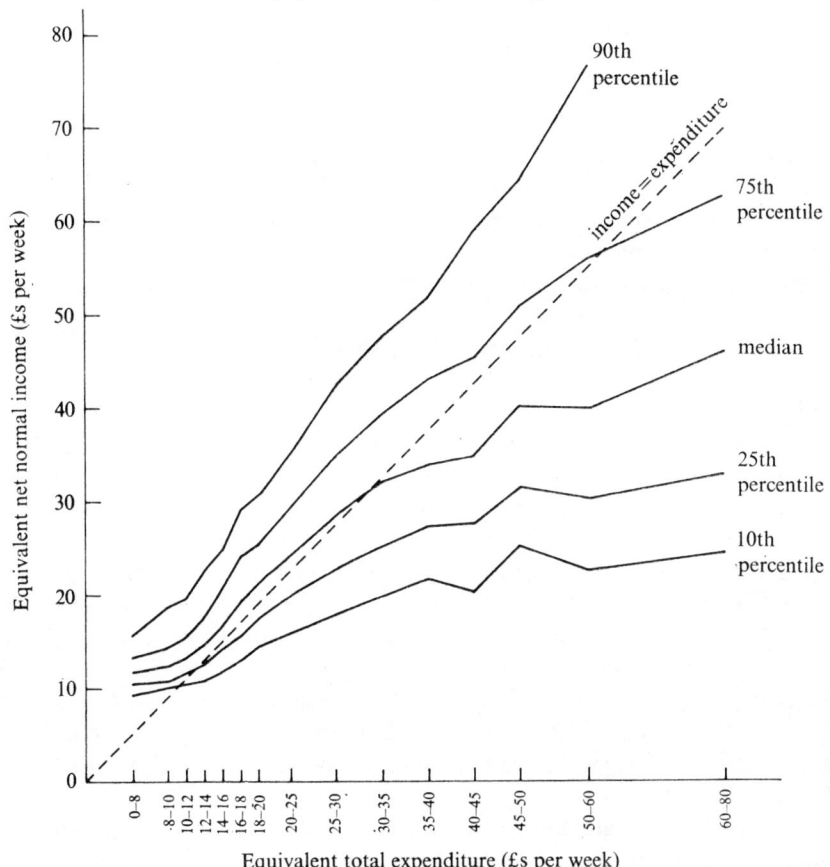

Source: As chart 4.1.

The variability is to a great extent the result of the way information on most household expenditure is collected in the budget diaries that are kept for only two weeks. Households only rarely make identical, or even similar, purchases week by week and, because of the irregularity of purchases, information is sought in interviews before diary-keeping begins on certain payments which are made infrequently and for which households are likely to have some records – rent and fuel bills, hire purchase, season tickets, licences, mortgages, credit repayment and insurance. However, only one-quarter by value of the items that make up total expenditure is covered in this way, and in consequence we find that almost one-fifth of households in the 1971 Survey recorded no expenditure on clothing and footwear, a tenth no purchases of durable household goods and almost 8 per cent no expenditure on transport and vehicles. Equally, there will be many households whose expenditure appears to be abnormally high because of the purchase of one or two larger items during their two weeks of diary-keeping.

In contrast, on the income side, there is some attempt to smooth out short-term fluctuations by calculating 'normal income' (which is described more fully on page 48 below). In brief, items such as bonuses and windfall payments are excluded, and, as we saw earlier, regular but infrequent payments, such as interest and dividends, are recorded over a twelve-month period. A comparison between households' total expenditure and their income without some of these adjustments on to a 'normal' basis (that is, comparing total expenditure with 'last week's income' – see page 48 below) revealed an even greater dispersion than that shown in charts 4.1 and 4.2.

Whilst these two charts display a similar degree of dispersion over most of their ranges, there is a sharp contrast at the lower income or expenditure end. In the case of households grouped by income (chart 4.1) the dispersion of total expenditures among the households with equivalent incomes below £10 per week is much greater than that of households with slightly higher incomes. Secondly, the values of the expenditure percentiles of these hundred or so households are all higher than the corresponding percentile values for households with rather higher incomes. In contrast, when households are grouped by total expenditure (chart 4.2), households with the lowest expenditures do not exhibit such 'perverse' behaviour; the dispersion of their incomes is similar to households with rather larger expenditures, and the values of their respective percentiles are below those in higher expenditure groups.

The excess of expenditure over income for the lowest income ranges in chart 4.1 (note the values of the 75th and 90th percentiles) suggests a degree of discrepancy not found elsewhere. No doubt elements of dissaving, under-recording of true income and overstatement of expenditure all make some contribution to these income–expenditure discrepancies. There might even be a presumption that dis-saving, rather than wholesale misrecording, is the primary reason for so many low income households spending in excess of their income. But it is difficult to explain on dissaving grounds alone why, in the lowest income households, expenditure is actually greater than in families with rather higher incomes. This points more strongly to misrecording and, in particular, understatement of income by a significant number of households in these groups.

This likelihood is reinforced when we consider the distribution of households with heads who are self-employed. We have already mentioned that the incomes of the self-employed are recorded retrospectively and other problems arise in assessing the precise level of these incomes. Of the households with both income and expenditure below the poverty line shown in table 4.3 the self-employed account for 3 per cent, whereas they form 8 per cent of the group with income below but expenditure above supplementary benefit level. In contrast, only 4 per cent of households with low expenditure but higher income had self-employed heads. This would seem to confirm that for some households total expenditure may more closely approximate to their true incomes.

While the question of whether to base poverty estimates on income or expenditure data, or on some combination of both, can only finally be resolved by more complete records of household finances, on the evidence considered above our tentative assessment might be as follows. There is a preference, *a priori*, using data from the Family Expenditure Survey, to measure poverty by income rather than total expenditure: the Survey yields a stable long-term measure of 'normal' income, while total expenditure – most items of which are measured over only a fortnight – is subject to sharp short-term fluctuations. However, some households in the low income categories have inordinately high expenditures, which may reflect an essentially transient low income among otherwise high income families, or an under-recording of income. The elimination of such households would reduce somewhat the 7·1 per cent recorded as in poverty on an income basis. The order of magnitude of this reduction can be roughly estimated from the data used in preparing chart 4.1. Among the 'aberrant' families, who appear to be concentrated essentially in households with incomes up to £10 a week, as many as 80 recorded total expenditures above the median value (approximately £12·00) of the next higher income group, £10–£12 a week. This represents 16 per cent of the 502 households in the three lowest income groups which, constituting 7·0 per cent of the total sample, approximate to the poor. Applying this result would reduce the proportion of households in poverty to approximately 6 per cent and the proportion of individuals to about 4·1 per cent.

THE POPULATION UNIT

Personal income is received, in the first instance, by a single individual, either in return for direct labour, or from ownership of assets, or through rights to State benefits. But some people do not enjoy incomes in their own right and, since these are mainly dependent children or married women not in employment, information about individuals' incomes tells us little about the extent of poverty. (Poverty measured on an 'individual' basis would be many times greater than measured on a household or family basis.) It has at times been advocated that each person should be guaranteed an income in his or her own right by the State, but this is not the current practice in this or other countries. In brief, most persons without any income, and many with only a little income, benefit in some way or another from the incomes of other individuals with whom they live and it would be misleading to ignore such income sharing. The question arises, however, how should individuals be grouped together to take account of this sharing.

For practical purposes there are two possibilities – the inner 'nuclear' family, or the household. Statistics derived from income tax records are presented in terms of the tax unit, which in effect is the inner family. That is, married couples are treated as one unit, and both they and single persons (including the widowed, divorced or separated) are grouped together with their dependent children if any. Information from sample surveys, however, is usually presented in terms of households, and this is so in the case of the published *Family Expenditure Survey Reports*. A household is defined as comprising all persons 'living at the same address having meals prepared together and with common housekeeping'. A household may therefore consist of more than one tax unit, whilst a tax unit is likely to constitute only one, or part of one, household.

Measuring poverty on the basis of the tax unit will yield more instances of low income than measurement based on households, since, in larger households containing more than one tax unit, there is scope for pooling income between relatively rich and relatively poor tax units. Thus, subdividing those households comprising more than one tax unit – about a quarter of the total – must increase the observed number of units with relatively small incomes. What cannot be predicted without detailed knowledge of individuals' incomes is by precisely how much the proportion of observed units below a given income level will rise. Our first task, therefore, is to quantify the effect of choosing one population unit rather than another. At a second stage we can consider whether or not there are grounds of principle or practicability for preferring one to another.

TABLE 4.5.   *The proportion in poverty based on tax units, 1971*

	Tax units	Individuals	
	(%)	(%)	(millions)
Income below poverty line	12·5	8·8	4·7
Income above poverty line	87·5	91·2	49·2
Total	100·0	100·0	53·9

Source: Special tabulations of 1971 Family Expenditure Survey.
Note: See notes to table 4.1.

Table 4.5 shows the proportion of tax units and individuals within them who are in poverty; also the number of individuals affected.[1] The propor-

[1] Table 4.5 is based on income without adjustment for the expenditure discrepancies discussed in the previous section, since data on tax unit expenditures were not available.

tion of tax units classified as below the poverty line is almost twice the proportion of households so classified (table 4.1) and the number of individuals below the poverty line on the basis of tax units, about 4·7 million, is some 80 per cent higher than the numbers in poverty, about 2·6 million, based on households. The choice of unit has a remarkably significant effect on the numbers in poverty. It is interesting to note, however, that the effect of this choice on the other principal dimension of poverty, the comparative living level of the poor, is less marked.[1]

It is apparent that there is a preponderance of single people amongst tax units with incomes below the poverty line; in fact they account for approximately 70 per cent of all poor tax units. The incidence of low income among single-person tax units is much the same whether we consider those living on their own and forming their own households, or those sharing households with other tax units, but the latter – who are transformed into independent units by the switch from households to tax units – outnumber the former in the ratio of two to one. And, since the majority of those that shared households did so with tax units that had higher incomes, single people sharing households appear to account for the bulk of the difference between the two estimates of poverty. For none of the other types of tax unit (married couples with and without children, and single adults with children) is low income mitigated on the same scale when the income of the whole household is considered.

We must next consider the relative merits of these two bases, households and tax units, for poverty measurement. Is one measure more accurate than another? Does one concept yield results that more closely approximate to commonsense notions of poverty? Or, does the choice perhaps depend on the context?

As far as accuracy is concerned, both sets of estimates are derived from the same income data in the Family Expenditure Survey. However, the assessment of needs on the basis of supplementary benefit rules cannot be achieved with equal accuracy for tax units and for households. In practice the supplementary benefit scale is applied to inner families (tax units) rather than households, and provides a separate allowance for the actual rent paid by each tax unit. In cases where two or more families comprise a single household it is not possible to identify from the Family Expenditure Survey each family's contribution to the rent. Rather than allocate the household's rent arbitrarily between the tax units, an average rent figure was estimated for each type of family, using the annual survey of supplementary benefit cases undertaken by the Department of Health and Social

---

[1] See Fiegehen and Lansley, 'The measurement of poverty'. The results given here in table 4.5 differ from those in that article because the former are based on 'normal' weekly income, the latter on 'last week's income' (see below); the latter also used an average of the two sets of supplementary benefit scales in operation in 1971, whilst here the scales used are those appropriate to each household's appearance in the Family Expenditure Survey.

Security.[1] It is possible that these average rents overstate the amounts that tax units sharing households actually pay, though it seems improbable that more than, say, half a million people out of the 4·7 million in poverty could be wrongly classified for this reason.

The main source of difference between the two sets of results lies, therefore, in the extent to which it is implicitly assumed that individuals share their incomes. Certain payments are made explicitly by one person to another, such as a housekeeping allowance paid to a wife by her husband. Also, some goods or services are financed from the income of one person and are consumed by several, such as rent and heating bills paid by a husband for the benefit of his wife, children and other members of his household. No doubt a greater degree of income sharing takes place amongst the members of an inner family than between two tax units forming a single household, but little is known about the pattern of such sharing, and neither the tax unit nor the household is wide enough to embrace all instances of income sharing.

Despite these difficulties, a view may be taken about the relative suitability of the two units in the present context. In measuring poverty we are concerned with living standards. The household is defined for the Family Expenditure Survey as consisting of those sharing a certain minimum of consumption and taking joint decisions about certain expenditures. For the purpose of measuring poverty in terms of living standards and incomes, it would seem appropriate to take account of such income sharing and to make estimates on a household basis. On the other hand, income sharing is not the only factor to be considered; it is also relevant whether or not the actual composition of each household is the one preferred by its members. The pattern of household formation is constrained by individuals' incomes and wealth, and by an imperfect housing market. Such constraints have particular force in the context of poverty, since, other things being equal, those with the lowest incomes are most likely to be restricted in their choice of household. The fact that some people are poor when assessed by their own tax unit's income, but are not considered poor when taken as part of their household, may be a consequence of their inability to maintain a separate household. But we have no way of knowing how many of the 2·1 million people who apparently escape poverty by membership of a larger household would prefer to live independently.

Moreover, a measure of poverty based on inner families is relevant for the government's social policy. Partly because not enough is known about income sharing, it is difficult to speculate about the 'fairness' or otherwise of income allocation between members of a household. The adequacy of income sharing within the inner family is also unknown, but, since it is a

---

[1] Unpublished data were kindly supplied by the Department of Health and Social Security (see also appendix IV).

smaller and more homogeneous unit, the degree of doubt may in this case be less. This is one reason why the State adopts the inner family rather than the household as the focal point for social (including redistributive) policies.

In any event, our findings show that the choice between the tax unit and the household has important implications for the apparent extent of poverty. If it is reasonable to assume that incomes are shared among individuals within a household and that poverty may be measured on this assumption, then the task of eliminating, or at least alleviating, poverty appears much less arduous than if more restrictive sharing assumptions are made and the inner family unit is adopted. However, if public policy wishes to maintain the independence of the inner family (including that of single adults) then, in terms of the number of people involved, the task is clearly very much greater.

THE TIME-PERIOD

Poverty is a situation where certain basic economic needs remain unsatisfied, and such needs are often expressed in terms of requirements over a fairly short period, usually a week. However, it may be felt that a family which has inadequate income for one week is not poor in the same sense as a family which has insufficient income for, say, several months: a fall in income below the poverty line for one week does not necessarily mean that a family's living standard drops below the poverty level, whereas a fall over a longer period clearly does.

For individuals whose weekly incomes are constant over the year plainly it makes no difference whether income for a single week, a quarter, or the entire year is considered; the number of these individuals falling below the minimum level remains unchanged. In practice, however, many incomes fluctuate from week to week, or from month to month, and for a variety of reasons. First, a large number of people enter and leave the labour force during the year, and even more people change their jobs. Secondly, earnings may fluctuate as a result of bonuses, overtime and short-time working; or unemployment and sickness, events particularly associated with poverty, may interrupt normal employment. Thirdly, family circumstances, which determine needs and sources of income, may change during a year: a household income which adequately supports, say, two adults and two children for part of a year may prove insufficient if a third child is born, or the number of earners may increase when a married woman or young adult starts work, lifting the family out of poverty. Such developments pose problems as complex and important as those raised by the choice of population units. Indeed, without proper formulation and due qualification, no unambiguous answer can be given to the question: how many people are in poverty at a given time?

Income data are collected by the Family Expenditure Survey for a number of time units. The two principal concepts on which attention is focused here are 'normal income' and 'last week's income'. Income other than earnings from employment and short-term social security benefits are treated identically in both concepts. For incomes received intermittently, such as interest and dividends, total receipts during the last twelve months are converted to a weekly equivalent. Similarly, a weekly figure for income from self-employment is based on a retrospective assessment, usually for the last accounting year. Regular incomes, such as pensions, are taken at their current actual rate. But earnings from employment and short-term social security benefits are treated differently: actual receipts from these sources are included in 'last week's income', but, if earnings in the week (or month) preceding the Survey are influenced by factors such as bonuses or short-time working, the employee's own assessment of his normal earnings is substituted in 'normal' income; and, if a person has been out of work for thirteen weeks or less, his normal earnings when last employed are substituted for 'last week's' actual benefits.

TABLE 4.6.   *The proportion in poverty measured by 'last week's' income, 1971*

	Households	Individuals	
	(%)	(%)	(millions)
Income below poverty line[a]	8·4	6·5	3·5
Income above poverty line[a]	91·6	93·5	50·4
Total	100·0	100·0	53·9

Source: As table 4.5.

[a] Based on a comparison between 'last week's' income and supplementary benefit levels at the date of interview.

Estimates of the numbers in poverty presented in preceding sections of this chapter were based on 'normal income'. Similar estimates using 'last week's income' are shown in table 4.6. It should be noted that, whilst the latter relates to earnings and some social security benefits for one week only – though not to a particular week[1] – no precise duration can be attached to the other concept of 'normal income'. In fact this relates to an income flow over a period longer than a week though shorter than a year; perhaps it is not misleading to think of it as relating to roughly three to six months.

The use of 'last week's' rather than 'normal' income increases the numbers of households and individuals below the supplementary benefit level,

[1] Since the Family Expenditure Survey sample comprises approximately equal numbers of households in each week throughout the year, it yields estimates of the numbers in poverty that are an average for all weeks in the year.

the increase being proportionately greater for the latter than for the former: on the basis of 'last week's income' 8·4 per cent of households accounting for 6·5 per cent of the population had low incomes. This is hardly surprising: normal weekly income may be greater or less than last week's income for those in employment, but in the majority of cases normal earnings when last employed will be greater than short-term unemployment or sickness benefits. Of the million or so people shown to be poor on the basis of 'last week's income' but not that of 'normal income', most were in households comprising a couple of working age with or without children. And only one kind of household, comprising one adult and one or more children, displayed a rise in the proportion in poverty when 'normal' rather than 'last week's' income was used.

CONCLUSIONS

More than anything else this chapter has demonstrated the importance of exercising great care when interpreting measures of poverty even when there is agreement about the concept to be quantified. Starting with an estimated 7·1 per cent of households consisting of 4·9 per cent of individuals in poverty on the conventional definition (those with incomes below supplementary benefit scales), the chapter has revealed just how sensitive such figures are to variations in methods of measurement.

If we take total expenditure rather than total income as our measure of a household's living standards, there is an apparent rise in the proportion of poor households to 9·4 per cent. However, a fairly detailed analysis of these two criteria suggested that retention of household income, with some statistical refinement, may be preferable to the use of expenditure by itself, in view of the latter's greater variability.

Other alternatives also lead to a rise in the estimated proportion with low incomes. If the estimates are based on a short-term measure – 'last week's income' – rather than a longer-term measure of 'normal income', there is an apparent rise to 8·4 per cent of households. Perhaps more significant is the effect of basing the measure on the inner family, the tax unit, rather than the household; this leads to an apparent increase in the proportion of poor individuals to 8·8 per cent. Both the scale and the implications of this adjustment are different from the others considered. The numbers in poverty are raised by over three-quarters, largely as a consequence of the separate consideration of single-person tax units living in larger households. The implication is that, if implicit assumptions about household income sharing are not made, the task – and cost – of alleviating poverty would be much greater than in fact it is.

CHAPTER 5

THE LIFE-CYCLE AND CAUSES OF POVERTY

INTRODUCTION

In this chapter we examine to what extent certain household and personal characteristics explain the existence of poverty in 1971. We begin by considering the typical life-cycle of a household and how the risk of poverty alters with the household's development. With the aid of information from the 1971 Family Expenditure Survey, we then attempt to relate instances of poverty to a number of 'proximate' causes, such as the head of the household being out of work, retired, or having sole responsibility for the family. Finally we examine the effect of social security benefits on poverty.

We adopt the same criterion of poverty as in the preceding chapter – the level of entitlement to supplementary benefits. However, we choose only one set of the alternative formulations used there; households in poverty are here defined as those whose combined normal income, net of income tax and national insurance contributions, falls below their supplementary benefit entitlement. A summary of the pattern that emerges when alternative formulations are used is presented in appendix V, but it does not differ greatly and does not alter the main conclusions.

POVERTY AND THE LIFE-CYCLE

In his study of York in 1899, Rowntree drew attention to the fact that an individual passes through alternating periods of 'want and comparative plenty';[1] since then there have been a number of attempts to describe the typical life-cycle pattern.[2] Rowntree postulated a cycle of poverty for a typical 'labourer', illustrated in his diagram reproduced as chart 5.1. He described the sequence as follows. 'During early childhood unless his father is a skilled worker, he will probably be in poverty; this will last until he, or some of his brothers or sisters, begin to earn money and thus augment their father's wage sufficiently to raise the family above the poverty line. Then follows the period during which he is earning money and living under his parents' roof...this period of comparative prosperity

This chapter has been prepared mainly by G. C. Fiegehen.

[1] Rowntree, *Poverty: a study of town life.*
[2] H. Lydall, 'The life cycle in income, saving and asset ownership', *Econometrica*, vol. 23, April 1955; A. B. Atkinson, 'Low pay and the cycle of poverty' and *The Economics of Inequality*, London, Oxford University Press, 1975, pp. 198–202.

may continue after marriage until he has two or three children, when poverty will again overtake him. This period of poverty will last perhaps ten years, *i.e.* until the first child is fourteen years old and begins to earn wages…While the children are earning, and before they leave home to marry, the man enjoys another period of prosperity – possibly, however, only to sink back again into poverty when his children have married and left him, and he himself is too old to work, for his income has never permitted his saving enough for him and his wife to live upon for more than a very short time.'[1]

Chart 5.1. *Rowntree's life-cycle*

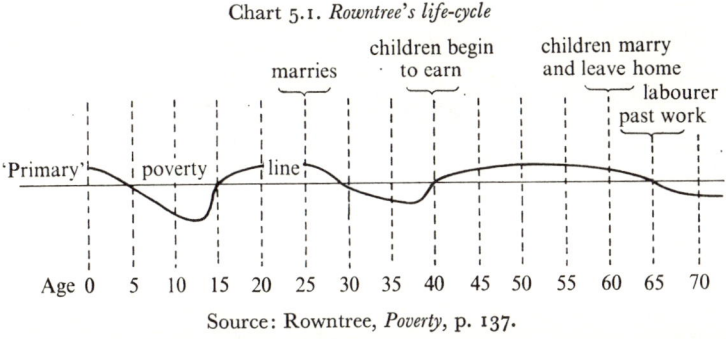

Source: Rowntree, *Poverty*, p. 137.

Rowntree used this cycle to emphasise that the persons shown by his inquiry to be in a state of 'primary' poverty *'represent merely that section who happened to be in one of these poverty periods at the time the inquiry was made'*.[2] Although many would pass on to a period of comparative prosperity, their places below the poverty line would be taken by others who at the time of his inquiry were in relative prosperity.

Our interest here lies in determining whether significant links persist between the normal life-cycle of households and the risk and amount of poverty. In other words, we distinguish between poverty caused by such unforeseen interruptions of income as unemployment, illness or the absence of one parent, and poverty of the kind which may be associated with more typical features of the life-cycle.[3]

In a 'modal' pattern of household development the principal stages are marriage, the rearing of children, the departure of children from the family unit, retirement and the death of one partner. This sequence is reflected in the rise and fall in the average number of persons per household, which increases from 2·5 when the head is under 25 to a peak of 4·0 when he is in the age-group 35–44, from which it declines to 1·6 where the head is over 75 (see chart 5·2).

[1] Rowntree, *Poverty*, pp. 136–7.
[2] Ibid., p. 137 (his italics).
[3] Cf. Dudley Jackson, *Poverty*, London, Macmillan, 1972.

Chart 5.2. *Demographic characteristics of the life-cycle of households*

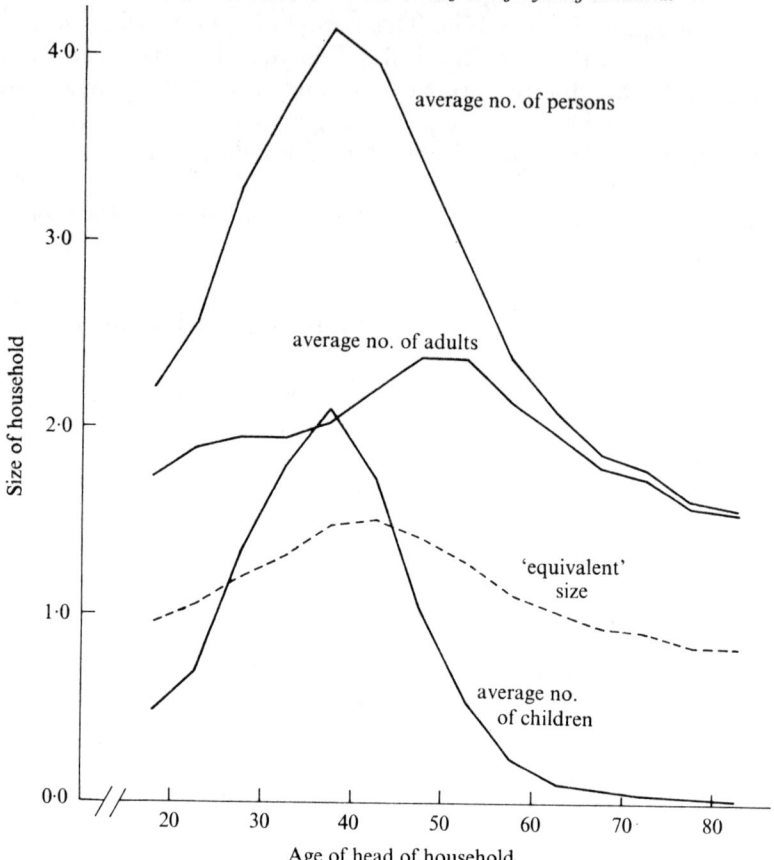

Source: Special tabulations of the 1971 Family Expenditure Survey.

Notes:

(i)   Left-hand point on each curve based on 23 households with heads aged under 20, and subject to large sampling error.

(ii)   A child defined as a person aged 18 or under in full-time education, or earning less than £8 per week, living with one or more adults.

(iii)   'Equivalent' size of household measured by weighting the numbers of adults and children by the equivalence scales on p. 40 and plotted in terms of equivalent couples unlike the other curves.

It is possible that most of those covered by Rowntree's survey passed through poverty at some stage in their lives. This is unlikely today. Even if a modal life-cycle of the kind shown in chart 5.1 persists, because of improvements in living standards the troughs of the cycle, at least for households with a median income, should now lie above any contemporarily prescribed poverty line. However, if the life-cycle of lower income households (such as those where the head is in low wage employment throughout his life) parallels that of the median household, then it is quite possible that for these families the troughs will carry them below a poverty line. On the other hand, it might be that the special kinds of hazard referred to above – unemployment, sickness, etc. – are mainly responsible for poverty. We consider, therefore, whether a modal pattern of family development exists, and whether the fortunes of lower income families are determined by such a cycle.

The modal life-cycle

No attempt is made in the Family Expenditure Surveys to trace the life histories of families in the sample. Such an exercise would be impracticable in a voluntary survey which already seeks a great deal of information. Our consideration of the life-cycle is necessarily based, therefore, on households in the Family Expenditure Survey classified by age of head of household. We examine the effects of the cycle first on economic needs and, secondly, on economic resources.

Needs depend to a large extent on the numbers of adults and of children in the household. For adults the average rises slowly from under 2·0 when the head of household is under 25 to about 2·4 when he is aged 45–54. For children the average rises to a sharp peak when the head of household is about 40 and then declines equally sharply. Since a child is defined as a person under 19 in full-time education (or earning less than £8 per week), the number of children per household falls as their ages increase from 15 to 18 and the number of adults increases unless the 'child' leaves home. This partly accounts for the decline in the average number of children after the head of household reaches 40, whilst, as chart 5.2 shows, the average number of adults continues to rise for some years. For an assessment of needs we are more concerned with the size of households in terms of adult equivalents:[1] the chart shows that household needs measured in this way are greater in middle life than earlier or later, but the variation is smaller than that in the average number of persons per household.

Average income reaches a peak when the head of the household is between 45 and 54 (see chart 5.3). In part this reflects the life-cycle earnings pattern of individuals, in part the fact that the number of wage earners per household reaches a peak at this stage. As can be seen, average household income falls quite sharply after this period.

Our principal interest is the relation between income and needs; accordingly chart 5.3 also shows variations over the life-cycle in income per equivalent couple. It is very clear that the most prosperous households, allowing for different needs, are those with heads in their late forties and early fifties. The oldest families are least well off, followed by 'young'

---

[1] Using equivalence scales (see footnote to p. 40).

Chart 5.3. *Household incomes and the risk of poverty over the life-cycle*

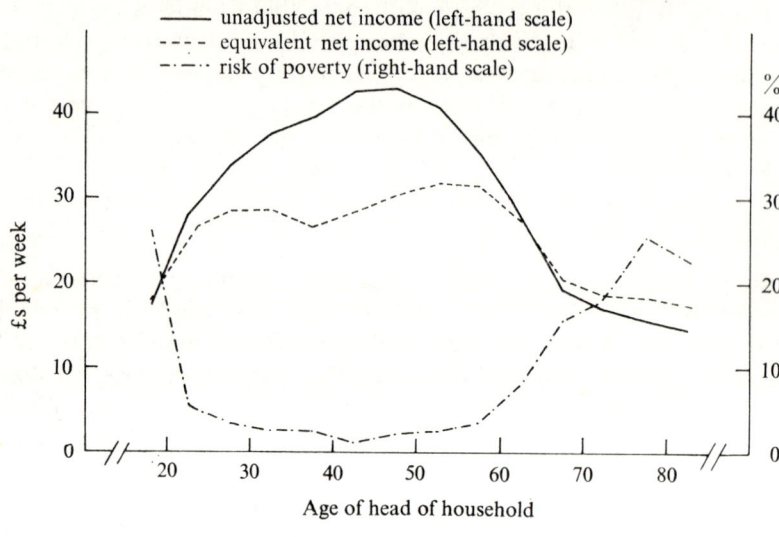

Age of head of household

Source: As chart 5.2.

Notes:
(i) Left-hand point on each curve based on 23 households with heads aged under 20, and subject to large sampling error.
(ii) Risk of poverty measured by proportion of households with head in each age-group where net normal income below supplementary benefit level.

families with heads under 20. The modal life-cycle as portrayed by the curve for income per equivalent couple confirms much of Rowntree's expectations depicted in chart 5.1: a period of comparative prosperity around the late twenties when there are few children, followed by a less affluent period in the thirties, which in turn is succeeded by the better times of middle and late middle age, and eventually by the final economic trough associated with old age. Discrepancies between Rowntree's pattern and our findings are perhaps most pronounced at the youngest end of the scale at around 20, when Rowntree depicted comparative prosperity. No doubt the fact that Rowntree was concerned with individuals – many of whom are without family responsibilities at such an age – while we have shown the position for heads of households, explains this difference.

The life-cycle for low income households

The picture presented above on the average household's pattern conceals a great deal of variation, in both demographic and economic characteristics, between households with heads in each specified age-group. We are concerned with the extent to which certain households experience a life-cycle that, when they are in the troughs, takes them into poverty.

Chart 5.4. *Percentiles of equivalent household income by age of head of household, 1971*

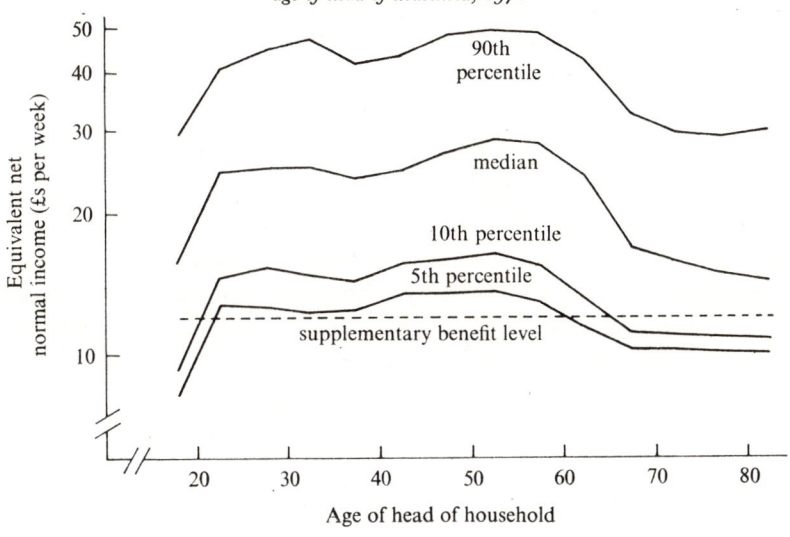

Source: As chart 5.2.

Notes:
(i) Left-hand point on each curve based on 23 households with heads aged under 20, and subject to large sampling area.
(ii) Net normal income shown on a logarithmic scale.

The values of income per equivalent couple were calculated for the 5th, 10th, 50th and 90th percentiles of households with heads in each age-group and are shown in chart 5.4. The modal life-cycle pattern appears to be slightly more pronounced for the highest 90th percentile and less pronounced for low income households. The life-cycle for the 10th, and especially the 5th, percentile households may suggest a sequence which is qualitatively different from that of the mode; the recession in economic fortunes experienced by more affluent households in their late thirties and early forties appears to occur earlier at lower income levels. However, even the 5th percentile does not fall below the supplementary benefit level at this stage.

The manner in which the risk of poverty varies with the age of the head of household is shown in chart 5.3: the risk is high for households with heads under 20, comparatively low for ages up to the mid-fifties, and very high thereafter. A high poverty risk in 'young' families may well reflect a combination of factors: an early marriage, with a husband in low wage employment and a wife prevented from working by the presence of very young children. A low poverty risk in the middle years suggests that normal demographic factors are no longer of great significance in this context. In particular, whilst child rearing limits the affluence of most families, it does not seem to give rise to much poverty. During these years it is likely – though not certain – that such 'accidental' factors as unemployment, sickness and broken families are mainly responsible for poverty. Finally, in later years the most important systematic cause of poverty is retirement.

PROXIMATE CAUSES OF POVERTY

The examination of the life-cycle helps us to distinguish the main characteristics of the poor and to identify the proximate causes of their poverty. We use the term 'proximate cause' because we are unable to examine the underlying reasons why a household has low income; we are restricted to those characteristics on which the Family Expenditure Survey provides information. Thus, while some poor households may have heads who are unemployed, the root cause of their unemployment – and therefore of their poverty – may lie in insufficient overall demand, local economic decline, unsuitable education and training, or other factors. However, the characteristics we are able to examine do throw some (interesting) light on the nature of poverty in Britain in the 1970s.

High risk and high accountability

In tables 5.1–5.4, various household and personal characteristics are distinguished and the sample is analysed in terms of two criteria: the risk of poverty – the proportion of households with that characteristic which are poor – and accountability – the number of poor households with that characteristic as a proportion of the total number of households in poverty.[1] The first step is to consider the characteristics which show one group of the population to have a particularly high risk of poverty. For example, regional location (table 5.2) has a much weaker effect than whether the head of a household is male or female (table 5.3). The chance of a household being in poverty ranges only from 5 per cent in Northern Ireland to 10 per cent in Wales,[2] whereas 18 per cent of households in which the head is a woman are in poverty compared with 4 per cent of those in which the head is a man.

We must also consider the extent to which a characteristic accounts for the totality of poverty. It is possible for a characteristic to be associated with a high risk of poverty, but to account for little poverty in total because it is relatively rare – and vice versa. For instance, households in rural areas display the highest risk of poverty among the various types of administrative area (table 5.2), but they account for the smallest number of poor households.

---

[1] Housing tenure of the poor is not included here but examined in chapter 6, because it is thought to be more a reflection than a cause of low incomes.
[2] See pp. 61–2 for a discussion of regional differences.

TABLE 5.1. *Characteristics of poverty, 1971: household composition (Percentages)*

	Risk of poverty[a]	Accountability for poverty[b] among: Household	Accountability for poverty[b] among: Individuals	Proportion of all households in Survey[c]
Persons in household				
1	20·7	50·9	26·2	17·5
2	6·4	29·0	29·8	32·3
3	3·3	8·9	13·7	19·1
4	1·6	4·1	8·5	18·1
5	2·8	3·2	8·1	8·1
6	3·7	1·6	4·9	3·0
7	9·8	1·8	6·4	1·3
8	9·1	0·6	2·4	0·5
9	—	—	—	0·2
Adults in household				
1	20·4	57·2	36·9	19·9
2	4·4	38·7	54·7	62·4
3	1·7	3·4	6·4	13·7
4	1·4	0·8	2·0	4·0
Children in household				
0	9·7	80·7	58·2	58·9
1	3·0	6·5	9·7	15·3
2	2·6	5·7	10·8	15·5
3	2·8	2·6	6·2	6·5
4	6·7	2·4	7·1	2·5
5	10·4	1·4	4·9	0·9
6	16·7	0·8	3·1	0·3
Tax units in household				
1	8·6	91·5	86·3	75·9
2	2·6	7·1	11·1	19·1
3+	1·9	1·4	2·6	5·0
Retired persons[d] in household				
0	3·1	32·0	49·1	72·1
1	17·2	48·1	29·2	19·8
2	17·4	18·7	19·9	7·6
3	21·4	1·2	1·8	0·4

Source: Special tabulations of 1971 Family Expenditure Survey.

[a] Proportion of households with specified characteristics where net normal income below supplementary benefit level.

[b] Poor households or individuals with specified characteristics as a proportion of all households or individuals in poverty.

[c] 7143 households with a risk of poverty of 7·1 per cent, but excluding 96 households (661 individuals) containing more than four adults or more than six children, which are included in the published data. This exclusion does not substantially affect the results.

[d] Includes unoccupied over retiring age.

TABLE 5.2. *Characteristics of poverty, 1971: location (Percentages)*

	Risk of poverty	Accountability for poverty among:		Proportion of all households in Survey
		Households	Individuals	
Region				
North	7·3	7·1	7·1	6·9
Yorkshire and Humberside	7·9	9·7	11·6	8·7
North West	5·8	10·1	8·9	12·3
East Midlands	5·6	4·7	5·3	6·0
West Midlands	8·1	10·7	12·1	9·4
East Anglia	6·0	3·4	3·5	3·9
Greater London	7·3	12·6	11·3	12·2
Other South East	5·8	14·6	13·8	17·7
South West	7·4	6·9	6·7	6·6
Wales	10·3	6·5	6·4	4·5
Scotland	9·0	12·4	12·2	9·8
Northern Ireland	4·9	1·4	1·2	2·0
Type of area				
Greater London	7·3	12·6	11·3	12·2
Other conurbations	6·7	17·9	17·4	18·9
Other urban areas	7·2	46·7	46·1	46·3
Semi-rural areas	6·1	15·6	17·1	18·1
Rural areas	11·2	7·1	8·0	4·5

Source: As table 5.1.   *Note:* See notes *a*, *b* and *c* to table 5.1.

TABLE 5.3. *Characteristics of poverty, 1971: status of head of household (Percentages)*

	Risk of poverty	Accountability for poverty among:		Proportion of all households in Survey
		Households	Individuals	
Age:				
16–24 years	6·6	4·9	6·8	5·3
25–34 years	2·9	7·1	14·5	17·3
35–44 years	1·8	4·3	11·8	17·4
45–54 years	2·3	5·9	8·8	18·0
55–64 years	5·8	15·2	12·3	18·6
65–74 years	16·6	37·1	28·3	15·9
75 and over	24·4	25·4	17·5	7·4
Male	4·3	47·7	62·0	79·4
Female	18·0	52·3	38·0	20·6
Employee	1·3	11·6	14·4	64·0
Unemployed	20·2	4·5	10·3	1·6
Self-employed	5·6	6·3	12·0	8·0
Retired	19·0	41·2	33·0	15·4
Unoccupied				
Under retiring age	19·0	12·6	15·8	4·7
Over retiring age	26·5	23·7	14·5	6·3

Source: As table 5.1.   *Notes:*
    (i) See notes *a*, *b* and *c* to table 5.1.
    (ii) Unemployed defined as 'out of work but seeking employment'.

TABLE 5.4. *Characteristics of poverty, 1971: household income (Percentages)*

		Accountability for poverty among:		Proportion of all households in Survey
	Risk of poverty	Households	Individuals	
No. of types of income: 1	20·7	38·5	34·5	13·2
2	8·8	35·5	37·0	28·5
3	4·9	22·1	23·5	31·7
4	1·2	3·2	3·9	18·8
5	0·4	0·4	0·6	6·6
6 or 7	1·2	0·2	0·3	1·2
Main source:				
Employment or self-employment	1·2	12·4	23·3	74·0
Investment, property, etc.	5·1	3·9	3·2	5·5
Social security benefits	29·1	79·3	67·3	19·4
Other	26·2	4·3	6·1	1·2

Source: As table 5.1.

Notes:
  (i) See notes *a*, *b* and *c* to table 5.1.
  (ii) The following seven types of income were identified: wages and salaries from employment; income from self-employment; social security benefits; other pensions or annuities; income from investments and property (other than owner-occupied); imputed rent of owner-occupied or rent-free housing and rent from sub-letting; other income, e.g. allowances from outside the household, scholarships, luncheon vouchers, but not other income in kind.
  (iii) One household had no income at all.

This distinction between 'risk' and 'accountability' has policy implications too; it might be argued that anti-poverty measures should be directed towards those characteristics which both display a high risk and account for much of poverty. If such measures were directed solely to characteristics associated with significant amounts of poverty although some of them involved only a small risk of poverty, many non-poor families would benefit. On the other hand, concentration of assistance on high risk groups would be more efficient, but might help only a relatively small number of the poor.[1]

If we take 15 per cent (twice the average risk) as our criterion for both high risk and high accountability, we find that, of the characteristics shown in tables 5.1–5.4, the following have a significant influence on poverty: one person in a household, one adult in a household, the presence of one or two retired persons, a head aged 65 or over, a female head of household, a retired or unoccupied head, social security benefits as the main source of income and dependence on one type of income.

Other household characteristics and poverty

The results are interesting for the characteristics that are less significant as well as for those that stand out. In particular, the small effect of the number

[1] See also A. Sinfield, 'Poverty rediscovered' in J. B. Cullingworth (ed.), *Problems of an Urban Society*, vol. III; *Planning for Change*, London, Allen & Unwin, 1974, p. 133.

of children in the household is noticeable, in view of the extent to which a large number of children has in earlier generations been an important cause of poverty. Certainly, the risk of poverty rises from 3 per cent in households with one to three children to some 17 per cent in six-child households.[1] Households with more than six children were excluded from our analysis (see appendix I), but their inclusion would not have affected the relative importance of children as a cause of poverty; although the risk of poverty for these excluded households would probably be high, they would not account for a large proportion of households in poverty. An alternative classification of four or more children as a large family would give an accountability of over 15 per cent, but such a group would also have a lower risk of poverty. Increases in real wages and the introduction of family allowances have helped to reduce the risk of poverty for households with children in comparison with prewar years, but there has also been a substantial reduction in the number of very large families.[2] It is important, however, to distinguish the role of a large number of children in causing poverty from the extent to which children account for the poor. Although the additional needs of large numbers of offspring do not seem to be responsible for much poverty, table 5.5 shows that children, who

TABLE 5.5.   *The population in poverty, 1971: children, adults of working age and retired*

	In sample[a]	Total household population		In poverty		Risk of income poverty
		Numbers	Proportion	Numbers	Proportion	
		(000s)	(%)	(000s)	(%)	(%)
Children[b]	5,905	15,648	29·0	628	24·0	4·0
Working age[c]	11,829	31,347	58·2	787	30·1	2·5
Retired[d]	2,593	6,872	12·8	1,198	45·9	17·4
Total	20,327	53,867	100·0	2,613	100·0	4·9

Sources: Special tabulations of the 1971 Family Expenditure Survey; CSO, *Annual Abstract of Statistics 1975.*

a Excludes 661 individuals in 96 households containing more than four adults or more than six children, who were included in the published data. This exclusion does not substantially affect the results.

b Aged under 19, in full-time education or earning less than £8 per week.

c All individuals other than children or retired.

d Includes unoccupied over retiring age.

comprise 29 per cent of the total household population, account for 24 per cent of all individuals in poverty, or some 600,000 in all.

1 Four out of 24 households that had six children were found to be poor.

2 In Great Britain the proportion of families of six or more people declined from 8·2 per cent in 1951 to 6·0 per cent in 1971 (CSO, *Social Trends*, no. 6, 1975). This trend is fairly typical of industrialised countries. In the United States families with four or more children constitute 12 per cent of all families, but 11 per cent of households in poverty. ('Poverty in America', chapter 21 in A. B. Atkinson (ed.), *Wealth, Income and Inequality*, Harmondsworth, Penguin Books, 1973, p. 380.)

Unemployment – for many years named as a major cause of poverty – is (or rather was in 1971) no longer a particularly important characteristic of poverty. Households with unemployed heads have a risk of poverty of more than 20 per cent, but they account for only 4½ per cent of households and a tenth of individuals in poverty. The risk of poverty associated with unemployment has declined since the 1930s, probably because of national insurance, and since the 1960s, possibly as a result of earnings-related unemployment benefits. Some poor households with unemployed heads may also be able to draw on redundancy payments, another innovation of the 1960s, but being received as a lump sum these are excluded from 'normal' income. Such households may temporarily be able to maintain a higher standard of living than indicated by their income, but among the small number of households in this category we found no evidence that expenditure exceeded income to any greater extent than among those in poverty generally. Whether or not the accountability of unemployment has declined also depends on the period in question; in relation to the early 1930s it is likely to have decreased, compared with the 1950s it may possibly be higher.[1]

The analyses presented in table 5.2 do not suggest any great dispersion in regional and area risks, but it remains possible that, with a finer classification of areas than is available from the Family Expenditure Survey, certain types of geographical location – such as depressed inner city areas – would be a feature of poverty. Some comment is required, however, on the ordering of regions in terms of their risk of poverty, and in particular on the fact that Northern Ireland emerges with the lowest risk, although average household income there was the lowest in any region of the United Kingdom in 1971. There is a higher sampling error than for other regions attached to the estimate for Northern Ireland, since it accounts for a small proportion of all households, but this does not appear to be the whole explanation. An additional analysis by region of average income, family size, age structure, composition of income and similar factors suggested that the regional pattern of poverty is probably associated with the operation of the supplementary benefit scheme. To those households already classified as poor in each region we added those which were receiving supplementary benefits but not classified as poor. This gave a total of households which were 'potentially poor', since without benefits the incomes of these households would be below the poverty level. This led to an ordering of regions that was somewhat different from that in table 5.2. Northern Ireland emerged as having the third largest proportion of

1 Abel-Smith and Townsend suggest that unemployment accounted for 3·1 per cent of poor households in 1953/4 (*The Poor and the Poorest*, p. 30). In 1971 the level of unemployment was comparatively high, approaching a figure of 1 million by the end of the year. Even so, since 1974 the proportion of the poor who are unemployed is likely to be still higher and the risk itself may have risen with the generally increased level and duration of unemployment.

households potentially poor (after Wales and Scotland), although it had the least actual poverty. The West Midlands, on the other hand, had the third lowest potential poverty, but the third highest risk of actual poverty. Other comparisons between the extent of potential and actual poverty suggested that differences in the risk of poverty between regions were associated as much with the extent to which the poor were eligible for supplementary benefits – those in full-time employment are excluded – and the extent to which those eligible claimed their benefits as with differences in the general level of prosperity of each region. Northern Ireland appears to be a case where the social security system mitigated to a greater extent than elsewhere the effects of regional economic depression.

Old age: the main cause of poverty

Perhaps the main conclusion from tables 5.1–5.4 is that old age appears to be the principal cause of poverty. This is also reflected among the other characteristics having both high risk and high accountability. Of the one-person households who were poor, eight out of ten were also classified as retired, or unoccupied and over retiring age. A third of all poor households were women living alone over retiring age, and this group also accounted for most of the poverty found amongst households with heads aged 75 and over. Again, households with retired or unoccupied heads over retiring age accounted for 95 per cent of those poor households where social security benefits were the main source of income.

The high risk and high accountability of old age is shown clearly in table 5.5. The risk of poverty for elderly and retired persons in general is 17 per cent, compared with 4 per cent and $2\frac{1}{2}$ per cent for children and other adults respectively, and the old account for 46 per cent of all poor persons. The more detailed breakdown of households by their composition in table 5.6 shows that the risk of being poor for the elderly living by themselves is as high as 30 per cent and for those living in households of one man and one woman it is 17 per cent. The elderly with the lowest risk of poverty were those living in other types of household, mostly those with three and four adults, who were presumably sharing households with grown-up and often married children; here the risk of poverty for the elderly was reduced to 7 per cent. Even so, this risk is above average for three- and four-adult households.

Other high risk groups

It is apparent from table 5.1 that nearly half of all poor individuals lived in households without a retired person. While the overall risk of poverty of those under retiring age was very low at 3 per cent, further inspection reveals the existence of other high risk groups that account for a fair

TABLE 5.6. *Poverty by type of household, 1971*

Household composition			Households		Risk of poverty[a]	Accountability for individual poverty[b]
	Adults	Children	In sample	In poverty	(%)	(%)
Head of	1M	–	145	42	29·0	4·3
household	1F	–	557	165	29·6	16·7
retired[c]	1M, 1F	–	576	97	16·8	19·7
	2M	–	13	–	–	–
	2F	–	81	7	8·6	1·4
Head of	1M	–	226	7	3·1	0·7
household	1F	–	320	44	13·7	4·5
not retired	1M, 1F	–	1450	31	2·1	6·3
	2M	–	39	1	2·6	0·2
	2F	–	76	2	2·6	0·4
All other	1	1	71	9	12·7	1·8
households	1	2	62	13	21·0	4·0
	1	3–6	39	10	25·6	5·0
	1M, 1F	1	727	18	2·5	5·5
	1M, 1F	2	887	13	1·5	5·3
	1M, 1F	3	384	9	2·3	4·6
	1M, 1F	4	129	6	4·7	3·7
	1M, 1F	5–6	65	9	13·8	6·7
	2M or 2F	1–6	28	3	10·7	1·0
	3	–	566	12	2·1	3·7
	3	1	218	2	0·9	0·8
	3	2	112	1	0·9	0·5
	3	3–6	84	2	2·4	1·4
	4	–	155	1	0·6	0·4
	4	1	66	2	3·0	1·0
	4	2–6	67	1	1·5	0·6
All households			7143	507	7·1	100·0

Source: Special tabulations of the 1971 Family Expenditure Survey.

[a] Proportion of households with the specified composition where net normal income below supplementary benefit level.

[b] Poor individuals in households with specified composition as a proportion of all individuals in poverty.

[c] Includes unoccupied over retiring age.

proportion of poverty, although less than the 15 per cent which we set originally as our measure of high accountability.

The analysis by household composition in table 5.6 shows that, next to the elderly living alone, households with one adult and two or more children have the highest risk of poverty – nearly one in four – and they account for 9 per cent of individuals with incomes below supplementary benefit level. Households with one adult and one child have a lower risk –

one in eight – and account for 2 per cent of poor individuals. Sole responsibility for children has always been difficult to combine with full-time employment and the high risk of poverty among this group is an inevitable consequence.[1] There has been an increase in the proportion of all households in the category 'woman with child' from 1·7 per cent in 1953/4 to 2·2 per cent in 1971.[2] If we accept the finding of Abel-Smith and Townsend that in 1953/4 no women with children were in households living below the basic national assistance scale plus rent, it would follow that the accountability of this group for poverty has increased considerably more than their incidence in the population; hence their risk of poverty has probably also increased. Two other categories of household are shown to have a high risk of poverty: those consisting of one woman, even if not retired, and one man, one woman with five or six children. The former account for only 4½ per cent of poor persons, however, and the latter for 6½ per cent.

Demographic and social factors apparently account for more poverty than purely economic factors (that is, unemployment and low pay). Retirement is a function of age, and the existence of single-parent families is attributable to differences in longevity, divorce, separation and illegitimacy. Even if the risk of poverty in these groups has not risen, their frequency in the population undoubtedly has. Longer life expectancy and more old people living alone have raised the numbers of retired households, and higher rates of divorce and separation have increased the numbers of one-adult households. Also, two other categories – single women under retiring age and large families – may find themselves poor for essentially demographic rather than economic reasons.

Economic or demographic causes of poverty

A closer inspection of the economic characteristics set out in tables 5.3 and 5.4 – number of types of income, main source of income and economic position of head of household – suggests that to some extent these also reflect demographic and sociological factors. For instance, households with only one source of income are shown as having a poverty risk as high as 21 per cent and accounting for 35 per cent of individuals in poverty. Some of these households will be those where wages constitute the sole source of income; however the table also shows that households where the principal income is from employment or self-employment have a very low risk of poverty and, though comprising about three-quarters of all households, account for no more than 23 per cent of individual poverty. Thus, it is

---

[1] The problems of one-parent families were the subject of a special inquiry, which showed the growing number of such families (see Department of Health and Social Security, *One-Parent Families. Report of the Committee* [Finer Report], Cmnd 5629, London, HMSO, 1974).

[2] Ministry of Labour, *Household Expenditure 1953–54*, p. 18, table 5; special tabulations of 1971 Family Expenditure Survey.

likely that the high risk of poverty in single-income households is largely accounted for by families which are entirely dependent on social security benefits. Households where this is the principal source of income have a very high risk of poverty, 29 per cent, and account for as much as 67 per cent of poor individuals. It is clear, however, that for the most part they are poor because of demographic or social factors, being retired or single-parent families.

Similarly, the variability in the risk of poverty when households are classified by the economic position of their head reflects for the most part demographic not economic factors. Households with retired heads have a 19 per cent risk of poverty and account for 33 per cent of the poor; the unoccupied over retiring age have a 27 per cent risk of poverty and constitute a further 15 per cent of the poor. It is also unlikely that many households with an unoccupied head under retiring age are poor for economic reasons; they run a 19 per cent risk of poverty and account for 16 per cent of the poor; they include some one-parent families (one-quarter) and those with a head who is chronically sick (one-sixth were receiving sickness or disability benefits) or no longer seeking work. In only one group, households with registered unemployed heads, can economic considerations be described as the cause of a high poverty risk – 20 per cent.

We cannot of course, dismiss economic factors as unimportant causes of poverty. The poverty of many old age pensioners can be attributed in part to a history of intermittent participation in the labour market, unemployment, or employment in low paid jobs – circumstances which would limit the likelihood of an occupational pension, or the accumulation of savings to help prevent poverty in old age. Similarly, poverty among single women and one-parent families may partially reflect employment in part-time or low paid jobs, or unequal opportunities to work.

A rough assessment of the relative importance of the various causes of poverty can be made with the help of table 5.7, which shows the proportion of all poor individuals in households grouped according to the economic status of the head and household composition.[1] For example, among households in poverty, we find that only about one-third of single parents were in employment; the major reason for poverty among single parents is probably the difficulty of taking up employment while having family responsibilities, which is broadly a demographic (and partly a social) influence. Of households in poverty with two adults and four to six children, we again find that only one-third had heads in employment. Any assessment of the relative importance of economic and of social and demographic causes of poverty is to some extent a matter of interpretation, but

[1] In view of the small samples in some cells, caution must be expressed about some of the figures presented.

TABLE 5.7. *Poor individuals in relation to household composition and economic status of head, 1971 (Percentages[a])*

Household composition	Economic status of head of household					All poor individuals
	High risk			Low risk		
	Retired[b]	Unoccu-pied[c]	Un-employed[d]	Self-employed	Employee	
High risk						
1–2 adults, retired[b]	42·1	n.a.	n.a.	n.a.	n.a.	42·1
1 adult with children	0·7	6·5	–	0·3	3·2	10·7
1 female, not retired	n.a.	1·9	–	0·2	2·4	4·5
1 male, 1 female, 4–6 children	–	1·4	5·5	1·4	2·0	10·3
Low risk						
1 male or 2 adults, not retired	n.a.	3·1	0·9	2·0	1·6	7·6
1 male, 1 female, 1–3 children	0·9	1·7	3·6	4·6	4·5	15·3
Others	3·8	1·2	0·3	3·5	0·7	9·5
All poor individuals	47·5	15·8	10·3	12·0	14·4	100·0

Source: As table 5.6.

[a] Proportions of poor individuals in specified categories of households out of total of 986 individuals in poor households.
[b] Includes unoccupied over retiring age.
[c] Excludes unoccupied over retiring age.
[d] Defined as 'out of work but seeking employment'.

TABLE 5.8. *Demographic and economic causes of poverty (Percentages)[a]*

Characteristics of head of household	Causes	
	Mainly demographic	Mainly economic
Employment hindered by:		
Retirement and/or old age	48	–
Being a single parent	10	–
Being female (not retired)	5	–
Other reasons (unoccupied)	7	–
Available for employment but:		
Unemployed	–	10
Employed, 4–6 children	3	–
Low income from:		
Self-employment	–	10[b]
Employment	–	7[b]
All poor individuals	73	27

Source: Table 5.7.

[a] Proportions of poor individuals in specified categories of households.
[b] Estimated as residual categories.

the poverty of such households with an unemployed head could be eliminated either by re-employment of the head or by the eventual growing-up of some children so that they ceased to be dependants. In this case we feel unemployment is the proximate cause of poverty.

Clearly some commonsense but partly arbitrary decisions are needed to establish a single proximate cause of poverty in all cases. Table 5.8 sets out our judgements based on the data in table 5.7. On this basis social and demographic influences can be said to be the proximate cause of poverty for 73 per cent of individuals, and economic influences (that is, an unemployed head or low earnings) the proximate cause for 27 per cent of individuals. If the poverty of single parents and single women in employment were attributed to economic causes (the adverse employment opportunities of women as compared with men) the proportions become 67 and 33 per cent.

TABLE 5.9. *Poverty and low pay, 1971*

Normal earnings of head of household	Households with head an employee		Risk of poverty[a]
	In sample	In poverty	
(£s per week)			(%)
0–9·99	289	46	*15·9*
10–14·99	139	5	*3·6*
15–19·99	423	6	*1·4*
20–24·99	729	1	*0·1*
25+	2990	1	—
All ranges	4570	59	*1·3*

Source: Special tabulations of the 1971 Family Expenditure Survey.

[a] Proportion of households with specified earnings ranges where net normal income below supplementary benefit level.

Our classification indicates that only 17 per cent of those in poverty are poor because of low earnings from employment. This group is, however, the residual category from table 5.7, of those who were in poverty neither because of their high risk household composition nor because of their high risk economic status. Although the poverty of some of these households may be largely due to low wages, table 5.9 shows that only 16 per cent of households with heads earning less than £10 a week were in poverty,[1] most of them having a wife not at work and one to three children.

POVERTY AND SOCIAL SECURITY BENEFITS

Following our examination of the relative importance of economic and

[1] In 1971 the lowest decile of full-time male earnings was £19·80 per week, and of full-time female earnings £10·50 per week.

demographic influences on poverty, it is natural to consider the extent to which the social security system alleviates poverty. It might be thought that, in principle, the social security system should prevent many of the instances of poverty we have found. However, the system was not designed to cope with all types of poverty, and we must first establish the proportion of cases in which it was clearly intended to provide assistance – namely, those unable to work or to find employment. In our sample, 74 per cent of the poor come from households where poverty is associated with retirement, or from households with unemployed or unoccupied heads (table 5.7). (If the intention of family allowances to meet the additional needs of larger families is included, the proportion rises to 77 per cent.) Thus, about a quarter of those in poverty cannot be helped by the social security system because they live in households with heads in employment and, although new types of benefit might be introduced to help them, their poverty cannot be ascribed to the failure of the system given the criteria by which it was designed to operate.

Of the three-quarters of the poor who are eligible for social security benefits, we find that for a great many of them – in fact 90 per cent – social security benefits were their largest single source of income.[1] Indeed, of all the categories of household distinguished in tables 5.1–5.4, those with social security benefits the largest source of income showed the highest risk of poverty (29·1 per cent). Thus, while the system provides sufficient assistance for the majority of those eligible for its benefits to take them above our poverty line, it leaves a substantial proportion below it. One reason for this is that some of those eligible fail to claim all the benefits to which they are entitled. Failure to claim supplementary benefits, in particular, appears to account for 37 per cent of individuals in poverty in our sample, even though many were receiving other forms of benefit. For about half this group their actual incomes (without supplementary benefits) were within 10 per cent of the supplementary benefit level. In terms of the rates of benefit then applicable for married couples, these households might have gained some £1·20 a week, but only by going through the fairly complicated and rigorous process of applying for benefits; it is possible that some did not think it worthwhile. But the other half of the group would have substantially increased their incomes by claiming benefits.

Another reason why those eligible for social security benefits had incomes below the supplementary benefit level may simply be that the benefit received was insufficient. Some of these cases would have been affected by the 'wage stop' rule still operating in 1971, but the majority of cases were retired or unoccupied individuals to whom it did not apply. Some cases

---

[1] The main benefits are national insurance retirement and widow's pensions, and sickness and unemployment benefits, family allowances and supplementary benefits.

may be due to misreporting of income, or to differences in interpretation between social security offices and the Family Expenditure Survey; for others, family circumstances may have changed between the calculation of benefit and participation in the Survey. However, we found, on the basis of the analyses in chapter 4, that for social security recipients their incomes tend to be more reliably recorded in relation to their expenditure than for most other groups.[1] Whatever the reason for the deficiency in income, it is worth noting that in the great majority of cases the deficiency was not very large; over 80 per cent of poor households receiving supplementary benefits had an income less than 10 per cent below our estimate of their entitlement; again there may be reluctance to go through complex procedures to obtain a small increase in benefits.

SUMMARY

Our assessment of the risk of poverty at successive stages in the household life-cycle suggested that old age remains the main systematic cause of poverty. Poverty during the earlier stages of the life-cycle is more often connected with contingencies such as unemployment, sickness or a single-parent family, although households with heads under 20 have a relatively high risk of poverty.

Statistical analysis of the household and personal characteristics collected by the Family Expenditure Survey showed that old age and retirement account for about half of all poor people in the United Kingdom and two-thirds of poor households. Other high risk categories include single-parent families, households with unemployed or unoccupied heads, households with over four children and women living alone. The risk of poverty does not vary greatly from region to region, or between urban and rural areas. Of the 'proximate' causes of poverty, two-thirds to three-quarters (depending on interpretation) may be regarded as social and demographic and the remainder as economic. About three-quarters of the poor were eligible for assistance in the form of social security benefits, but half of these had not taken up an apparent entitlement to supplementary benefits. Amongst the poor who were receiving supplementary benefits, four in five households had total incomes less than 10 per cent below their basic entitlement.

[1] See also appendix V, p. 155

CHAPTER 6

EXPENDITURE OF THE POOR

INTRODUCTION

We now turn to an examination of the expenditure patterns of the poor. Although individual living standards depend on a variety of personal and social factors, such as education, health, housing and environmental conditions, as well as income, an examination of the mix of goods and services consumed by the poor may throw some light on the quality of life of those in poverty and improve our understanding of the effects of low income.

Most of the analysis relates to 1971, but first we trace in a summary fashion the manner in which consumption patterns of the poor compared with those of the non-poor have changed over the past twenty years or so. This enables us to look at the hypothesis that the expenditure patterns of the poor today resemble those of the non-poor at some previous date. For the most part, those in poverty are defined in this chapter as the poorest 5 or 10 per cent of households (or individuals). But we also compare expenditure patterns among the poverty groups which emerge from the other criteria adopted in chapter 4 in an attempt to establish which criterion defines poverty in the most useful way.

Analysis of poor and non-poor consumption patterns may also help in the measurement and identification of poverty. Earlier research has repeatedly confirmed the validity of Engel's Law – that the proportion of income spent on food declines as income rises – and extended it to other necessities such as heat, light and basic clothing.[1] In this chapter we try to determine whether there are any relatively abrupt changes in expenditure patterns as income rises which might help to suggest where a line should be drawn between the poor and non-poor. But, as we shall see, this approach is unsuccessful.

We also investigate Rowntree's concept of secondary poverty – the idea that certain families enjoy an income which would be sufficient to maintain the prescribed standard, 'were it not that some portion of it is absorbed by other expenditure, either useful or wasteful'.[2] Finally, we examine some aspects of housing and poverty, because contrasts in the housing expendi-

This chapter has been prepared mainly by P. S. Lansley.

[1] See, for instance, H. S. Houthakker, 'An international comparison of household expenditure patterns', *Econometrica*, vol. 25, October 1957.
[2] Rowntree, *Poverty*, p. 87.

ture of the poor and the non-poor may reflect other factors as well as income differentials.

EXPENDITURE PATTERNS, 1953/4 TO 1973

A necessary assumption for examining patterns of consumption is that consumption can be approximately measured by current expenditure. This may not be wholly realistic for a particular household or a particular item at a given time, because consumption is also determined by past expenditure, which affects stocks held currently, by future expectations and possibly by free or subsidised goods and services. Thus the consumption of the poor may be higher than appears from the Family Expenditure Survey, especially if a household's period of low income has been, or is expected to be, brief.

The methods for deriving the patterns of expenditure are described in appendix VI and necessarily involve some approximations. There are four main reasons for this. First, data on expenditure patterns are not published for all types of household separately. Secondly, the published information is presented in the form of averages for groups classified by gross income; these had to be converted into 'equivalent income' and the results re-ranked to obtain the relevant percentiles. Thirdly, all items of consumption were converted to an equivalent basis by means of a single scale, whereas ideally allowance should be made for the specific needs of individuals for different goods and services. Finally, while the classification of households on the basis of net income would be more appropriate, the use of gross income was dictated by the published tables. However, the more detailed study of the 1971 data below demonstrates that none of these factors is sufficiently important to qualify the general conclusions.

Table 6.1 shows the pattern of equivalent household expenditure for the 5th, 10th and 50th percentiles for 1953/4, 1961, 1971 and 1973 at constant 1971 prices. Between 1953/4 and 1971 real expenditure of all the groups rose by about 40 per cent; this may be compared to the rise in real incomes after tax of over 50 per cent during the same period reported in chapter 3 (see table 3.3). At the median level the difference between growth of real incomes and of total expenditure arises mainly because of the increasing proportion of income saved in some form. This may also be part of the explanation for the 5th and 10th percentiles, but a more important factor here is the method of converting current incomes and expenditure to constant prices. In chapter 3 the same price index was used to convert incomes at all levels to real terms, and we noted that this might overstate the increase in the real incomes of the poor by under 5 per cent. In table 6.1 real total expenditure was obtained by adjusting each component of expenditure by the change in its appropriate index; this allows

TABLE 6.1.   *Household expenditure at constant prices,[a] 1953/4 to 1973 (£s, 1971 prices)*

	5th percentile[b]				10th percentile[b]				Median[b]			
	1953/4	1961[c]	1971	1973	1953/4	1961[c]	1971	1973	1953/4	1961[c]	1971	1973
Housing	1·69	1·96	2·74	2·32	1·56	1·91	2·34	2·56	2·71	2·24	3·20	3·31
Fuel, light and power	1·40	1·57	1·86	1·81	1·08	1·31	1·52	1·76	1·40	1·25	1·68	1·58
Food	3·97	4·37	4·64	4·67	4·25	4·86	4·92	4·93	5·52	6·55	6·31	6·52
Total necess-ities	*7·06*	*7·90*	*9·24*	*8·80*	*6·89*	*8·08*	*8·78*	*9·25*	*9·63*	*10·04*	*11·19*	*11·41*
Clothing	0·51	0·55	0·81	0·78	0·59	0·68	0·99	0·89	1·32	1·60	1·71	2·28
Alcoholic drink	0·17	0·27	0·26	0·43	0·18	0·31	0·45	0·48	0·32	0·53	0·96	1·30
Tobacco	0·33	0·47	0·45	0·65	0·60	0·68	0·75	0·85	0·77	1·09	1·13	1·24
Durables	0·30	0·36	0·64	0·70	0·31	0·47	0·74	0·80	0·87	1·19	1·76	2·04
Other goods and misc.	0·78	0·80	0·96	1·09	0·84	0·90	1·14	1·28	1·41	1·61	1·81	2·23
Transport and vehicles	0·29	0·33	0·64	0·94	0·39	0·59	1·03	0·95	0·89	1·71	2·82	4·08
Services	0·85	0·86	1·35	1·06	0·68	0·82	1·04	1·10	1·61	1·42	1·99	2·19
Total non-necessities	*3·23*	*3·64*	*5·11*	*5·65*	*3·59*	*4·45*	*6·14*	*6·35*	*7·19*	*9·15*	*12·18*	*15·36*
TOTAL	10·29	11·54	14·35	14·45	10·48	12·53	14·92	15·60	16·82	19·19	23·37	26·77

Sources: Ministry of Labour, *Household Expenditure 1953–54*; Department of Employment, *Family Expenditure Survey Reports* (various years).

[a] Expenditure per equivalent couple converted to 1971 prices using the components of the retail price index.

[b] Households ranked by equivalent gross normal income.

[c] Based on a small sample.

directly for the somewhat faster rise in the cost of living over the period for poorer households than for those at the median. Some of the discrepancy may also derive from the greater improvement that has probably taken place in the recording of income data; also we used the whole sample in estimating incomes and only about three-quarters of it in estimating expenditure. However, increased saving by middle income households and faster price increases for goods forming a large part of the budget of the poor probably explain most of the difference between estimates of the rise between 1953/4 and 1971 in real incomes and in total expenditure.

Between 1971 and 1973 there were marked contrasts between the groups shown in table 6.1, with expenditure by the median household rising a further 15 per cent and by the 10th percentile a further 5 per cent, while that of the 5th percentile hardly changed. It is possible that the alteration in the Family Expenditure Survey definition of a child, which raised the age limit from 16 to 18 in 1973, has distorted the comparisons; indeed the estimates of incomes in 1971 and 1973 in chapter 3 also suggested the possibility of distortion occurring with the change in definition. Consequently, in discussing changes in expenditure patterns we shall refer mainly to 1971.

In terms of constant 1971 prices, food expenditure has risen at about the same rate for each group, but expenditure on housing and fuel, light and power shows a much faster increase for the lower percentiles – nearly 50 per cent compared with under 20 per cent for the median. This would be consistent with the poorer groups devoting a greater share of the rise in their real incomes than the median group to improving their housing conditions, but there could be other explanations, for example that the cost of housing to the poorer groups has risen more rapidly than to the median household. We shall examine these possibilities later in the chapter.

TABLE 6.2. *Household expenditure patterns at current prices,[a] 1953/4 to 1973 (Percentages)*

	5th percentile[b]				10th percentile[b]				Median[b]			
	1953/4	1961[c]	1971	1973	1953/4	1961[c]	1971	1973	1953/4	1961[c]	1971	1973
Housing	13·1	15·5	19·1	16·9	11·6	13·8	15·6	17·2	12·4	10·4	13·7	13·1
Fuel, light and power	11·5	13·0	13·0	11·7	8·5	9·9	10·2	10·6	6·8	6·1	7·2	5·6
Food	41·6	38·6	32·3	34·4	42·7	39·2	33·1	33·6	34·4	34·0	27·0	26·2
Total necessities	66·2	67·1	64·4	63·0	62·8	62·9	58·9	61·4	53·6	50·5	47·9	44·9
Clothing	7·0	5·7	5·6	5·4	7·8	6·5	6·6	5·8	10·9	9·8	7·3	8·6
Alcoholic drink	2·0	2·4	1·8	2·7	2·1	2·4	3·0	2·8	2·3	2·7	4·1	4·5
Tobacco	3·8	4·5	3·1	3·9	6·6	6·0	5·0	4·7	5·3	6·2	4·8	4·0
Durables	4·0	3·6	4·5	4·5	4·0	4·2	5·0	4·8	7·1	7·0	7·5	7·2
Other goods and misc.	7·2	6·8	6·7	6·8	7·6	7·0	7·6	7·6	7·8	8·0	7·7	7·8
Transport and vehicles	2·8	3·1	4·5	6·2	3·7	5·0	6·9	5·8	5·1	9·2	12·2	14·6
Services	7·0	6·8	9·4	7·5	5·4	6·0	7·0	7·1	7·9	6·6	8·5	8·4
Total non-necessities	33·8	32·9	35·6	37·0	37·2	37·1	41·1	38·6	46·4	49·5	52·1	55·1

Source: Appendix table VI.2.

[a] Expenditure per equivalent couple.
[b] Households ranked by equivalent gross normal income.
[c] Based on a small sample.

Over the period 1953/4 to 1971, the proportion of expenditure on necessities – housing, fuel, light and power, and food – has declined for all three groups (table 6.2). Whilst this was to be expected, the fall for the lowest 5th and 10th percentiles was less than that for the median household: 2–4 compared with 6 percentage points. By 1971 the 5th percentile still devoted 64 per cent of expenditure to the necessities, compared with 48 per cent by the median household. A significant decline of about 10 per cent in the share of total expenditure on food occurred for all groups. The differences were in housing, and fuel, light and power, where the proportion of expenditure rose for the poorer groups but changed little for the median household.[1]

In chapter 3 we concluded that, when allowance is made for changes in direct taxation, there has probably been little relative change between 1953/4 and 1973 in the incomes of the poor as compared with the median, either in their favour or to their disadvantage. This finding seems to be supported by the data on comparative total expenditure in table 6.3, at least up to 1971. This table also sets out the changes in the comparative levels of expenditure on each main item by the lowest groups in relation to the median. As a result of the trends already described, there has been a substantial rise in the comparative level of their housing and fuel expenditure, and very little change in that on food. The decline in comparative expenditure on transport reflects an extension of car ownership down the income scale to embrace the median group; between 1953/4 and 1973 transport costs in the median household increased from 5 to 15 per cent of total expenditure (table 6.2). Comparative expenditure by the poor on clothing is low in all years, reflecting the role it plays as a luxury item in the consumption of the more affluent. A relative decline in expenditure by the poor on alcoholic drink is also recorded, but it is difficult to comment because of known recording biases in this item.

The data do not provide an unequivocal answer to the question of time-lags in expenditure patterns. We would need to go further back than 1953/4 for the median household to spend in real terms the same total as the lowest 5th percentile in 1973, £14·45 per week. Nevertheless, there is no great disparity between total real expenditure of the 10th percentile in 1973, £15·60, and the median in 1953/4, £16·82, so that a comparison of the expenditure patterns of these two groups is instructive.

It is of course a remarkable fact in itself that in 1973 the 10th percentile had an expenditure level of the same order of magnitude as the median household twenty years ago. Broadly speaking, table 6.1 shows that the expenditure pattern of the 10th percentile today is also fairly close to that of the median twenty years ago, but there are certain differences which are

[1] A fall in average household size from 3·2 persons in the 1953/4 Survey to 2·8 in 1973, and a corresponding fall in the number of children, would be associated *ceteris paribus* with a rise in the share of items such as housing and fuel which have relatively large economies of scale, and a fall in the share of items such as food where the opportunity for economies of scale is less.

TABLE 6.3. *Comparative expenditure levels of the poor
at constant prices, 1953/4 to 1973 (Percentages)*

	5th percentile/median				10th percentile/median			
	1953/4	1961[a]	1971	1973	1953/4	1961[a]	1971	1973
Housing	63	87	86	70	58	85	73	77
Fuel, light and power	100	126	111	114	77	105	90	111
Food	72	67	74	72	77	74	78	76
Clothing	38	34	47	34	45	43	58	39
Alcoholic drink	53	52	27	33	58	58	47	37
Tobacco	43	43	40	52	77	63	66	69
Durables	34	30	36	34	36	40	42	39
Other goods and miscellaneous	55	50	53	49	60	56	63	57
Transport and vehicles	33	19	23	23	44	52	37	23
Services	53	60	68	49	42	58	52	50
Total	61	60	61	54	62	65	64	58

Source: Table 6.1.

[a] Based on a small sample.

significant. Real expenditure of the contemporary poor on clothing and on services appears to be appreciably less than that of the median household twenty years ago and on fuel, light and power appreciably greater. A lower consumption of services could be attributable to a price increase above the average for the period, but a lower consumption of clothing occurred in the face of a comparatively small price increase, and a greater consumption of fuel, light and power despite an above-average price increase.

Such differences suggest that taste (or long-standing 'class' habits) may contribute to consumption patterns. The tendency for the poor to maintain their proportionate expenditure on fuel, light and power, despite large price rises, does much to explain why the overall share of their expenditure on necessities has fallen less than that of the median household. Moreover, this is reinforced by their expenditure on housing. Although the cost of housing has increased more than that of any other item, in real terms the share of such expenditure by the 10th percentile is at approximately the same level as that of the median household of twenty years ago.

RELATIVE EXPENDITURE PATTERNS, 1971

Expenditure by poor and other households

Expenditure differences between the poor and non-poor are now examined in more detail for 1971. We seek to determine the impact, if any, on the observed contrasts in expenditure behaviour of the poor and non-poor, when:

(a) households are ranked by different criteria;
(b) specific as opposed to income equivalence scales are used;
(c) alternative definitions of poverty are adopted.

TABLE 6.4. *Expenditure patterns, 1971, for households ranked by different methods*

	Equivalent total expenditure, using common scales and whole sample[a]	Equivalent gross income		
		Using common scales		Using specific scales[c] and whole sample[a]
		Whole sample[a]	Dual criterion sample[b]	
5th percentile		(percentages)		
Housing	22·0	17·1	18·5	15·8
Fuel, light and power	12·5	12·1	14·4	11·7
Food	38·0	33·5	38·1	34·1
Clothing	2·2	6·9	3·2	7·2
Alcoholic drink	1·5	1·9	2·0	2·4
Tobacco	4·2	3·7	4·7	4·1
Durables	2·2	2·8	2·1	3·0
Other goods and misc.	7·5	7·3	7·5	7·6
Transport and vehicles	2·9	5·1	3·0	4·6
Services	7·0	9·5	6·5	9·4
Total	100·0	100·0	100·0	100·0
10th percentile				
Housing	19·5	17·1	20·2	15·2
Fuel, light and power	11·1	15·5	13·3	15·2
Food	37·8	31·7	36·0	32·7
Clothing	2·2	4·9	4·2	4·9
Alcoholic drink	5·1	2·9	2·0	3·3
Tobacco	3·6	3·3	3·3	4·1
Durables	2·4	5·0	2·9	4·9
Other goods and misc.	6·9	6·0	7·3	6·0
Transport and vehicles	4·8	6·8	3·8	6·7
Services	6·5	6·7	7·0	6·9
Total	100·0	100·0	100·0	100·0
Median				
Housing	13·9	13·3	13·4	12·9
Fuel, light and power	7·2	6·1	6·9	6·4
Food	29·9	27·0	29·6	27·0
Clothing	8·2	8·9	8·4	8·8
Alcoholic drink	4·6	4·3	4·2	5·1
Tobacco	5·0	4·4	5·0	5·2
Durables	4·1	7·1	5.1	6.7
Other goods and misc.	7·7	8·1	8·0	7·9
Transport and vehicles	11·8	12·4	11·9	11·8
Services	7·6	8·4	7·5	8·1
Total	100·0	100·0	100·0	100·0
Total expenditure		(£s per week)		
5th percentile	*10·51*	*14·07[d]*	*11·26*	*14·13[d]*
10th percentile	*12·48*	*15·44[d]*	*12·41*	*15·37[d]*
Median	*22·09*	*23·93*	*22·01*	*23·93*

Source: Appendix table VI.3.

[a] 7143 households, about 99 per cent of the full sample.

[b] 46 per cent of the full sample of households, with a ratio of total expenditure to gross income in the range 0·75 to 1·25.

[c] Equivalence scales calculated separately for each type of expenditure.

[d] In principle these totals should be the same in the two columns; the discrepancies are due to rounding in the estimation of equivalence scales.

Expenditure patterns per equivalent couple for poor and non-poor households in 1971 (estimated with the help of various statistical approximations) are shown in table 6.4. The largest discrepancies come from ranking by total expenditure (as in the first column) rather than by income and, given the variability of expenditure week by week, this is not surprising. In the second column households are ranked by gross income per equivalent couple, using a common set of income equivalence scales for the various items of expenditure. Discrepancies between this column and the figures for 1971 in table 6.2 reflect differences in the numerical methods and approximations employed, and the fact that rather less satisfactory techniques have to be used when deriving patterns from published data (table 6.2) than here from the special tabulations. The third column presents the expenditure patterns of poor and non-poor households when they are ordered on the basis of the 'dual' criterion, whereby only those households with a ratio of total expenditure to gross normal income within the limits of 0·75 to 1·25 are considered; again the ranking is by gross income per equivalent couple. Whilst the expenditure patterns in the first three columns were all derived using the same income equivalence scale for each commodity, the figures in the last column were obtained by converting the individual items of expenditure to an equivalent basis by a series of specific equivalence scales varying between the items.[1]

TABLE 6.5. *Mean deviations between expenditure patterns,[a] 1971 (Percentage points)*

	Historical[b]	Equivalent total expenditure using common scales and whole sample[c]	Equivalent gross income	
			Using common scales and dual criterion sample[c]	Using specific scales and whole sample[c]
For 5th percentile	0·81	2·09	2·11	0·46
For 10th percentile	1·35	3·58	2·29	0·48
For median	0·50	1·10	0·82	0·39

Sources: Tables 6.2 and 6.4.

[a] Deviations from pattern using equivalent gross income, common scales and whole sample.

[b] Pattern shown in table 6.2 for 1971, derived from published tables of the *Family Expenditure Survey Report for 1971* and covering 74 per cent of the full sample of households.

[c] See notes to table 6.4.

The discrepancies between the expenditure patterns yielded by the various methods are summarised in table 6.5, which shows the mean deviations for the relevant percentiles between the pattern in the second column of table 6.4 and the other four methods.[2] In all cases, the various

[1] These scales, together with other details of the various methods used to derive the expenditure patterns presented in table 6.4, are described in appendix VI.

[2] The mean deviation between a given pair of expenditure patterns is measured as the average discrepancy, in percentage points and ignoring signs, between the percentages shown by the two series for each commodity group.

methods disturb the expenditure pattern of the median household significantly less than that of the poor and, among the latter, changes in the pattern for the 10th percentile are larger than for the 5th. The overall differences between the patterns derived from the published data and from the special tabulations are relatively small. The largest differences result from the alternative criteria by which households are ranked – gross income or total expenditure – and from whether the whole sample is considered or only the 46 per cent to which the 'dual criterion' applies. The choice of income or specific equivalence scales has least overall impact on expenditure patterns and on comparisons between different income levels, even though household composition and size vary appreciably between income levels (chart 3.1 above).

Even the wider discrepancies between the columns in table 6.4 are not sufficient to cloud the basic picture of differences between the expenditure behaviour of poor and non-poor groups. True, housing – and necessities in general – seem rather more important, and clothing and transport less important, in poor households ranked by expenditure rather than income. Nevertheless, the same general picture emerges: a relatively large proportion of expenditure by the poor on necessities and comparatively low expenditure on other items.

Table 6.6 shows that for both the 5th and 10th percentiles comparative expenditure by the poor is highest on fuel, light and power. The scales employed (both income and specific) no doubt understate the economies of scale available in the consumption of this item, especially for households with more than one child. For these reasons, equivalent expenditure on fuel, light and power by the median household, which contains more children than 5th and 10th percentile households, will be somewhat larger than indicated.[1] But the difference in fuel expenditure also reflects the high proportion among the poor of retired people, the disabled and mothers with young children, who spend much time at home and require additional heating. Also the housing of the poor tends to have less efficient heating systems, and it is known that expenditure per unit of fuel consumed falls as consumption rises, so that households using one form of fuel for heating, typically the better-off, can heat their homes more efficiently than those using a mixture.

Whilst comparative expenditure of the poor on housing and food is above average, it is appreciably less so than for fuel, light and power. At the other end of the scale, comparative expenditure by the poor is lowest on transport, which in part reflects lower requirements by the aged poor

---

[1] Also, the Family Expenditure Survey makes no allowance for the rebates received when prepaid gas and electricity meters are cleared – in 1971 equal to about 6 per cent of average weekly household expenditure on gas and about 3 per cent on electricity (see *Family Expenditure Survey Report for 1971*, London, HMSO, 1972, p. 3). Expenditure on these fuels is, therefore, overstated and this applies mainly to lower income consumers.

and in part the costs of owning a car in median households. Other categories with low comparative expenditure by the poor are alcoholic drink, durables and clothing. There is a need to reconsider the traditional view that, as a single item at least, clothing should be regarded as a necessity; for most of the population it may also be regarded as an item of affluence.

TABLE 6.6. *Comparative expenditure patterns of the poor, 1971 (Percentages)*

	Equivalent total expenditure, using common scales and whole sample	Equivalent gross income		
		Using common scales		Using specific scales and whole sample
		Whole sample	Dual criterion sample	
5th percentile/median				
Housing	75	77	71	72
Fuel, light and power	82	116	107	108
Food	60	72	66	75
Clothing	13	45	20	49
Alcoholic drink	16	26	24	28
Tobacco	40	49	49	47
Durables	25	23	21	26
Other goods and misc.	47	52	48	57
Transport and vehicles	12	23	13	23
Services	44	66	44	68
Total	48	59	51	59
10th percentile/median				
Housing	79	83	85	79
Fuel, light and power	87	164	109	152
Food	72	76	68	78
Clothing	24	36	28	36
Alcoholic drink	27	43	27	42
Tobacco	53	49	38	51
Durables	33	46	32	49
Other goods and misc.	51	48	51	48
Transport and vehicles	23	35	18	38
Services	48	52	53	54
Total	57	64	56	64

Source: As table 6.4.

Note: See notes to table 6.4.

Comparative expenditure on individual items

To highlight the contrasts between the poor and non-poor, chart 6.1 shows in more detail items on which expenditure by the 5th percentile is over 100 per cent, between 75 and 100 per cent, between 30 and 75 per cent, and less than 30 per cent of expenditure on the same item by the median household.[1] The list of goods which the poor appear to consume

[1] Expenditure on fuel, light and power, and on durables was not available in detail in the tabulations to which we had access. Housing expenditure is considered in detail at a later stage. The ranking of households by gross equivalent income using income (not specific) equivalence scales may sometimes understate actual contrasts in poor–non-poor expenditure levels.

in quantities not much less than – and for certain items even more than – the median household contains one or two surprises. It has, of course, been generally accepted that the poor's consumption of such basic foods as bread, other farinaceous foods, margarine, lard and tea is relatively high. But it also appears that their expenditure on meat, fresh fish, milk, butter, cheese, eggs and fresh vegetables is not far below that of the median household. Comparatively low expenditure by the poor is now more a characteristic of 'convenience' foods (frozen vegetables, etc.).

Expenditure on newspapers, radio and television hardly differs between poor and non-poor; the absolute living levels of the poor are now high enough to enable them to enjoy at least cheaper 'stay-at-home' leisure activities. High expenditure on domestic services is in part explained by the fact that this includes laundries, laundrettes and repairs.

Items on which comparative expenditure by the poor is especially low are, of course, readily understood. The poor spend less than 30 per cent of the median on costly leisure pursuits, such as meals out, private motoring, cinemas, sports and holidays. Expenditure on toys and hobbies is also low, partly because it is non-essential, but also because, like children's clothing, it is inevitably of less importance in poor households where the number of children is small.[1] Low expenditure on private medical services reflects the fact that poor households do not use them. On the other hand, the poor's expenditure on non-national health service drugs is high in absolute as well as comparative terms, possibly reflecting the high proportion of the old among those in poverty.

Relationships between income and expenditure levels

A possibility broached in the introduction to this chapter was that any discrete changes in expenditure behaviour as income changed might prove helpful in drawing a line between the poor and the non-poor. In an attempt to test this possibility table 6.7 shows for households selected by the dual criterion expenditure patterns for the 5th percentile and each succeeding decile.[2] Shares of expenditure devoted to housing, fuel and food all fall with income levels, the last two consistently, the first after an apparent rise up to the 20th percentile. Shares devoted to other goods and to services fluctuate somewhat between income levels, but on the whole rise slightly with income. The share for tobacco is reasonably constant, though there is some indication that it is least at low incomes (no doubt as a result of budgetary constraints) and high incomes (perhaps reflecting greater awareness of health hazards), with a peak of approximately 6 per

---

[1] Because equivalent expenditure in chart 6.1 was not derived from specific scales, this factor has not been allowed for in the resulting comparative expenditure levels.

[2] It was thought that expenditure series for the dual criterion sample would yield stabler income elasticities.

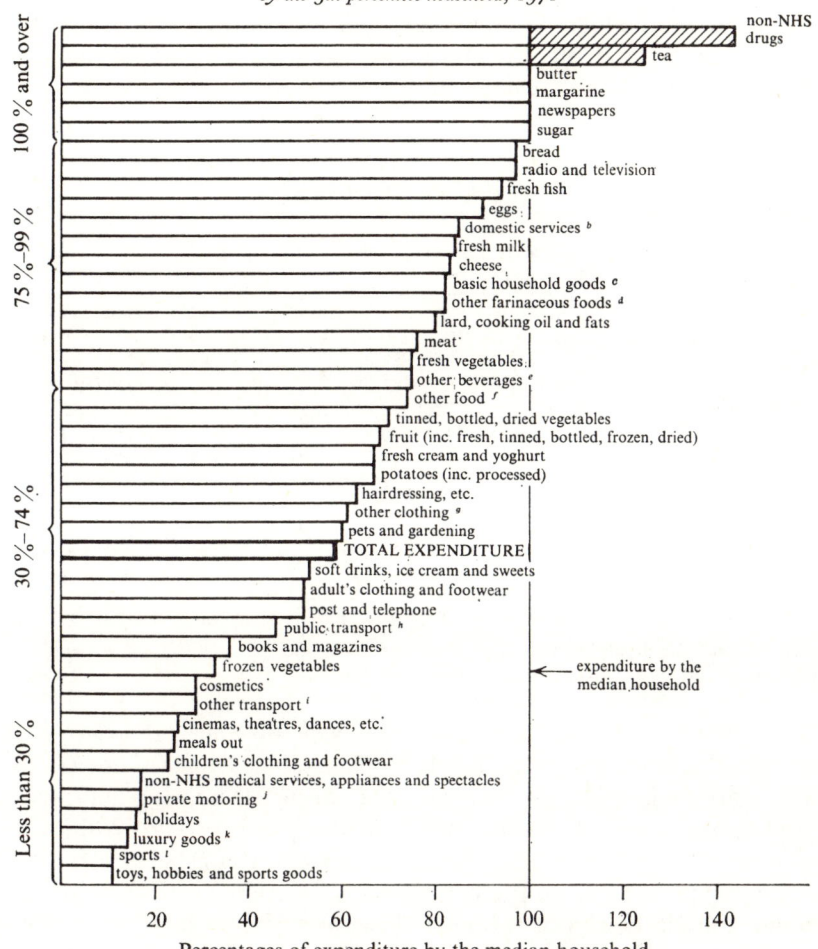

Chart 6.1. *Comparative equivalent expenditure on individual items[a] by the 5th percentile household, 1971*

Percentages of expenditure by the median household

Source: Special tabulations of the 1971 Family Expenditure Survey.

[a] School meals and national health service prescriptions excluded from group where expenditure less than 30 per cent of the median because many 5th percentile households receive these free; also gifts, fees and subscriptions which include especially heterogeneous expenditures.

[b] Baby sitters and nurseries, sweeps, window cleaning, laundries and laundrettes, household repairs.

[c] Basic toilet requisites, hot-water bottles, paper and paper goods, pens, ink and glue, etc., matches, soap, detergents and cleaning materials.

[d] Biscuits, cakes and pastries, breakfast cereals, flour, etc.

[e] Coffee, cocoa and drinking chocolate, other food drinks.

[f] Baby foods, jam, soups, flavourings, chutney, etc., prepared and semi-prepared foods.

[g] Clothing materials, headgear, haberdashery, shoe repairs and other clothing charges.

[h] Rail, tube, bus and coach fares.

[i] Air and sea fares, taxis and car hire.

[j] Purchases of cars and cycles, accessories and spares, AA membership, tax, insurance, petrol, oil, other costs.

[k] Leather and travelling goods, umbrellas, jewellery and watches, decorative fancy goods, smokers' requisites.

[l] Participant and spectator sports, subscriptions to clubs.

cent in the middle income range. Expenditure shares on the other items –
clothing, alcoholic drink, durables and transport – display a tendency to
rise with income though, except in the case of transport, the increase is not
uninterrupted.

TABLE 6.7.   *Equivalent expenditure patterns, 1971, for households selected by*
the dual criterion[a] (Percentages)

	Percentiles:									
	5th	10th	20th	30th	40th	50th	60th	70th	80th	90th
Housing	18·5	20·2	22·2	17·3	13·7	13·4	12·4	11·9	11·8	11·2
Fuel, light and power	14·4	13·3	10·7	9·2	7·5	6·9	6·3	5·7	5·5	5·2
Food	38·1	36·0	33·8	32·4	31·4	29·6	27·5	25·4	22·4	20·4
Clothing	3·2	4·2	5·2	6·8	8·4	8·4	9·7	11·2	10·9	10·9
Alcoholic drink	2·0	2·0	2·3	3·2	3·7	4·2	4·7	5·2	5·4	4·7
Tobacco	4·7	3·3	4·6	5·4	5·8	5·0	4·9	4·6	4·1	3·5
Durables	2·1	2·9	2·4	4·3	4·6	5·1	5·5	5·9	7·7	7·4
Other goods and misc.	7·5	7·3	6·9	7·6	7·7	8·0	8·2	8·0	7·9	8·4
Transport and vehicles	3·0	3·8	5·0	7·1	10·2	11·9	13·3	14·6	16·4	18·0
Services	6·5	7·0	6·9	6·7	7·0	7·5	7·5	7·5	7·9	10·3
Total	100·0	100·0	100·0	100·0	100·0	100·0	100·0	100·0	100·0	100·0
Total expenditure ($£$)	*11·26*	*12·41*	*14·73*	*17·13*	*19·58*	*22·01*	*24·74*	*28·21*	*33·48*	*40·41*

Source: Special tabulations of the 1971 Family Expenditure Survey.

[a] Based on households ranked by equivalent gross income where total expenditure lies
between 0·75 and 1·25 of gross normal income.

This picture is confirmed by income elasticities derived from constant
elasticity Engel curves.[1] The resulting elasticities, from the lowest to the
highest, are fuel, light and power 0·23; food 0·52;[2] housing 0·57; tobacco
0·73; other goods 1·10; services 1·30; alcoholic drink 1·73; clothing 1·77;
durables 1·82; transport 2·23. Thus, when as here constant elasticities are
assumed, expenditures on the first three items are inelastic with respect to
income, the elasticities of the next three are not too far from unity and
for the last four items appreciably greater than unity. Ranking the items
on the basis of these elasticities accords well with the comparative expenditure patterns of the poor observed earlier; relative to median households
the poor devote most expenditure to those items where demand is inelastic – fuel, food and housing – and least to items where demand is
elastic – alcoholic drink, clothing, durables and transport.

---

[1] These curves were of the log-linear form:

$$\log_e E_i/S = a + b \log_e Y/S$$

where E_i = expenditure on item i,
          Y = total expenditure
and S = household's equivalence scale.
The curves were fitted to data for the dual criterion sample using weighted least squares with the
group frequencies as weights.

[2] The income elasticity for food exluding meals out is 0·36, the elasticity for meals out being
2·00. All the elasticities are significant at the 1 per cent level.

However, despite the fairly consistent picture which emerges of changes in expenditure patterns over the income range, it does not appear from table 6.7 that any line can be drawn between percentiles on the basis of a significant and comparatively abrupt change in consumption patterns. Somewhat more involved analyses were no more successful in unearthing such a boundary between poor and non-poor expenditure patterns. Income elasticities were calculated for each item at successive percentiles – the proportionate change in expenditure on a given item being expressed as a ratio of the proportionate change in total expenditure. These did not reveal a systematic pattern but suggested a rather unstable relationship between income and expenditure elasticity on particular goods or services.[1] In any event the results failed to support the attempt to delimit poverty on the basis of a sharp break in expenditure behaviour.

We have seen earlier (page 36) that a different group of households is classified as poor depending on whether they are selected by the level of their income or of their total expenditure. Could it be that the pattern of expenditure of these two groups of households provides a clue as to which criterion is more appropriate in identifying those in poverty?

TABLE 6.8. *Equivalent expenditure, 1971, by the poor and non-poor on various criteria (£s per week)*

	Dual criterion[a]	High income, low expenditure[b]	Low income, high expenditure[c]	High income, high expenditure[d]
Housing	3·32	2·75	3·98	3·67
Fuel, light and power	1·39	1·18	2·03	1·65
Food	3·66	3·91	5·71	6·91
Clothing	0·23	0·20	1·44	2·52
Alcoholic drink	0·10	0·15	0·48	1·31
Tobacco	0·35	0·39	0·61	1·14
Durables	0·14	0·20	1·29	1·88
Other goods and misc.	0·63	0·73	1·47	2·17
Transport and vehicles	0·20	0·38	1·34	3·90
Services	0·69	0·75	2·14	2·73
Total	10·71	10·64	20·49	27·88
Gross normal income	11·68	17·49	11·85	35·01
Percentage of households[e]	*3·9*	*4·6*	*5·5*	*85·9*

Source: As table 6.7.

a Both net normal income and total expenditure below supplementary benefit scales.

b Net normal income above, but total expenditure below, supplementary benefit scales.

c Net normal income below, but total expenditure above, supplementary benefit scales.

d Both net normal income and total expenditure above supplementary benefit scales.

e These percentages differ from those in table 4.3 because the average of supplementary benefit scales operating during 1971 was taken here as the poverty line, not the scale actually in force on the date each household was interviewed.

[1] This does not necessarily imply that such instability was statistically significant, it may simply have reflected the variability of behaviour among households and the limited size of the sample available.

Table 6.8 attempts to cast some light on this. The poverty line taken is the official supplementary benefit scale, and households are divided into four groups:

(a) those with both normal income and total expenditure below the poverty line;

(b) those with normal income above the poverty line, but total expenditure below it;

(c) those with normal income below the poverty line, but total expenditure above it;

(d) those with both normal income and expenditure above the poverty line.

For each group of households the table shows the distribution of expenditure over the usual ten broad commodity groups. If a household with a normally low income shows relatively high total expenditure in the weeks of the Survey, this could indicate the purchase of some durable and infrequently purchased item, such as a refrigerator or an overcoat, but then 'staple' expenditure on rent or food would be at its 'normal' level corresponding to that household's normal income. On the other hand, if total expenditure is low in relation to normal income, it might be that postponable expenditure, such as on the durables just mentioned, was particularly low, but expenditure on many food items might also be low in today's conditions, when tinned and preserved foods are widely available, often at lower prices than fresh food. Neither of these possibilities is really confirmed by the data. On examining the expenditure patterns of the anomalous groups, it is seen that group (b) has an expenditure pattern very close to that of group (a); although group (b) has a recorded gross income 50 per cent above that of group (a), this seems to have had a negligible effect on its expenditure pattern. Group (c)'s gross normal income is much the same as that of group (a), but it has somehow managed to spend twice as much on average. The excess expenditure is by no means confined to durable items; on the contrary, 'staple' expenditure on rent and fuel is higher even than for the average household in group (d). Food expenditure by group (c) is rather closer to that of group (d), which has triple its gross income, than to that of group (a).

From the practical point of view of classifying individual households, we are interested in information that is representative of normal circumstances as well as being reliable. There is little doubt that correct information on incomes is more valuable than information on expenditure, since the latter must vary substantially from week to week, which makes it difficult to assess a household's standard of living from expenditure data alone.

SECONDARY POVERTY IN 1971

So far we have been concerned with differences between expenditure patterns of poor and non-poor households, where poverty is defined in terms of income or total expenditure. But an apparently adequate income does not necessarily mean that all basic needs are satisfied. Households with incomes above the poverty line may still be short of some necessities, and within non-poor households some individuals may consume less than they need. In chapter 4 it was shown that the proportion in poverty is much greater when based on the smaller inner family unit than on the household, but the Family Expenditure Survey does not analyse expenditure within a household or family. We can, however, examine the consumption of necessities in non-poor households to see whether this reveals any secondary poverty, where family income should be sufficient to provide for basic necessities, but does not do so because too large a share is absorbed by other expenditure.

Traditionally four items of expenditure have been regarded as necessities – food, housing, fuel (including light and power) and clothing – but only food seems worth considering here. Housing expenditure is too variable, an analysis of expenditure on fuel would give perverse results, and today clothing includes items that are not basic necessities. Food is the most important item in the budget of the poorest families and, because of its regular purchase, expenditure is probably a better guide to actual consumption than it is for most other commodities. It is a basic necessity, with an income elasticity significantly less than unity (an estimate of 0·52 was given on page 82 above).

TABLE 6.9. *Secondary poverty in 1971 (No. of households)*

Gross normal income per week[a]	Equivalent expenditure on food per week					All households
	Up to £2·99	£3·00– £3·49	£3·50– £3·89	£3·90– £4·39	£4·40+	
Up to £9·99	14	11	13	16	65	119
£10–£11·99	50	41	39	62	160	352
£12–£13·99	60[b]	55[b]	49	77	223	464
£14–£15·99	51[b]	31[b]	35	62	284	463
£16–£17·99	25[b]	18[b]	27	36	241	347
£18+	180[b]	145[b]	186	379	4508	5398
All households	380	301	349	632	5481	7143

Source: As table 6.7.

[a] Per equivalent couple.
[b] Households possibly in secondary poverty (see text).

The question is how many households there are that spend very little on food. Table 6.9 cross-classifies households by income per equivalent couple and by food expenditure per equivalent couple. Taking £3·50 a week as a minimum expenditure on food (corresponding to that of the 5th percentile ranked by total expenditure), there are 681 households, 9½ per cent of the total, which spend less than the minimum, but 565 of those households, 8 per cent of the total, have an income of over £12 per equivalent couple, approximately the supplementary benefit level. However, most of these households also tend to be low spenders in total. This may be due to bad record keeping, a period of holiday or illness, or irregular shopping habits. But there are some households with comparatively high income but low food expenditure which also have comparatively high total expenditure.

A more detailed examination of expenditure by each income-group of households with low expenditure on food reveals a broad common pattern. There is a tendency for the shares of expenditure on clothing and other goods, and to a lesser extent on transport and services also, to be below the average for the income-group, while shares of expenditure on housing and on fuel, light and power – especially the former – tend to be higher. It is possible that low food expenditure is to some extent attributable to high expenditure on other necessities, but it is also partly due to total expenditure being less (for whatever reason – perhaps sickness) than that of their income-group as a whole.

The evidence available is rather different from that which led to Rowntree's finding that 28 per cent of the working class in York in 1899 was in secondary poverty. But those calculations were thought to be too rough to give reliable results and the exercise was not repeated in his later surveys.[1] It is conceivable that on our definition – of a diet probably below the recommended intake – some secondary poverty does still exist, but we have no evidence that it is a major problem.

HOUSING OF THE POOR

There are several reasons why housing costs might have implications for poverty. First, after food housing costs are one of the largest items in the budgets of poor and non-poor households alike. Secondly, while the occupation of cheap accommodation is often a direct result of low income, the housing conditions of the poor may also be an important cause of poverty in the longer term. This has been discussed at length by other authors[2] and we concentrate here on the shorter-term effects of poverty on housing expenditure.

The relation between income and expenditure in the case of housing is more complex than for most goods and services. This is due to the existence

[1] B. S. Rowntree, *Poverty*, p. 86, and *Poverty and Progress: a second social survey of York*, Longmans Green, 1941, p. 461.

[2] See, for example, A. L. Schorr, 'Housing policy and poverty', in Townsend (ed.), *The Concept of Poverty*.

of separate forms of tenure operating under distinct sets of regulations, and to the fact that the cost of housing is subsidised in a number of largely uncoordinated ways. Housing choices and mobility are restricted by regulation as well as by income, and for most families rent or mortgage payments are an inflexible element in their budget; that is, families may find it difficult to adjust their housing expenditure as quickly as other forms of expenditure.

There are wide variations in the size and quality of accommodation obtained for a given amount spent on housing. Among tenants, for instance, costs vary between the public and the private sector, between furnished and unfurnished accommodation, and according to a range of regional, legal and historical factors; net housing costs also depend on whether a tenant is receiving a rebate or allowance. In the owner-occupied sector mortgage payments reflect the date of purchase, interest rates and (variable) tax relief as much as the 'quality' of the accommodation.[1] These relationships are rendered even more complex by inflation, which affects the various sectors in different ways and leads to high variability of housing expenditure within a given income-group.

Housing tenure

Over the past twenty years the structure of housing tenure has changed considerably. By 1971, 47 per cent of all households lived in an owner-occupied dwelling, 31 per cent rented from local authorities and only 19 per cent were in privately rented accommodation. But among those in poverty, only just over a quarter were owner-occupiers, 45 per cent rented from local authorities and 28 per cent were in privately rented accommodation (table 6.10).

TABLE 6.10. *Distribution by tenure group of all households and poor households, 1971 (Percentages)*

	All households	Risk of poverty[a]	Accountability for poverty[b] among:	
			Households	Individuals
Local authority rented	31	10	45	48
Other unfurnished rented	15	10	23	20
Furnished rented	4	10	5	5
Rent free	3	5	2	2
Owned with mortgage	27	1	4	7
Owned outright	20	8	22	18
All groups	100	7	100	100

Source: As table 6.7.

[a] Proportions of households in each tenure group where net normal income below supplementary benefit level.

[b] Poor households or individuals in each tenure group as a proportion of all households or individuals in poverty.

[1] Moreover, unlike rents, mortgage repayments contain an element of saving.

In rented accommodation, whether local authority or private and whether furnished or not, the chances of a household being in poverty are somewhat greater than average (10 as compared with 7 per cent). Those occupying rent-free accommodation or owning it outright had a risk of poverty close to the average; nonetheless, such has been the growth of home-ownership, that as many as a fifth of the poor owned their own homes outright in 1971. Poverty is least frequent among those in the process of buying their homes (the category 'owned with mortgage'),[1] no doubt because mortgage loans are only granted to those with sufficient income to finance the repayments. Only 1 per cent of households in this sector are classified as poor and, although it includes 27 per cent of the population, it contains only 4 per cent of households that are poor and 7 per cent of poor individuals.

TABLE 6.11.   *Characteristics of tenure groups, 1971*

	Persons per household (averages)	Median gross household income		Equivalent income[a] of lowest decile	
		Unadjusted	Equivalent[a]	Actual	Propn of median
		(£)	(£)	(£)	(%)
Local authority rented	3·05	30·66	23·30	12·40	53·2
Other unfurnished rented	2·44	25·95	23·10	11·40	49·4
Furnished rented	2·13	31·11	33·60	14·00	41·7
Rent free	2·78	27·50	24·00	11·70	48·7
Owned with mortgage	3·39	46·47	35·60	21·30	59·8
Owned outright	2·78	28·51	27·45	13·10	47·7
All groups	2·85	35·89	27·85	13·10	47·0

Source: As table 6.7.

[a] Per equivalent couple.

In the main these results reflect the pattern of average incomes in the different tenure groups. The median value of household income is significantly lower (about £30) in rented accommodation than in the 'owned with mortgage' sector where it was over £45 (table 6.11). But dispersion of income about these averages also influences the risk and extent of poverty within each category. Table 6.11 shows that in this respect the risk and extent of poverty in the 'owned with mortgage' sector is reduced not only by a high average income but also by a comparatively high income for the lowest decile in the group.

Housing expenditure[2]

Housing expenditure is narrowly dispersed between income levels. Of the

---

[1] The method of calculating the total housing costs of this category is explained in appendix IV.
[2] The Family Expenditure Survey definition of housing expenditure in the published tables used throughout this study is far from ideal for comparing housing expenditure and income. For

ten expenditure categories, housing is among the least variable over the income range (table 6.7), but variability within income-groups is much greater. Table 6.12 shows the dispersion of 'net rent' paid by individuals receiving supplementary benefits. This is the sum taken into account in the practice of adding 'reasonable' actual housing costs to the other basic entitlements when calculating supplementary benefits.

TABLE 6.12.   'Net rent'[a] paid by individuals receiving supplementary benefits, November 1971

	No. of individuals	Average 'net rent'	Proportion of mean paid by:	
			10th percentile	90th percentile
	(000s)	(£s per week)	(%)	(%)
Public tenants	1308	3·03	60·4	144·6
Private tenants	746	2·25	34·2	192·9
Owner-occupiers	417	1·38	38·4	179·0

Source: Department of Health and Social Security, *Annual Report for the Year 1971*, Cmnd 5019, London, HMSO, 1972, tables 118–20.

[a] Includes rent, rates and mortgage interest.

However, we have already noted that variations in housing expenditure will not accurately reflect differences in the actual consumption of housing; it is therefore interesting to examine rateable values as a possible alternative measure of housing consumed. Rateable values, although they have often been used in studies of this kind, are not ideal, as they cannot be entirely consistently assessed, but they are universally available and constitute the sole alternative quantitative guide to housing consumption.[1] For owner-occupiers the Family Expenditure Survey imputes a notional rental value which forms part of the recorded housing expenditure; consequently, rateable values are not wholly an independent measure, especially higher up the income scale, where the majority of owners and mortgagors are found.

With these qualifications in mind, the values in table 6.13 suggest that on average the poorest 5th and 10th percentiles receive lower rateable values per pound of housing expenditure than the median household. While these results are by no means precise, they suggest a number of alternative possibilities: that the poor may be getting less real housing value for money than the median household; that poorer households live in older properties in which maintenance and repairs form a larger proportion of total housing costs, so that net rateable values are lowered to

tenants housing expenditure approximates to actual outgoings, whilst for owners it is partly a notional amount. For rent-free households and owner-occupiers an 'imputed rent' is considered to reflect more closely a household's current consumption of housing than mortgage payments, which are highly variable and include an element of saving.

[1] For a discussion of the use of rateable values in this manner, see D. Nevitt and P. Roberti, 'In search of determinants of rents and gross values', *Policy and Politics*, vol. 2, March 1974.

allow for this; or that, in terms of rateable values, the accommodation of the poor is under-valued relative to that of better-off families. The discrepancy shows itself essentially in local authority housing; in other unfurnished rented accommodation there appears to be little difference in this respect between poor and median households. This perhaps provides most support for the third explanation advanced above. The relation between market values and rateable values, and between gross values and deductions for costs of repair and maintenance, have been the subject of a number of inquiries.[1] Recently the Layfield Committee noted that the scale of deductions for repairs and maintenance 'has been used to some extent as a device for increasing the advantage enjoyed by lower assessed properties'.[2] This seems to support the view that the information in table 6.13 does not by itself mean that the poor get less real value than the non-poor for their housing expenditure.

TABLE 6.13.   *Housing expenditure and rateable values, 1971 (£s)*

| | Percentiles[a] | | | |
	5th	10th	50th	90th
All sectors				
Housing expenditure (per week)	2·09	2·50	2·94	4·52
Rateable value (per annum)	74·30	86·30	119·50	164·00
Rateable value per £ of weekly housing expenditure	35·60	34·50	40·60	36·30
Local authority rented				
Housing expenditure (per week)	2·51	2·75	2·62	3·35
Rateable value (per annum)	87·50	90·00	118·60	124·20
Rateable value per £ of weekly housing expenditure	34·90	32·70	45·30	37·10
Other unfurnished rented				
Housing expenditure (per week)	1·91	1·95	2·55	4·09
Rateable value (per annum)	66·10	71·80	91·60	117·50
Rateable value per £ of weekly housing expenditure	34·60	36·80	35·90	28·70

Source: Based on special tabulations of 1971 Family Expenditure Survey.

a Households in the dual criterion sample (see note to table 6.7) ranked by equivalent gross income.

CONCLUSIONS

Consideration of a variety of aspects of expenditure by poor households tends to confirm the conclusion derived from the income data in chapter

[1] J. Revell, *The Wealth of the Nation*, Cambridge University Press, 1967, pp. 298–330. F. G. Forsyth and A. Stuart, 'The determination of rates and their impact on households', appendix 3 to Ministry of Housing and Local Government, *Committee of Inquiry into the Impact of Rates on Households* [Allen Report], Cmnd 2582, London, HMSO, 1965.
[2] Department of the Environment, *Local Government Finance. Report of the Committee of Enquiry*, Cmnd 6453, London, HMSO, 1976, p. 197.

3 that there has been a great *absolute* improvement in their standards of consumption; roughly speaking, a household at the 10th percentile of the distribution in 1973 was enjoying the same standard as a median household in 1953/4. But the *relative* position of the poor has changed little over the past twenty years, and the share of necessities in total expenditure has declined faster for median households than for the poor. There have been some alterations in expenditure patterns, due partly to changes in relative prices (or relative efficiency as in the case of heating), but also to some extent to changes in tastes. In particular, poorer households now seem to spend a relatively larger share of the total on housing and the related expenditure on fuel, light and power than the median household of twenty years ago, but a rather smaller proportion on clothing. The more detailed analysis for 1971, using a number of alternative measures of expenditure, concluded on a note of caution about using expenditure to measure and identify poverty. But the analysis left open the possibility that there may be families not classified as poor on the basis of the supplementary benefit standard who nevertheless are not satisfying basic needs. Whatever the reasons for this, it may qualify to some extent the picture of a substantial fall in the number of poor households over the past twenty years.

As one would expect, the risk of poverty is higher among households in rented accommodation, both local authority and private, than in housing owned with a mortgage, but there is an above-average risk among those occupying accommodation which is owned outright; they are mainly the retired. There is too much variation in housing expenditure for us to draw any conclusions about its significance as either a cause or a consequence of poverty. Nor can we infer from rateable values that poor households get less value for money for their housing expenditure, because of the possibility that the housing of the poor is less onerously assessed.

CHAPTER 7

FAMILY COMPOSITION, EXPENDITURE PATTERNS AND EQUIVALENCE SCALES FOR CHILDREN

INTRODUCTION

Any discussion of the adequacy of family incomes and any attempt to count the numbers in poverty involve some comparison of standards of living between families of different size and composition. There is therefore a need for some equivalence scale to put on a par the incomes needed by families of different composition to attain a given standard of living and to show how much additional income a given family requires to 'compensate', in some sense, for the additional expense of an extra member. For some comparisons made in this study numbers in poverty have been estimated on the basis of the equivalence scales implied in the official supplementary benefit allowances. But the kind of 'behaviouristic' scales derived in this chapter on the basis of observed consumers' expenditure patterns have also been used in this and other studies of poverty.

The determination of such behaviouristic scales has other applications. Many important policy measures are geared to variations in needs as determined by differences in family size and composition, and there is much reason and advantage in basing estimates of those variations on a detailed analysis of observed expenditure behaviour. Thus, in the context of measuring poverty, it is instructive to compare the official supplementary benefit scales with such 'observed' scales, and similar comparisons are relevant to the size of personal income tax allowances.

There is also a need for equivalence scales when measuring the relation between household income and household expenditure on particular commodities – that is in the formulation of Engel curves. Engel curves seek to display the net relation between income and expenditure on a specific commodity, and in estimating this relation it is desirable to eliminate the effects of variations in household size and composition, which would otherwise cloud the picture. For instance, it would be possible – but quite wrong – to deduce that a higher income led to lower food consumption from comparing a sample of large families having relatively low incomes, but spending heavily on food because of the needs of their large families, with a sample of small families with relatively high incomes, but spending little on food because they had few children. One way of eliminating the effect of family size and composition is to estimate the Engel curve for

This chapter has been prepared by N. C. Garganas.

samples of families of given composition (say two adults and two children) but of varying incomes. The disadvantage of this method in practice is that the numbers of households of particular types are too few in most sample studies of expenditure patterns to establish the Engel curve with an adequate degree of certainty. In these circumstances it is usually desirable to analyse the full sample of households, whilst making some allowance for differences in family composition; equivalence scales can be used to allow for such differences by comparing expenditure per equivalent adult on a specific commodity with household income per equivalent adult. When standardising a family's expenditure on to an equivalent basis, each item of expenditure may require a different equivalence scale, since the relative needs and preferences of adults and children vary from one item to another. One can also conceive of a general income equivalence scale which reflects the combined, or average, effect of such specific equivalence scales.

The aim of this chapter is to provide some new estimates of both specific and income scales on the basis of observed consumer behaviour, and more particularly to investigate how such scales vary with income levels.

THE METHOD ADOPTED

The method of analysis draws upon and extends previous work in this field, and in particular seeks to overcome certain difficulties encountered in earlier attempts to measure equivalence scales. A review of these earlier methods is presented in appendix VII.

Although there has been a certain amount of progress as a result of sporadic attempts over the past 50 years to estimate equivalence scales, no entirely satisfactory method has yet emerged. Among the problems that have caused difficulty is the question whether or not, as a matter of principle, income and specific equivalence scales can be simultaneously estimated from family budget data. Forsyth suggested that this was not possible unless restrictive assumptions were attached *a priori* to the values of the specific scales for one of the commodities.[1] A possible method which circumvents this problem in principle is explained in appendix VII, but it seems to require larger samples than are usually available. In practice some restrictions on certain coefficients appear to be necessary. For example, one may assume (as explained below) that the consumption of adult clothing or tobacco is unaffected by any specific requirements of children, so that the number of children affects the household's expenditure on these commodities only via a general income effect.

The approach adopted in early studies by Nicholson and Henderson provides a convenient point of departure for an exposition of the method

[1] F. G. Forsyth, 'The relationship between family size and family expenditure', *Journal of the Royal Statistical Society* (series A), vol. 123, part 4, 1960.

used here.[1] Both these authors sought to estimate directly the income equivalence scale of a particular type of individual, say a child, by considering as an indicator of the family living standards a 'standard' commodity (or group of commodities) which does not feature in children's consumption, such as adult clothing. This approach assumes that a given level of expenditure on adult clothing by the average two-adult family having no children will be attained by a family with children only at a rather higher income level, and that the proportionate excess income required can be regarded as a measure of the 'cost' of those children. In turn, this provides the basis of an income equivalence scale.

Nicholson and Henderson were concerned exclusively with the 'cost of children', that is with estimating income equivalence scales for children. We have attempted to extend the analysis to yield estimates of both income and specific scales by developing an approach used by Prais and Houthakker.[2] The estimation procedure consists of two basic steps: first, the income equivalence scales of children are isolated and measured along the lines explained above; then, those income equivalence scales are employed to standardise the incomes of different types of family on to the basis of an adult couple family and estimates of children's specific equivalence scales for particular commodities are obtained from comparisons of standardised Engel curves.

Estimating income equivalence scales

For clarity a diagrammatic exposition of the derivation of income scales precedes a more detailed illustration based on actual observations (a procedure also followed in the case of specific scales). Chart 7.1 shows the Engel curves of a 'standard commodity' for two types of family: one comprising a man and a woman – taken as the standard of reference (that is, its income scale is definitionally set equal to unity) – and the other having one child. The standard commodity is one theoretically consumed exclusively by adults, such as alcoholic drink, tobacco, or adult clothing. For such commodities the Engel curve for couples with a child usually lies below that for childless couples, as shown in the chart. In other words, at any given level of household income the average childless couple spends more on, say, alcoholic drink than a couple with a child, since the lower requirements of the childless family mean they have more income to spare

[1] J. L. Nicholson, 'Variations in working class family expenditure', *Journal of the Royal Statistical Society* (series A), vol. 112, part 4, 1949, p. 359; A. M. Henderson, 'The cost of a family', *Review of Economic Studies*, vol. 17, April 1950, p. 127 and 'The cost of children', *Population Studies* vol. 3, September 1949, p. 130 and vol. 4, December 1950, p. 267. These studies were in turn based on a suggestion by E. Rothbarth ('Note on a method of determining equivalent income for families of different composition', appendix IV to C. Madge, *War-time Pattern of Saving and Spending*, Cambridge University Press, 1943.)

[2] S. J. Prais and H. S. Houthakker, *The Analysis of Family Budgets*, Cambridge University Press, 1955 (2nd edn, 1971).

for such items. To determine the income equivalence scale for the first child, a particular income level, say Y_0, is chosen for the childless couple, and from the relevant Engel curve the corresponding value of expenditure on the standard commodity is determined – E_0 in chart 7.1. It is then possible to find from the Engel curve of the couple with a child the level of income, Y_1, at which household expenditure by such a family on the standard commodity is equal to E_0. The proportionate difference in income levels, $(Y_1-Y_0)/Y_0$, provides an estimate of the income equivalence scale for a first child at the income level Y_0 of the standard family.

Chart 7.1. *Derivation of income equivalence scales*

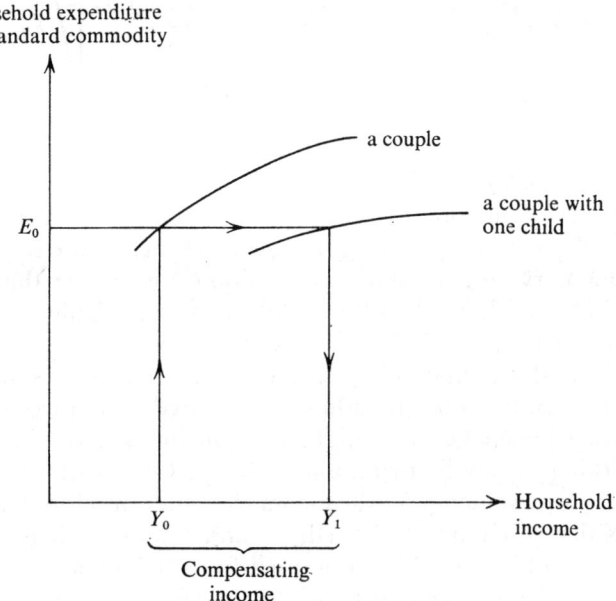

Earlier investigations of the shape of the Engel curve suggest that, where the range of incomes is limited, there may often be little to choose between alternative formulations. Nevertheless, estimates employing semi-logarithmic, double logarithmic and linear functions were fitted to the data to determine whether the choice of functional form has any substantial effect on the estimated equivalence scales. Using the semi-logarithmic form as an example and letting subscripts denote family size, the equations for the two family types depicted in chart 7.1 are:

$$E = a_0 + b_0 \log Y \qquad (1)$$

$$E = a_1 + b_1 \log Y \qquad (2)$$

where a_0, b_0, a_1 and b_1 are constants to be estimated from the observations. For any given value of household income, Y_0, the corresponding expenditure on the standard commodity by childless couples is now given by $E_0 = a_0 + b_0 \log Y_0$, and the income Y_1 at which a couple with one child can afford the same expenditure on the standard commodity is found from (2) to be

$$\log Y_1 = \frac{(E_0 - a_1)}{b_1} = \frac{(a_0 - a_1 + b_0 \log Y_0)}{b_1} \tag{3}$$

After some manipulation, the child's income equivalence scale (in terms of an equivalent two-adult household) may be expressed as:

$$c_0 = \frac{Y_1 - Y_0}{Y_0} = \left[\exp \frac{a_0 - a_1 + b_0 \log Y_0}{b_1} \right] \Bigg/ Y_0 - 1$$

$$= \left[\exp \frac{a_0 - a_1}{b_1} \right] Y_0^k - 1 \tag{4}$$

where $k = b_0/b_1 - 1$.

It can be seen from equation (4) that, in general, the income equivalence scale will vary with the specified income level, Y_0.[1] If the slope of the semi-logarithmic curve for the standard family, b_0, is greater than that for the couple with a child, b_1, then the child's income equivalence scale will rise with increases in Y_0; it will fall if b_0 is smaller than b_1.

It will be understood that in practice the choice of a standard commodity – an item consumed only by adults – is limited. The three obvious possibilities, used by Nicholson and Henderson in their original studies, are adult clothing, alcoholic drink and tobacco. Others that have been used at times are 'excess income' – the income left after provision for expenditure on necessities (used by Rothbarth) – and family savings. All these are open to some objection. Data obtained from budget surveys for expenditure on drink and tobacco substantially underestimate actual consumption as revealed by excise returns and those for household savings are erratic. Expenditure on adult clothing is rather more reliable, except for the fact that it is not incurred very frequently, so that a family budget inquiry covering a short period only is bound to show substantial variations amongst families in expenditure on this item. An even more important reservation is that the nature of expenditure on adult clothing may be different for parents and for childless couples. For example, the arrival of a child may oblige parents to stay at home more and if, as a result, they

[1] It should be emphasised that the equations are fitted only as a means of providing interpolated values of expenditure levels in the regions of the incomes Y_0 and Y_1; if these incomes are not too far from the sample means it will make little difference to the final answer which form of curve is chosen. The expression corresponding to (4) will usually differ according to the form chosen, though for the double logarithmic form the outcome is the same as (4).

decide to spend less on clothes and more on, say, furniture, then a measure based on their expenditure on adult clothing will understate their economic well-being. These reservations can only be recorded as matters that require further attention, but they are perhaps in the nature of refinements that can properly be left aside in the present state of knowledge.

In the event the sum of expenditure on three items – adult clothing, drink and tobacco – was adopted as the standard commodity for our principal estimates. In addition, however, scales were estimated using expenditure on adult clothing only, and also combined expenditure on adult clothing and alcoholic drink. This helped to identify the data which yield the most consistent and acceptable results, and to determine whether or not the choice of standard commodity has a significant effect.

TABLE 7.1. *Engel functions[a] for children's income equivalence scales*

	Regression coefficients[b]	
	a	b
Couple without children	-3434	487
Couple with one child	-2483	358
Couple with two children	-2714	383

Source: NIESR estimates.

[a] Functions in semi-logarithmic form for expenditure on the combined standard commodity – adult clothing, alcoholic drink and tobacco.
[b] Based on variables expressed in pence per week and natural logarithms.

The results of applying the above procedure, taking expenditure on adult clothing, drink and tobacco combined as the standard commodity, and using the semi-logarithmic form of the Engel curve, are set out in table 7.1. If Y_0 is chosen as 3000 pence (approximately the average total weekly expenditure for childless couples in 1971), the income equivalence scale for the first child as given by (4) is:

$$c_{01} = \left[\exp \frac{-3434 + 2483}{358} \right] 3000^{(487/358 - 1)} - 1$$
$$= 1.25 - 1 = 0.25$$

The income equivalence scale for two children is obtained in the same way, and emerges as $c_{02} = 1.35 - 1 = 0.35$. These results imply that, in terms of total income requirements, one child is equivalent to 0.25 of an adult couple (or half an adult), and two children to 0.35 of an adult couple (or say three-quarters of an adult). It would appear that for couples with two children the income scale per child, 0·175 (half 0·35) is less than for couples with one child, 0.25. This appears to reflect such factors as the younger age of the second child and economies of scale in consumption.

Estimating specific equivalence scales

The income scales derived above were next used to convert the income of each family on to a common basis, in this case per equivalent couple. The Engel curves for various types of family can then be presented to show the relation between households' expenditure on a specific commodity and income per equivalent couple. Once household incomes were standardised in this manner, we chose a particular level of income per equivalent couple, Y_0, and measured the difference at that income level between consumption of the commodity in question by couples with one child, E_1, and consumption by couples without children, E_0. The proportional difference in consumption $(E_1-E_0)/E_0$ is then a measure of the child's specific equivalence scale for this item. As noted above income scales may vary with income levels and it would be desirable to take account of this in any further work. At this stage, however, we used the scales estimated at the level of average income for the sample.

The procedure for standardising the Engel curves and determining the

Chart 7.2. *Effect of standardising household incomes on Engel curves for a necessity*

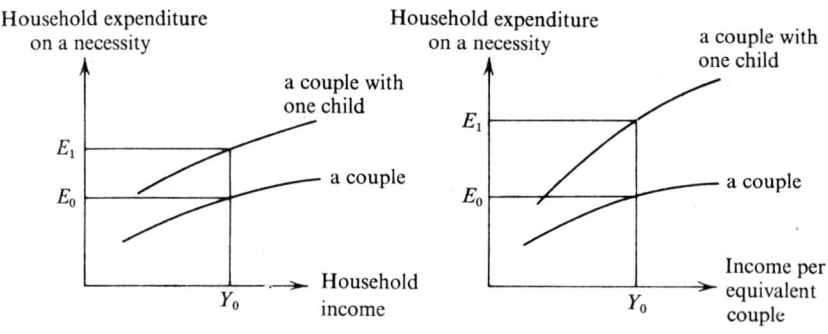

Chart 7.3. *Effect of standardising household incomes on Engel curves for a luxury*

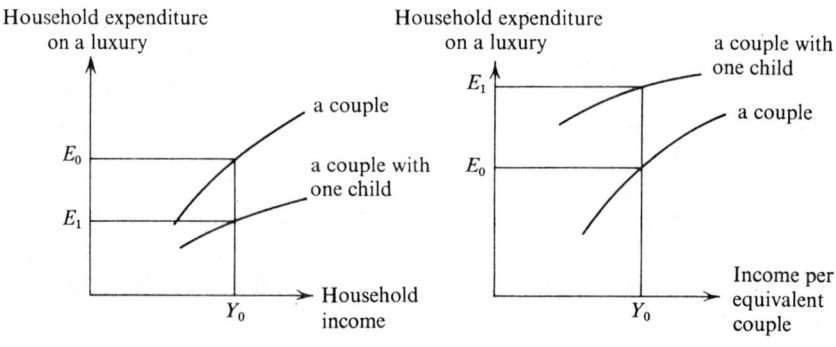

specific equivalence scales is illustrated diagrammatically in charts 7.2 and 7.3. The effect of standardising household income using the calculated income equivalence scales is to shift the Engel curve for larger families to the left, leaving that for couples unchanged. In the case of necessities (chart 7.2), where expenditure of the larger family is greater than that of the smaller family at given household income levels, the effect of standardising is to enlarge this excess, so that the specific equivalence scales for necessities will almost invariably be positive. At a given household income the observed difference between consumption of a necessity by a childless household and by one with a child derives from a positive additional specific requirement for the item by the child, which is partially offset by the mild negative income effect that the child has on the family's general living standard.

In the case of luxuries, the Engel curve for a couple with one child tends to be below that for a childless couple (see chart 7.3); that is household expenditure on the item is less by the larger family than by the smaller at each level of household income. In this case, the positive specific requirement by the child is more than offset by the stronger negative income effect which the child has on the household's general living standards.[1] By correcting for the income effect (standardising on to the basis of an equivalent couple), the specific requirement of the child for the commodity can be seen explicitly.

In general terms – and assuming again two family types, a couple and a couple with one child – the Engel functions for a specific commodity (assuming a semi-logarithmic form) can be written as $E = a_0 + b_0 \log Y$ for the standard couple and $E = a_1 + b_1 \log[Y/(1 + c_0)]$ for the couple with one child, where c_0 is the child's coefficient in the income scale. Then, at any given value of income Y_0, expenditure by the childless couple on that commodity is $E_0 = a_0 + b_0 \log Y_0$, and the level of expenditure on the item which can be attained by a couple with a child at this standardised income level is $E_1 = a_1 + b_1 \log Y_0$. The specific coefficient $c_i = (E_1 - E_0)/E_0$ is then derived from these expressions.

The technique may be illustrated by deriving the specific scales for children in the consumption of food. First, the income equivalence scales previously estimated were used to standardise the incomes of families with one or two children on to the basis of an equivalent couple. Expenditure on food was then regressed on total expenditure per equivalent household for families without children, with one child and with two children, with the following results:

---

[1] These propositions follow from the accepted definition of a necessity as a commodity having an income elasticity below unity and of a luxury as having an elasticity above unity, combined with the assumption that expenditure per person depends approximately on income per person (see Prais and Houthakker, *The Analysis of Family Budgets*, p. 127).

$$E_0 = - 2463 \cdot 48 + 398 \cdot 96 \log Y$$

$$E_1 = - 1766 \cdot 65 + 331 \cdot 01 \log(Y/1 \cdot 25)$$

$$E_2 = - 3167 \cdot 14 + 526 \cdot 59 \log(Y/1 \cdot 35)$$

Estimates of the specific equivalence scales obtained from these results at an income of £30 per week per equivalent couple (which is close to the mean value for childless couples) are for the first child $c_{i1} = 884/731 - 1 = 0.21$, and for the first two children together $c_{i2} = 1050/731 - 1 = 0.44$.

To conclude this general expository section, it is instructive to present an alternative set of diagrams which show the joint derivation of income and specific equivalence scales by the method adopted in this chapter. First, the income equivalence scale of one child is derived by means of a standard commodity as already shown in chart 7.1. A compensating income of $Y_1 - Y_0$ is required to give a family with one child the same living standard as a couple without children having an income Y_0. That is, childless couples at income Y_0 and couples with one child at income Y_1 both consume the same quantity of the standard commodity and, by definition, a child's specific equivalence scale for the standard commodity is zero. (The arrows in the chart are intended to show the order in which the various quantities are derived – starting at Y_0 and referring to the two Engel curves Y_1 is duly reached.)

Charts 7.4 and 7.5 then illustrate the derivation of a child's specific equivalence scale for a necessity and a luxury respectively. Here expendi-

Chart 7.4. *Derivation of a specific equivalence scale for a necessity*

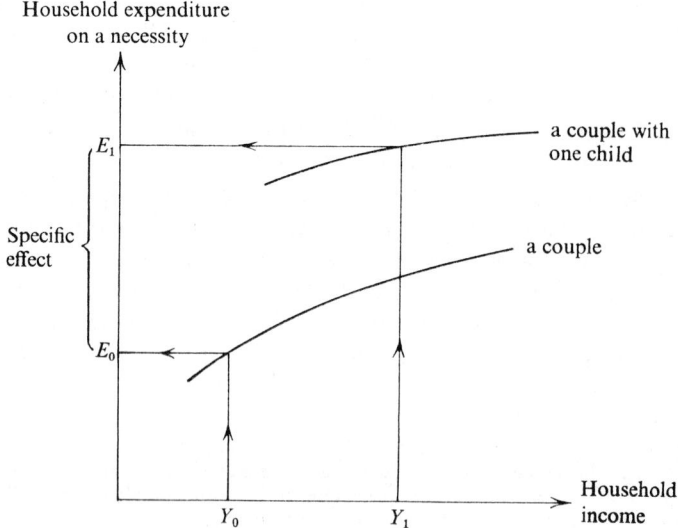

Chart 7.5. *Derivation of a specific equivalence scale for a luxury*

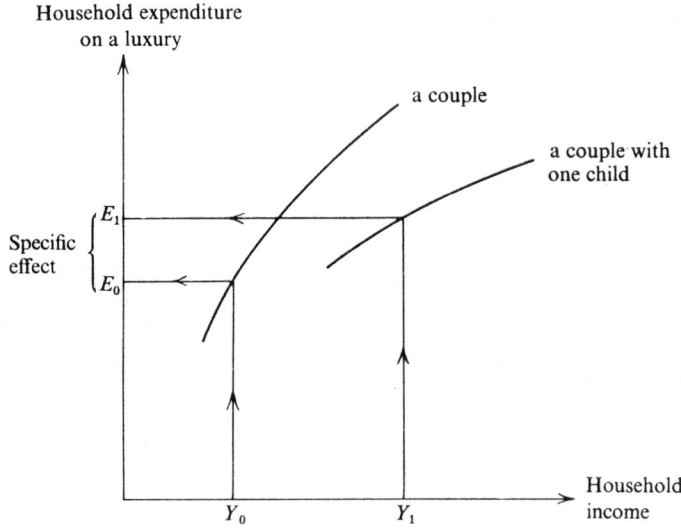

ture on the items in question is compared at income Y_0 for the childless couple and at income Y_1 for the couple with a child, this being the household income which, per equivalent couple, gives the latter family the same living standard as a couple. In other words, once the income effects of differences in family size had been taken into account, the contrasts in expenditure on the item in question, shown on the vertical axes of charts 7.4 and 7.5, reflect only the different specific requirements of the two kinds of family, and so provide a measure of the specific equivalence effects of a child.

THE RESULTS AND THEIR INTERPRETATION

The method outlined above was applied to data from the *Family Expenditure Survey Report for 1971* to yield estimates of income and specific scales for various numbers and ages of children. Four basic types of family were considered: a non-retired adult couple (the standard household), and families with one, two and three children under 18 years of age. Two age-groups of children were also distinguished – up to 4 years and 5–14 years. Where the samples were large enough, equivalence scales were estimated for families with the relevant numbers of children in each of these age-groups. On average there were 500 households in each sub-sample analysed. A finer age classification of children – perhaps also by sex – may be desirable, but this would reduce the number of observations in each sub-sample to a point where the estimates of equivalence scales cannot be precise enough.

Income equivalence scales

The sum of expenditures on adult clothing, tobacco and alcoholic drink (the 'composite commodity') was the principal standard commodity. Alternative estimates derived from expenditure on adult clothing alone, on alcoholic drink alone and on adult clothing plus alcoholic drink were also made to determine the sensitivity of the results to the choice of standard commodity.[1] Semi-logarithmic, double logarithmic and linear Engel curves were fitted to these expenditures for each of the selected

TABLE 7.2.   *Estimates of children's income equivalence scales: semi-logarithmic form*

Total expenditure	Couple with one child aged		Couple with two children aged			Couple with three children aged	
	0–4	0–18	0–4	5–14	0–18	5–14	0–18
(£s per wk)			*Adult clothing*				
20	0·06	0·08	0·06	0·14	0·15	0·32	0·23
30	0·22	0·23	0·25	0·51	0·30	0·40	0·56
50	0·46	0·47	0·55	1·18	0·52	0·50	1·11
			Alcoholic drink				
20	0·05	−0·01	−0·03	0·28	0·13	−0·30	−0·26
30	0·04	0·23	0·16	0·35	0·36	1·91	0·62
50	0·02	0·61	0·44	0·45	0·70	16·60	3·35
			Adult clothing and alcohol				
20	0·15	0·13	0·13	0·29	0·23	0·35	0·23
30	0·09	0·21	0·16	0·46	0·30	0·48	0·49
50	0·03	0·31	0·21	0·71	0·39	0·66	0·90
			Composite commodity				
20	0·12	0·08	0·08	0·29	0·21	0·11	−0·11
	(−0·05/	(−0·12/	(−0·24/	(0·00/	(0·03/	(−1·00/	(−0·76/
	0·25)	0·24)	0·24)	0·47)	0·35)	0·48)	0·20)
30	0·13	0·25	0·21	0·52	0·35	0·64	0·56
	(0·03/	(0·13/	(0·06/	(0·35/	(0·23/		(0·30/
	0·26)	0·42)	0·72)	0·94)	0·52)		2·05)
50	0·15	0·50	0·40	0·87	0·55	1·68	2·20
	(−0·03/	(0·19/	(−0·01/	(0·35/	(0·26/		(0·69/
	0·52)	1·20	3·22)	2·95)	1·11)		64·81)

Source: NIESR estimates.

Notes:
 (i) The type of household taken as standard (i.e. with scale 1.00) is that of a couple without children and total expenditure levels relate to such a household.
 (ii) The estimates for families with two or three children refer to the combined effect of all children in the household, not to the effect per child.
 (iii) Figures in brackets are confidence intervals at the 95 per cent level.
 (iv) The composite commodity consists of adult clothing, alcoholic drink and tobacco.

[1] Estimates based on expenditure on tobacco and household savings were not pursued, since the relevant Engel curves displayed too much residual variability.

types of family.[1] Income equivalence scales for children derived from these Engel functions are presented in tables 7.2, 7.3 and 7.4. They were calculated for each of the standard commodities and functional forms at three income levels – £30 per week (the approximate average in the standard family), £20 and £50.

TABLE 7.3. *Estimates of children's income equivalence scales: double logarithmic form*

Total expenditure	Couple with one child aged		Couple with two children aged			Couple with three children aged	
	0–4	0–18	0–4	5–14	0–18	5–14	0–18
(£s per wk)			*Adult clothing*				
20	0·16	0·16	0·37	0·44	0·25	0·47	0·41
30	0·23	0·21	0·26	0·47	0·27	0·43	0·44
50	0·33	0·28	0·13	0·51	0·30	0·39	0·47
			Alcoholic drink				
20	−0·15	−0·04	−0.05	0·29	0·14	−0·21	−0·16
30	0·04	0·17	0·24	0·33	0·28	1·37	0·37
50	0·34	0·51	0·75	0·39	0·47	8·48	1·53
			Adult clothing and alcohol				
20	−0.01	0·07	0·18	0·31	0·20	0·26	0·18
30	0·13	0·19	0·16	0·39	0·26	0·50	0·38
50	0·33	0·34	0·13	0·48	0·34	0·87	0·68
			Composite commodity				
20	0·00	0·03	0·05	0·33	0·17	−0.05	−0·18
	(−0·20/	(−0·19/	(−0·27/	(0·04/	(0·01/		(−0·88/
	0·16)	0·19)	0·22)	0·52)	0·31)		0·16)
30	0·16	0·22	0·22	0·42	0·30	0·65	0·40
	(0·04/	(0·10/	(0·06/	(0·26/	(0·20/		(0·20/
	0·33)	0·38)	0·70)	0·77)	0·42)		0·54)
50	0·41	0·50	0·48	0·55	0·47	2·33	1·78
	(0·12/	(0·18/	(0·04/	(0·18/	(0·21/		
	1·03)	1·28)	3·16)	1·95)	0·95)		

Source: NIESR estimates.

Note: See notes to table 7.2.

Several features encourage confidence in the results. First, whilst there are discrepancies between the income scales as measured by the three functional forms at income levels away from the mean there is a reassuring degree of agreement at the mean income level. For instance, at this level in the case of a single child, the semi-logarithmic, double logarithmic and linear forms based on the composite standard commodity yield income scales of 0·25, 0·22, and 0·24 respectively. Secondly, with few exceptions, it

[1] Weighted least squares were applied to grouped data. Group means were weighted by the corresponding household frequencies to allow for the varying numbers of families in each group. Households were grouped by net income but the calculations used total expenditure, not income, as the determining variable. Nevertheless for convenience the term 'income' rather than 'total expenditure' is used in the text.

TABLE 7.4. *Estimates of children's income equivalence scales: linear form*

Total expenditure	Couple with one child aged		Couple with two children aged			Couple with three children aged	
	0–4	0–18	0–4	5–14	0–18	5–14	0–18
(£s per wk)			*Adult clothing*				
20	−0·05	0·02	0·10	0·02	0·12	0·33	0·21
30	0·25	0·22	0·19	0·47	0·27	0·37	0·49
50	0·48	0·38	0·26	0·82	0·39	0·40	0·72
			Alcoholic drink				
20	−0.02	−0.06	0·04	0·35	0·12	0·33	0·21
30	0·04	0·21	0·11	0·32	0·27	0·37	0·49
50	0·08	0·42	0·17	0·30	0·39	0·40	0·72
		Adult clothing and alcohol					
20	0·05	0·06	0·15	0·23	0·22	0·34	0·18
30	0·13	0·21	0·14	0·45	0·28	0·46	0·43
50	0·19	0·33	0·14	0·63	0·32	0·55	0·63
			Composite commodity				
20	0·01	−0·02	0·09	0·23	0·20	0·08	−0·41
30	0·17	0·24	0·18	0·51	0·32	0·55	0·45
50	0·30	0·45	0·24	0·73	0·41	0·99	1·14

Source: NIESR estimates.

Note: See notes (i), (ii) and (iv) to table 7.2.

appears to matter little which of the four specifications of the standard commodity is chosen. Using the semi-logarithmic form, income scales for the first child at the £30 income level emerge as 0·23, 0·23, 0·21 and 0·25 on the bases of adult clothing, alcoholic drink, adult clothing and alcoholic drink, and the composite commodity respectively. Thirdly, the resulting scales accord well with intuitive ideas of how household needs change as family size increases. At the mean income level, on the bases of the composite commodity and the semi-logarithmic form, the income scales for one child, two children and three children are 0·25, 0·35 and 0·56 respectively, indicating that second and third children increase a family's needs less than the first.[1] No doubt this reflects economies of scale available to larger families as a result of sharing such items as housing, durables and goods needed for child care. Fourthly, the results confirm that children's needs rise with their age, and they provide a measure of that rise. The scales for the children up to 4 years old are lower than for those aged 5–14, whilst estimates for the broader group aged up to 18 lie in between.

A somewhat surprising feature of the results is the suggestion that income equivalence scales for children rise with the level of family income. As an illustration, scales for one child based on the composite commodity and

[1] The results do not suggest that the third child adds less to family needs than the second, but there are large sampling errors attached to the estimates.

the semi-logarithmic form are 0·08, 0·25 and 0·50 at income levels of £20, £30 and £50 respectively. Sampling errors prevent any precise and definite view about this on the basis of these estimates. One may also wonder whether the specification of the equation contributes to this effect. Because of the obvious importance of this matter, some further calculations were undertaken.

The household sample was divided roughly in half – those with total expenditure of £29 a week or less, and those with over £29 a week. Engel curves for the composite commodity were fitted to the two sub-samples – each of which contained families with two, one or no children – using both semi-logarithmic and double logarithmic forms. Table 7.5 contains the results and suggests that, for the selected types of family, children's income equivalence scales are higher in higher income families than in lower income families.

TABLE 7.5. *Children's income equivalence scales at different income levels*

	Couple with one child aged			Couple with two children aged		
	0–4	5–14	0–18	0–4	5–14	0–18
Semi-logarithmic form: Income £29 per week or less	..	0·31 (0·19/ 0·38)	0·13 (−0·09/ 0·24)	0·07 (−0·18/ 0·24)	0·34 (0·07/ 0·48)	0·24 (0·06/ 0·36)
Income over £29 per week	0·11 (0·00/ 0·37)	..	0·48 (0·18/ 0·75)	0·20 (0.03/ 1·70)	1·64 (0·36/ 1·78)	0·47 (0·25/ 0·78)
Double logarithmic form: Income £29 per week or less	..	0·25 (−0·76/ 0·35)	0·10 (−0·15/ 0·20)	0·04 (−0·21/ 0·23)	0·35 (0·08/ 0·52)	0·20 (0·04/ 0·31)
Income over £29 per week	0·19 (0·09/ 0·63)	..	0·51 (0·16/ 0·76)	0·26 (0·06/ 1·67)	1·38 (0·23/ 1·28)	0·40 (0·22/ 0·66)

Source: NIESR estimates.

Notes:
(i) See notes to table 7.2.
(ii) Income levels also relate to standard households: those with income £29 per week or less would have mean total expenditure of £21 per week; those with income over £29 per week would have mean total expenditure of £39 per week.

Our findings may be attributable to the possibility that families with higher incomes contain older children than those with lower incomes: for example children in the 5–14 age-group may be nearer to 14 in the higher income groups and nearer to 5 in the lower income groups. Whether or not this is the case could be resolved with the help of larger samples. Another possibility is that higher income families have accumulated stocks of adult clothing (and other items) which enable them to devote more current expenditure to childrens' needs. Our knowledge of such matters is as yet rudimentary and much further work is necessary before one can accept without qualification our finding that richer families find children relatively more costly than poorer families.

This is an appropriate stage to consider the degree of statistical confidence which may be attached to our results. Confidence intervals at the 95 per cent level were calculated for the principal scales in tables 7.2, 7.3, 7.4 and 7.5.[1] The interpretation of these limits can be illustrated by the double logarithmic equation for the couple with two children aged 0–18 years in table 7.5. The values in brackets indicate (to use approximate language) that there is a 95 per cent chance that the true value of the appropriate income scale lies between 0·04 and 0·31 for lower income families and between 0·22 and 0·66 for higher income families. Since these ranges overlap, one cannot, on this evidence alone, exclude the possibility that there is no difference between the true scales. However, there are a number of independent comparisons that can be made from these results and, whilst no formal pooled probability has been calculated, it may be conjectured that the differences would on the whole be judged as significant. Further

TABLE 7.6.   *A comparison of children's income equivalence scales*

Sources	Date	Age of children	First child	Second child	Third child
This study (tables 7.2 and 7.7)	1971	0–4	0·13	0·08	..
		5–14	0·29	0·23	0·12
		0–18	0·25	0·10	0·21
Nicholson, 'Variations in working class family expenditure', p. 384	1937–8	0–14	0·25	0·21	..
Henderson, 'The cost of a family', table VIII	1937–8	0–14	0·16	0·15	..
C. Bagley, *The Cost of a Child*, London, Institute of Psychiatry, 1969, p. 10.	1963	not specified	0·24	0·19	0·14[a]
Supplementary benefit scales[b]	1971	0–4	0·17	0·16	0·14
		5–15[c]	0·21	0·20	0·18
		0–17[d]	0·21	0·20	0·18
L. D. McClements, 'Equivalence scales for children' (unpublished), 1975, table 2	1971	0–1		0·10[e]	
		2–4		0·18[e]	
		5–7		0·20[e]	
		8–10		0·23[e]	
		11–12		0·24[e]	
		13–15		0·27[e]	
		16–18		0.36[e]	

[a] For three or more children.
[b] Scales including rent allowances as used in chapter 4.
[c] Based on scales for age-groups 5–10, 11–12 and 13–15 years.
[d] Based on scales for all children's age-groups.
[e] For any child.

[1] Dr K. F. Wallis, of the London School of Economics, developed the formulae for computing these confidence intervals.

CHILDREN'S EQUIVALENCE SCALES

calculations based on larger samples, or pooled samples embracing a number of Family Expenditure Surveys, would improve the precision of the results.

It is interesting to compare the income equivalence scales obtained above with the findings of other studies. Such a comparison is given in table 7.6. Making what allowance one can for the lack of precise comparability of age-groups, it is clear that there is a fair degree of agreement between the scales, especially for the first two children aged 5–14 years. For children aged up to 4 years our scales tend to be somewhat lower than others.

Specific equivalence scales

Using the principal estimates of income equivalence scales derived above, specific equivalence scales were estimated for the usual ten broad commodity groups, although the scales for alcoholic drink and tobacco were zero by assumption and the scales for clothing were based on total expenditure on clothing by all members of the household (for expenditure on adult clothing alone, children's scales would, of course, again be zero). The estimated parameters of the resulting regression equations, which on the whole seem to be well determined with low sampling errors, yielded the estimates of children's specific equivalence scales for the various commodity groups shown in table 7.7.

TABLE 7.7. *Estimates of children's specific equivalence scales for broad commodity groups*[a]

	Average expenditure by standard household	Couple with one child aged			Couple with two children aged			Couple with three children aged	
		0–4	5–14	0–18	0–4	5–14	0–18	5–14	0–18
	(£s per week)								
Housing	4·14	0·15	0·14	0·14	0·01	0·27	0·18	0·33	0·45
Fuel, light and power	1·83	0·18	0·21	0·26	0·32	0·25	0·18	0·76	0·44
Food	7·23	0·08	0·26	0·21	0·30	0·56	0·44	0·86	0·74
Clothing	2·53	0·29	0·23	0·33	0·50	0·89	0·54	1·17	0·81
Alcoholic drink[b]	1·51	–	–	–	–	–	–	–	–
Tobacco[b]	1·27	–	–	–	–	–	–	–	–
Durables	2·24	0·74	0·74	0·55	0·07	0·75	0·33	0·43	0·22
Other goods and miscellaneous	2·41	0·83	0·23	0·44	0·32	0·38	0·35	1·13	0·78
Transport and vehicles	4·65	0·29	0·40	0·30	0·20	0·59	0·46	0·41	0·33
Services	3·24	0·19	0·34	0·27	0·05	0·79	0·36	0·53	0·79
Total[c]	31·06	0·29	0·29	0·27	0·21	0·53	0·35	0·68	0·56

Source: NIESR estimates.

[a] Based on semi-logarithmic Engel curves and calculated at the average income for the standard couple; see also notes (i) and (ii) to table 7.2.

[b] These scales zero by assumption.

[c] Income equivalence scales calculated as a weighted average of the specific scales, with the budget shares of the commodities as weights.

These estimates display several interesting features. First, the scales, being calculated to show the effect on consumption of all children in the family (not the additional effect of an extra child), tend to rise with the number of children, reflecting the greater needs of larger families. For example, in the case of food, one child aged 5–14 is equivalent to 0·26 of a couple, two children are equivalent to 0·56 of a couple and three children to 0·86 of a couple. The principal exception is in the case of durables, where it appears that expenditure is particularly high for one child – even a young child – but no further increase is required for subsequent children. This makes good, if rather obvious, sense in terms of the cycle of family life. The evidence confirms, secondly, that for most commodities specific equivalence scales are higher for older children than for younger ones. Taking again the case of food, the scale for two children both aged 5–14 is 0·56, nearly double the scale, 0·30, for two children up to 4 years old. Thirdly, there is a suggestion of economies of scale in consumption, the scales for two children being somewhat less than twice those for one child of the same age. As already noted, evidence of the presence of such economies of scale is clearest in the case of household durables; it is also marked in transport and vehicles. It is reassuring that the income equivalence scales calculated as a weighted average of the various specific equivalence scales (using weights proportional to the shares of the various expenditures in the respective family budgets) are similar to those derived by the method described in the previous section.

SUMMARY

This chapter has set out and applied a new method of estimating equivalence scales for families of different size and composition. The object has been to obtain estimates of the 'cost of children' of different ages and so help in the identification of families in poverty. It is reassuring that the income scales estimated in this chapter are apparently in good agreement both with previous estimates based on a behaviouristic approach and with the scales implicit in the official supplementary benefit allowances. However, in view of the size of the statistical confidence intervals attached to our estimates, it is possible that the agreement between the various scales is overstated; further calculations using larger samples (for example by pooling several years of Family Expenditure Surveys) might bring to light important differences. It seems desirable in principle, when income scales are employed to compile numbers in poverty (as in chapter 3), to use a set of scales based on behaviouristic estimates, as presented in this chapter, as an alternative to the supplementary benefit scales; but the scales are so close that, in any practical analysis of large samples of families, one can hardly expect any great difference in the total estimates of numbers in poverty.

An interesting feature of our results is the suggestion that children's scales rise with the level of income; the causes and implications of this require further analysis.

We also derived a set of specific equivalence scales for ten commodity groups. These are of interest in showing, for example, in which commodities there are economies of scale, and in which the specific requirements of children are particularly high or low; they thus contribute to an understanding of the elements contributing to the total cost of children. Such equivalence scales are also required in the analysis of historical developments in comparative living levels, and in the analysis of expenditure patterns based on Engel curves.

CHAPTER 8

CONCLUSIONS

It is as well to emphasise in our concluding chapter the limited objectives of this study, which were to investigate certain economic aspects of poverty, using the results of the regular official sample surveys of households known as the Family Expenditure Surveys. Its point of departure was a recognition that other studies have only partially filled gaps in our knowledge of poverty which have become apparent in the postwar period. This concluding chapter assembles our salient findings on the extent of poverty, how it has changed, and what we have learnt of its causes and effects.

The debate about policy has been concerned partly with the practical matter of what are the most cost-effective means of reducing poverty and partly with the more academic question of what is meant by poverty. Is it more appropriate to measure poverty by an absolute standard, or in relation to the current standard of living of the population as a whole? Should concern be directed primarily to economic resources, or is it essential to take account of deprivation in a wider, sociological or psychological sense? Such conceptual questions have been considered in the present study in a descriptive rather than a normative way. Chapter 2 surveyed briefly various concepts of poverty, such as income insufficiency or economic inequality, drawing attention to their various properties, with the primary intention of providing an analytical framework for the subsequent chapters. Despite weaknesses, data from the Family Expenditure Surveys were found sufficiently reliable, with adequate response rates, for us to make estimates of the extent of poverty using a number of measures. We could not detect any sharp changes in expenditure patterns along the income scale that might have been used to pinpoint poverty in some behaviouristic sense, but perhaps this is hardly surprising. And whilst secondary poverty, in the sense of adequate income but deficient food consumption, may well be a serious matter, the analysis encountered a number of fundamental difficulties which prevented any conclusive appraisal based on the statistical information available to us. However, it proved informative to measure the numbers in poverty both by using the supplementary benefit scales as an absolute standard and by comparing the incomes of the poorer groups with those of the median household.

This chapter has been prepared mainly by A. D. Smith.

THE DECLINE OF POVERTY

Despite the reservations that are bound to attach to all statistical measures of poverty, any information that yields a clearer picture should be helpful in its alleviation. Our principal finding on the extent of poverty is that, on the basis of a constant 1971 absolute living standard, numbers in poverty declined from about a fifth of the population in 1953/4 to about a fortieth in 1973. A fall by a factor of eight in only twenty years is a notable improvement. But in relative terms we found little change: the net income of the poorest 5th percentile was about the same proportion of the median income in both years, so that the decline in the numbers in poverty so measured reflects essentially the growth of the economy rather than a redistribution of income.[1] The need for information on this topic may well increase during the next few years, since it may be doubted whether rates of economic growth either in Britain, or perhaps in other industrialised 'western' countries, will return to the rates sustained over most of the postwar period; hence we may experience slower progress in the further eradication of poverty.

ALTERNATIVE MEASURES OF POVERTY

Governments are at one in their desire to reduce, and if possible eliminate, poverty. There may be disagreement about the kind of measures through which this goal should be sought, about the broad distribution of income and wealth, and perhaps about the priority to be given to anti-poverty measures, but not about the need to treat poverty.

Whatever definitions or criteria of poverty may be preferred, few would deny the desirability of estimating the number of people who fall below some contemporarily prescribed minimum living standard. In the United Kingdom this means attempting to assess the numbers living in households with incomes below supplementary benefit levels. Such a measure has some general validity as a test of the success or failure of the government's anti-poverty programme since, in principle, the supplementary benefit scales have been accepted by Parliament as the minimum living standard to which everyone is entitled.

Using the information from the Family Expenditure Survey, we estimated that in 1971 7·1 per cent of households in the sample, containing 4·9 per cent of individuals (2·6 million), received net normal incomes below the current level of supplementary benefits. This can be broadly

---

[1] Comparisons of changes in the total incomes of the poor and the non-poor should take account of the fact that prices of necessities (which take a large share of the expenditure of the poor) rose more than those of non-necessities, so that in real terms incomes of the poor grew slightly less than those of the median household.

described as the amount of poverty that is unacceptable by contemporary standards and is essential information in determining the scale of action required to eliminate poverty in the sense of income deficiency.

In applying the supplementary benefit scales to the income distribution in 1971, we examined the effect of using different definitions. We found that the most important element in the definition was the choice of the 'population unit'. Measuring poverty on the basis of the 'nuclear' family rather than the total household has the effect of raising the estimated numbers in poverty by more than three-quarters, to about $4\frac{3}{4}$ million. It has, of course, long been understood that the smaller the unit adopted the higher the proportion of units and individuals that fall into the category of the poor because of a reduction in the implicit allowance for income sharing. Or, to put it in a more familiar way, the basis of family life is that provision is made for those who are inactive, infirm, or unable to support themselves because of their youth or old age; if we assess such individuals separately according to their own means, the apparent extent of poverty is bound to rise. It is perhaps a matter of some interest that the rise is larger than some people had thought.

The effect of measuring poverty over different time-periods was also examined. Again, the direction of this effect was known *a priori*, but it is interesting that measurement on the basis of a single week ('last week's income') – instead of a rather longer period ('normal income') – can raise the estimated proportion in poverty by almost 2 percentage points, equivalent to about 1 million people. The difference between measuring poverty by household income and by total expenditure – a choice which proves rather difficult to make on grounds of principle or practicality – is approximately the same. In this case, the proportion in poverty is raised from 7·1 per cent of households on the income criterion to 9·4 per cent on an expenditure basis. Fluctuations from week to week in household expenditure and the omission of items such as life insurance and mortgage repayments from the definition of total expenditure in the Surveys result in a greater proportion of households with total expenditure below supplementary benefit level than is the case using income net of direct taxes. Since there is an attempt to smooth out short-term fluctuations in 'normal income' this would appear a more appropriate basis for these estimates, after adjustments for understatement of income by some households.

We also considered the effects of alternative definitions on the estimated change in the extent of poverty during the postwar period. Whilst a measure of contemporary poverty is important for future policy, an indication of changes in poverty is necessary for assessing the effectiveness of past attempts to eradicate poverty – which will in itself influence future action. In any case, a measure of changes in poverty is of fundamental interest, since fears have sometimes been expressed that poverty in this country is now greater than in the immediate postwar period. A typical expression of such apprehension was that voiced by the Child Poverty Action Group; focusing attention on numbers of people with incomes up to 110 per cent of the supplementary benefit level, the Group concluded that poverty had almost doubled between 1960 and 1972.[1] Over a somewhat longer period, 1953/4 to 1973, the present study suggests that such poverty has fallen. In any case, when attempting to measure changes in poverty over time, there is the 'need for information on the same basis for different years, the need for agreement about the change in the poverty standard relative to the general level of incomes, and for interpreting the evidence in the light of demographic and other developments'.[2]

While a definition of poverty in relation to the supplementary benefit standard has an important role to play in measuring the present extent of poverty and the effectiveness of current anti-poverty measures, it is less suited to measuring changes in poverty over time. Although this minimum national living standard is raised periodically, the changes do not bear any immediate or exact relation to developments in average living standards.

An alternative method of measuring changes in the extent of poverty is to identify changes in the income differential between the poor and non-poor, that is the ratio between the incomes of those in poverty and of the median household; it is perfectly reasonable for a policy objective to be formulated in terms of a narrowing of the income differential between those at the bottom of the income scale and the average. A comparison of the 5th percentile household with the median household in 1971 suggested that, on this basis, the poorest received a gross income equal to no more than $22\frac{1}{2}$ per cent of the median. However, when various adjustments were made to obtain a more realistic picture of the comparative economic well-being of the lowest 5th percentile and the median, a rather different picture emerged. These adjustments were: an allowance for the fact that low income households typically contain fewer people – and fewer children – by calculating equivalent income per standard household; a deduction for income tax and national insurance, which, of course, bear more heavily on median households; consideration of the comparative living standards of poor individuals rather than households. When these adjustments are made, the income of the poorest 5th percentile relative to the median rises from $22\frac{1}{2}$ to 49 per cent – a very much more encouraging picture.

Moreover, comparative incomes of the poor seem to have been more or

[1] F. Field and P. Townsend, *A Social Contract for Families*, London, Child Poverty Action Group, 1975.
[2] A. B. Atkinson, 'Poverty and income inequality in Britain', Essex University, Department of Economics Discussion Paper, 1971, pp. 60 and 61.

less constant between the early 1950s and the 1970s at about 48 to 49 per cent of the median level – a constancy which may be the mirror-image of an unchanged proportion of the population in relative poverty. While indicating that there has been no apparent decline in relative poverty over the period, this measure fails, however, to reveal how many individuals are suffering very acute poverty. It appears that, even in 1971, some members of the population received real incomes which were below the national assistance scales deemed necessary as long as twenty years ago.

WHO ARE THE POOR?

The data from the Family Expenditure Survey have enabled us to identify a number of characteristics of poor households which probably play an important causal role in poverty though, not surprisingly, it has proved difficult to identify the real roots of poverty with any precision. The number of households in the sample was too small to distinguish the 'net' poverty effect of a given characteristic, but we can build up a picture of certain typical kinds of households in poverty.

The results confirm what has been suspected for some time, that two factors which were associated with poverty in earlier years now rank some way down the list. While the risk of poverty for households with an unemployed head is high, such households did not account for a particularly large proportion of the poor in 1971.[1] Secondly, although the risk of poverty for households with large numbers of children (five or more) may be high, the numerical importance of such poverty is now even less significant. Both the risk and the numerical importance of poverty are especially high for the retired and for single-parent households. Whilst this confirms the relevance of official attention to certain fairly well defined poverty groups, such cases account for little more than half the total amount of poverty. Moreover, whilst it is tempting to ascribe these kinds – and therefore most – of poverty to essentially demographic and sociological factors (such as age, female longevity and separated families), economic considerations (such as low pay) also make a significant contribution.

A complementary way of distinguishing kinds of poverty is to determine the extent to which its incidence may be ascribed to the life-cycle of a family – relatively predictable changes over time in a typical household's needs and income – or to individual and 'accidental' events which bear little or no relation to the normal family life-cycle. The evidence suggests that in the modal household life-cycle equivalent income has two 'peaks' (when the head of the household is aged about 25–30 and about 50–60);

[1] The higher unemployment levels experienced in recent years may have added to the significance of such poverty – but probably not sufficiently to rank it alongside the major causes of poverty.

it is lowest when the head is over 65, but it also falls slightly in the age-group 30–40. The general pattern accords fairly well with Rowntree's original account of the life-cycle. At lower income levels the picture is not so very different. Equivalent income in low income households is lowest when family heads are very young, and – like the modal household – when they are old; prospects are best in the intervening years. The results suggest that in middle-age child rearing is now a less significant factor than such influences as broken families, sickness and unemployment.

While it may be desirable to focus attention on specific kinds of poverty – old age, single-parent families, etc. – in an attempt to identify and eradicate causes, or to specify the form in which assistance is most appropriately provided, it is not necessary to translate this into a system consisting exclusively of selective assistance. Our results have shown that most poverty arises where there exists a specific identifiable risk, but there is still a need for a comprehensive policy to meet the essential symptom of poverty – low income.

In this context it is important to distinguish between the working and the non-working poor. Some people are unable to earn sufficient income because of old age, sickness or disability, because family responsibilities prevent them from working, or because they are unemployed. Although in principle these groups are entitled to supplementary benefits to remedy any deficiencies in the amount and coverage of national insurance, poverty may occur because they do not claim their entitlement, or because they are disqualified from receiving full benefits. In principle it is possible to abolish poverty among these groups by extending eligibility for national insurance benefits to all categories of risk, raising these benefits to supplementary benefit levels, and abandoning rules that disqualify certain claimants. The main constraint is cost not feasibility.

Alleviating poverty among the working population is more difficult. In order to avoid a disincentive to work, supplementary benefits are not provided for those in employment with earnings that yield a living standard below the poverty line. There are two possible approaches for relieving poverty in these families – to supplement income in relation to the needs of dependants, and to establish minimum earnings levels – both raise complex issues extending beyond the scope of this study.

THE EFFECTS OF POVERTY

The effects of poverty are reflected in such diverse forms as housing conditions, educational attainment, medical standards and social behaviour. Using the Family Expenditure Surveys we have been able to consider only one kind of effect, but a very important one, the impact of poverty on expenditure and expenditure patterns. As part of our examination of alternative methods of measuring poverty total expenditure was used to estimate the numbers in poverty and explore the possibility of using expenditure on selected items for the same purpose. In addition, expenditure patterns were examined to see if they would throw more light on the effects of poverty.

The principal conclusion is that, in consequence of the rise in living standards, the proportion of expenditure devoted by poor households to the necessities – food, housing, fuel, light and power – has declined considerably between 1953/4 and 1971, but at a slower rate than for the median household. (One reason for this is that the prices of necessities rose faster than those of other goods.) The poor continue to devote a higher proportion of their income than more affluent households to necessities – in conformity with Engel's Law – and the dispersion between households of expenditure on food, housing, fuel, light and power is much less than for expenditure on other commodities.

Surprisingly, expressed in terms of standard household units, expenditure on fuel, light and power by the poor appeared to be about as much as, or perhaps even more than, that of the average household. This may reflect the special needs of many of those in poverty: for example, the elderly living alone – because of the high costs of heating a house for only one or two persons – and families with young children. It may also be partly due to less efficient heating systems, which mean that the cost of fuel per unit of heat generated is higher for such households than for the better-off.[1]

A finer commodity breakdown suggested that the poor's consumption of meat, fish, dairy products and fresh vegetables, as well as of bread, is close to that of the median household, but the poor buy substantially less of the more expensive convenience foods. Although spending little on luxury goods, many poor households seem to be able to afford television.

FUTURE RESEARCH REQUIRED

The present study has underlined the need for a coordinated approach to the problem of poverty and, more especially, for integrating the results of a rather narrow study of this kind into a wider framework of knowledge about the extent, nature, causes and treatment of poverty. It is also necessary to assimilate our findings with current and future research into the general distribution of incomes. For it is clear that many policies influence simultaneously the whole spectrum of incomes and those of

---

[1] Special allowances are available for supplementary benefit recipients who need extra heating because of exceptional circumstances, such as poor health, restricted mobility or damp accommodation; they may be entitled to a discretionary extra weekly allowance known as the heating addition, or sometimes fuel debts may be met by a single exceptional needs payment, which may also be provided for purchasing blankets and replacing or repairing heating appliances. The cost in 1975 was £95 million.

the poor, and an understanding of the income distribution is an essential condition for determining how poverty is to be alleviated.

In the area with which this study has been concerned we are rather better equipped to comment on future research requirements – having assessed what already exists. Moreover, when identifying the gaps which have become evident to us, we feel free to release ourselves from a self-imposed constraint – that consideration be given only to areas which might be illuminated by the Family Expenditure Survey.

Further work on the conceptual basis of measuring poverty does not, in our view, merit high priority in future research. While there is always some scope for improving measurement tools, we suspect that they have been developed to a pitch at which diminishing returns to future work would set in. One exception might be further research on behaviouristic measures of poverty; our experience here suggests, however, that whilst such paths may seem important they will not be easy.

Some aspects of the features of poverty merit further attention. In particular, is it reflected in low income, low expenditure, or both? Whilst income–expenditure discrepancies in poorer families were examined in detail in this study, the outcome was inconclusive. Week to week fluctuations in expenditure would seem to invalidate any ranking of households by total expenditure. Although 'normal' income attempts to overcome this problem, for some households actual income appears to be much higher than recorded income. Further exploration of the problem almost inevitably would require a more detailed cataloguing of the incoming and outgoing financial flows in samples of poor households, as well as a comprehensive statement of household assets and liabilities at both the beginning and the end of the relevant period. More needs to be known about, and allowance made for, income in kind, fringe benefits, and both financial and material stocks. It is difficult to see how a proper understanding – and improved measures – of poverty can be achieved without such knowledge.

Of course, for many households income–expenditure discrepancies can be explained in terms of the time-periods over which poverty is measured. The shorter the period the greater the possibility of divergence, since there is a good chance of maintaining expenditure levels for short periods out of savings. But the question of the period of measurement also has great intrinsic interest. The longer it is the smaller the apparent extent of poverty, since in many households income or expenditure will fall below a given level for a comparatively short time only.

We have also seen that the way in which families run the risk of poverty changes in a systematic way over the life-cycle. But our knowledge of the dynamics of household poverty – of the extent to which households generally and kinds of households in particular move in a systematic or random fashion into and out of poverty – is non-existent.

The threat or the actuality of poverty may also have a significant effect on patterns of household income sharing; such sharing may in turn greatly influence the extent to which poverty is observed and exists. This study has amply confirmed the validity of this observation, but it has been unable to draw upon any specific knowledge of the extent and nature of sharing economic resources within the family or household, nor to illuminate these activities. This area of research deserves some priority.

The expenditure behaviour of the poor merits further attention on account of the fundamental policy assumption that alleviation of poverty is best achieved by ensuring a minimum income level for each family according to its composition, which it is then free to use as it wishes. Further exploration of secondary poverty, essentially the misallocation of low incomes, is necessary for judging the validity of this assumption.

Research on these lines would require sources additional to the Family Expenditure Survey. Ideally, two alternative kinds of household sample would seem to be needed: for the essentially dynamic aspects of poverty a cohort type analysis, in which the fortunes of a sample group of households are traced over time; for the other areas where further research is merited, smaller samples than used by the Family Expenditure Surveys might suffice, provided that the survey was oriented specifically towards poverty, and an attempt made to cover the homeless and the institutional population (the use of 'area samples' needs to be considered). However, before the feasibility of such alternative sources of data is considered, it would seem advisable to explore the extent to which existing sources could be made to yield relevant information. It is not inconceivable that significant amounts could be found in the General Household Survey,[1] the follow-up income survey to the 1971 Census of Population, the survey by the London School of Economics and Essex University,[2] the New Earnings Survey[3] and national insurance records, used separately or jointly.

Finally, we would suggest that published official information on the poor needs to be supplemented. Estimates are now published in *Social Trends* of the numbers of families and individuals with incomes below supplementary benefit level,[4] but if we are to judge the seriousness of their poverty, we need also to know their average income. Our preference would be for annual estimates of the incomes of the poorest 5th and 10th percentiles, adjusted as in chapter 3, both in real terms and as a proportion of average or median income. Further, while present statistics distinguish

---

[1] Office of Population Censuses and Surveys, *The General Household Survey*, London, HMSO (annual).

[2] An elaborate survey of household resources and standards of living carried out in 1968/9 under the direction of B. Abel-Smith and P. Townsend, the full report of which is still in the course of preparation.

[3] Department of Employment, *New Earnings Survey*, London, HMSO (annual).

[4] See CSO, *Social Trends*, no. 6, tables 5·31, p. 116.

those receiving benefits from those who do not, estimates of those below the supplementary benefit level should also distinguish those who are eligible for benefits from those who are not, in order to permit an assessment of the effectiveness of anti-poverty policy. This additional information would require only marginal, if any, additions to statistical resources already applied in this area.

THE FAMILY EXPENDITURE SURVEYS

In this book we have drawn extensively upon the government's Family Expenditure Surveys. These collect information about many of the socio-economic characteristics relevant to an analysis of poverty and provide detailed information on expenditure patterns as well as on incomes. We have used both the published *Reports* of the various Surveys conducted since 1953/4, and a number of special (unpublished) tabulations relating to the 1971 Family Expenditure Survey, which were made available by the Department of Health and Social Security.[1]

The first large scale survey of family budgets was conducted in 1937/8[2] and related to a sample of manual wage earners in agriculture, industry and commerce; industrial households contributed 8905 usable budgets and agricultural 1491. The next full scale enquiry into consumption patterns was implemented in 1953/4. It originated in a 1951 recommendation by the Cost of Living Advisory Committee (now the Retail Price Index Advisory Committee) that household expenditure patterns should be examined in order to provide new weights for the index of retail prices.[3] This survey covered 19,881 households and yielded 12,911 usable budgets.[4] The annual series of Family Expenditure Surveys commenced in 1957. Up to 1966 it was based on an annual sample of 5000 addresses and each year produced about 3000–3500 budgets from cooperating households. In 1967 the sample was doubled and has since yielded over 7000 budgets a year.[5]

Although the Survey is concerned primarily with household expenditure, certain information is also collected about the characteristics of each co-operating household, including its income.[6] In measuring the distribution

---

[1] The information in its original form relates to individual households and is stored on tape; the Department of Health and Social Security provided us with grouped information in the required form.

[2] Ministry of Labour, 'Weekly expenditure of working-class households 1937–38'; see also Prais and Houthakker, *The Analysis of Family Budgets*.

[3] Ministry of Labour, *Cost of Living Advisory Committee: interim report*, Cmd 8328, London, HMSO, 1951.

[4] Ministry of Labour, *Household Expenditure 1953–54. Report of an Enquiry*. London, HMSO, 1957.

[5] Since the sample changes from year to year, the Surveys yield no direct information about the response of particular households to changing conditions.

[6] The Survey is used for a variety of purposes in addition to its original role of yielding weights for the index of retail prices: it is used in the calculation of special price indices for one-person and two-person pensioner households, to study the redistributive effects of direct and indirect

of income and estimating the extent of poverty in a given year, as well as in tracing developments over time in these phenomena, a number of problems are associated with the use of the Family Expenditure Surveys; partly these reflect the intrinsic nature of the data collected and partly the manner in which the information is published. The methodology and sampling techniques used in the Surveys have been examined in detail elsewhere.[1] In this appendix we confine ourselves to singling out features relevant to the analysis of poverty. They fall under the following headings and are discussed in the ensuing three sections: the extent of relevant information in the Surveys, the accuracy of the information and problems of historical comparison. The final section of this appendix describes the special tabulations of the 1971 Family Expenditure Survey.

THE INFORMATION COLLECTED

The Family Expenditure Survey is a continuous sample of private households in the United Kingdom. Each week addresses randomly selected from the electoral register in various administrative areas (themselves selected from a stratified rotating sample) are visited by an interviewer. The households at these addresses are invited to participate in a survey of spending patterns, and those who agree are interviewed to obtain details of household members, including their incomes. Information on regular and less frequent expenditures is also sought at the interview, but most items are recorded in budget diaries which each member of the household aged 15 or over keeps for the following two weeks. A small payment is made on completion of the diaries. The information collected is checked and coded by the Office of Population Censuses and Surveys before being published by the Department of Employment.

The Survey is based on households (rather than families) – a household being defined as one person living alone, or a group of people living at the same address, having meals prepared together and with common housekeeping. Members of a household are not necessarily related and may include several families.

Income

In the published tables, households are usually grouped by gross normal income before the deduction of national insurance contributions and income tax. The definition of gross normal income has been consistent

taxation and of a wide range of social benefits, and for national income and expenditure estimates.

[1] See, for example, Government Social Survey, *Family Expenditure Survey. Handbook on the sample, field-work and coding procedures* by W. F. F. Kemsley and the various Department of Employment, *Family Expenditure Survey Reports*.

since its introduction in the 1960 Survey. It includes earnings from employment and self-employment (including the value of luncheon vouchers); pensions and income from annuities; income from investments and property; weekly paid social security benefits; other allowances and benefits; other non-earned income. Households living in owner-occupied or rent-free accommodation are assigned a weekly imputed income based on the rateable value of the dwelling with a corresponding addition to expenditure. However, certain additions to the household's resources are excluded: in particular windfall payments such as legacies, maturing insurance policies and gambling winnings; proceeds of the sale of a house or durables; capital gains; withdrawals of savings; the value of educational grants and scholarships not paid in cash and of concessionary goods and services received free or at reduced prices; other income in kind. These exclusions are made since they do not represent part of *normal* income, even though they may have a substantial effect on household expenditure in a particular period.

There is in fact no uniform time-period over which normal income is measured. Income from investments is taken as the weekly equivalent of all receipts over the last twelve months, and income from self-employment as that of the last complete twelve months' accounting period. In contrast, pensions and social security benefits are measured at their current rate. The object is to define income available to finance expenditure, ignoring short-term fluctuations. Consequently, two important adjustments are made to earnings from employment and social security benefits received whilst away from work. First, each employee is asked whether he considers his previous week's or month's earnings were normal. If not, his own assessment of normal earnings is substituted for the actual receipts in the last pay period. Secondly, if a person has been out of work for thirteen weeks or less, his normal earnings when last employed, rather than last week's actual benefits, are included in his normal income.

We use normal incomes defined in this way, and in chapter 4 we compare them with last week's earnings or benefits actually received. In chapters 3, 4 and 5, we also examine household incomes net of income tax and national insurance contributions.

Expenditure

We use the term total expenditure as it is defined in the published *Reports* – that is expenditure on the current consumption of goods and services. Households are asked to report all their payments whether on current consumption items or not. The following payments are then excluded: purchases of financial assets, life insurance premiums, pension contributions and other payments which are essentially savings; mortgage repayments and other payments for purchase of or alterations to dwellings; income tax and national insurance contributions and gambling losses. The consumption of housing by those owning their own houses or living rent free is expressed by a notional expenditure of imputed income.

Expenditure and payment data gathered at the interview and in the two-week budget diaries are brought together, checked for overlap and converted to a weekly equivalent. The information collected at the interview is intended to capture regular but less frequent payments, such as rent and fuel bills, rates, insurance, licences, season tickets. Nevertheless, all variability in expenditure patterns due to the timing of purchases cannot be eliminated and, as has been seen in chapter 4, considerable discrepancies remain between households' incomes and their recorded payments.

Most of our expenditure analysis is concerned with ten major expenditure categories, but it also proved possible to compare expenditure levels of the poor and the non-poor for a number of individual items (see chart 6.1).

The published tables

In chapters 3 and 6 comparisons over time using the Family Expenditure Surveys have been based on tables in the published official *Reports*. These tables were not originally intended to yield information for the measurement of poverty, and their use for this purpose gives rise to a number of problems. One major source of difficulty is that households are classified by gross household income in the tables showing expenditure patterns and a variety of other features. Comparisons between the various income-groups, both in a given year and between years, are made difficult because of differences in the average size and composition of households in the various groups. One way of making some allowance for such differences would be to group households on the basis of income *per capita*. Even better for our purposes would be a classification on the basis of equivalent household income, employing a set of equivalence scales to allow not only for household size but also for composition. Unfortunately households are not classified in this way in the published tables.[1]

The *Reports* usually contain a table which groups households simultaneously by composition and by income, although the composition breakdown has varied somewhat from year to year.[2] Certain tables also show, for some though not all types of household, expenditure patterns for households classified by income and composition.[3] With some manipulation, and in conjunction with use of a set of equivalence scales,

[1] This may reflect official reluctance to choose a particular set of equivalence scales (see Ministry of Labour, *Household Expenditure 1953–54*, p. 21, para. 94).

[2] In 1953/4 and 1967, for example, some of the groups distinguished were particularly heterogeneous. Such information was not published for the years 1957–60, or for 1962.

[3] Usually only the most common types of household – one adult, and one man and one woman with 0–3 children.

it is possible to convert these published data approximately on to the basis of equivalent household income. Access to the special tabulations for 1971 enabled us to confirm the adequacy of the methods used to derive information in this form.

ACCURACY

It has sometimes been asserted that the Family Expenditure Survey is not properly representative of the United Kingdom population and, in particular, that the poor are under-represented. Two questions have to be dealt with: how representative is the Survey and what reliability can be attached to the information collected?

Is the Survey representative?

There are two reasons why the results of the Survey may not be representative. First, the sampling frame, being based on private households, excludes people living in hotels, hostels, hospitals and similar institutions, the homeless and members of the armed forces not living in private households. It also excludes students to the extent that they are absent from their parents' homes at the time of the Survey. In the 1971 Census 3 per cent of the population of Great Britain (1,620,000 people) were living in institutions rather than households (table I.1). Whether it makes sense to assess the poverty of these individuals in the manner we have adopted in this book must depend very much on their particular situation; without a special survey it is not possible to judge whether their proportion in poverty is similar to that for households.

TABLE I.1.   *The institutional population of Great Britain, 1971*

	Proportions of total
	(%)
Hotels:	
Resident guests	3·6
Visitor guests	8·3
Staff and relatives	6·9
Total	(18·8)
Hospitals	34·3
Homes for the old and disabled	11·0
Children's homes	2·9
Educational establishments	14·9
Places of detention	3·4
Defence establishments	6·3
Others	8·4
Total	100·0
Total number	*1,618,155*

Source: CSO, *Social Trends*, no. 6, 1975, table 2.3.

Secondly, response to the Survey, which has averaged about 70 per cent, is associated with a certain amount of bias in the sample achieved. A comparison by Kemsley of the 1971 Census of Population and the 1971 Family Expenditure Survey revealed a lower than average response rate among smaller households and those with a self-employed head. There was also a marked decline in response as the age of the head of household increased.[1] We used Kemsley's results to recalculate the extent of poverty as estimated in chapter 4, reweighting the sample for differential response according to the age of head of household and the numbers of individuals and children in the household. The proportion of people in poverty was increased by at most 0·3 per cent. An adjustment for differential response by tenure group, on the other hand, reduced the proportion by a similarly small figure.

Since no income data are collected in the Census it was not possible to test directly for the possibility of response bias in this respect. However, we were able to reweight the results by the number of cars in the household and, as just noted, by the type of tenure of the household. For both these characteristics there is some association with income, but again no significant change was found in the total proportions in poverty.

We conclude therefore that, although differential sampling bias may lead to samples of low income households being slightly unrepresentative in terms of other characteristics, this is probably no more so than for the rest of the population. Although it is possible that low income households, as such, have a lower response rate, we have found no evidence to support this. Factors such as the likelihood of someone being at home when the interviewer calls and willingness to cooperate appear to be more important.

Reliability of the information

While many attempts are made to ensure accuracy, it is known that there are some biases in the collection of data on account of both the method of collection and misreporting. This is evident from a comparison of Family Expenditure Survey data grossed up to a national basis and corresponding figures taken from the national accounts and earnings surveys. Certain kinds of expenditure are known to be under-recorded, particularly on alcohol, tobacco, meals out, confectionery, ice cream and soft drinks. This may be due to a combination of factors: diarists cutting expenditure during the period when they are monitoring their behaviour, errors of memory in recalling small expenditure items, an allocation of some expenditure to business rather than household accounts, or deliberate

[1] CSO, 'Family Expenditure Survey. A study of differential response based on a comparison of the 1971 Sample with the Census' by W. F. F. Kemsley, *Statistical News*, no. 31, November 1975. Census returns for households in the 1971 Family Expenditure Survey were extracted and those of cooperating and non-cooperating households compared.

understatement. There is also evidence that some types of income are under-recorded. Earnings appear to be slightly understated – mainly by women in part-time employment – and so are incomes from self-employment and investments.[1] The reliability of income and expenditure data is discussed further in chapter 4, where it appears that the extent of low income is probably overstated when account is taken of the level of expenditure of some low income households.

On the basis of our analysis of the variation in response rate and the reliability of income information, we would conclude that, on balance, the Family Expenditure Survey may tend to overstate the extent of low income (that is income below a given level) rather than to understate it. However, it may equally well understate the amount of income received at all levels.

Sampling errors

Sampling also gives rise to errors in the data, though the Family Expenditure Survey is not a particularly small sample: the number of cooperating households was 12,911 in 1953/4, 3486 in 1961, 7239 in 1971 and 7126 in 1973. Sampling error is smallest for estimates of expenditure by large groups of households on items purchased frequently, when the expenditure does not vary greatly between households. Standard errors are larger for small groups of households, for items purchased infrequently and for expenditure varying widely between households. This adds to the difficulty of studying small groups at the extremes of the income distribution. Estimates of standard errors for the various items of income and expenditure are given in the *Family Expenditure Survey Reports*.

HISTORICAL COMPARISONS

There were some important differences between the definitions in the 1953/4 and subsequent Surveys, as well as some minor changes in the codes. The most important were as follows.

First, Surveys since 1957 have sought more detailed income information than in 1953/4. In 1953/4 wage and salary earners were asked to state the gross amount they were paid before deductions such as national insurance contributions and income tax; since 1957 they have been asked for the actual amount received ('take-home' pay) and, separately, for the various deductions. There are also now detailed questions about the various sources of earned and unearned income.[2] Information from 1957 onwards is probably more accurate than for 1953/4 as a result of this, and it has

[1] A. R. Thatcher, 'The distribution of earnings of employees in Great Britain', *Journal of the Royal Statistical Society* (series A), vol. 131, part 2, 1968, concluded that earnings recorded in the Family Expenditure Survey are on average a few per cent less than in other sources.

[2] Ministry of Labour, *Family Expenditure Survey Report for 1957–59*, London, HMSO, 1961, p. 2.

become increasingly so with improvements in the experience and training of the interviewers. The 1953/4 Survey noted that absolute accuracy could not be claimed for the income details and referred to the likelihood of understatement.[1] While there is evidence of understatement in later years also, it is likely to have been smaller.

Secondly, from 1960 onwards questions have been put about the 'normal' wage or salary as well as the actual wage or salary last received,[2] and households are now classified on the basis of their gross normal income.

Thirdly, following the raising of the school-leaving age from 15 to 16 in 1972, the definition of a child was changed in 1973 from a person under 16 to an unmarried person under 18. Thus analyses by household composition in the 1973 Survey are not strictly comparable with similar analyses for earlier years. For example, some households classified in 1973 as one man, one woman, and two children would have been classified in earlier Surveys as three adults and one child.[3]

Whilst changes in survey design are easy to record, it is much more difficult to assess changes in differential response rates. The only extensive analysis of response rates relates to 1971.[4] However, the 1953/4 *Report* suggested that its sample was deficient in the elderly and in single-person households. These are two of the categories that Kemsley's article showed were under-represented in 1971, and it would seem from this evidence that relative response patterns have not changed greatly. Furthermore, the increase in the sample size in 1967 and gradual improvements over time in the implementation of the Survey, especially at the interviewing stage, will have led to greater consistency and accuracy.

SPECIAL TABULATIONS FOR 1971

In this study we have also used special tabulations from the 1971 Family Expenditure Survey. These have been drawn upon in chapters 4–7 in analyses of the numbers in poverty in 1971, their characteristics and expenditure patterns, also in the estimation of equivalence scales. For this purpose a special computer tape was prepared, containing information

---

[1] Ministry of Labour, *Household Expenditure 1953–54*, p. 15, para. 73.

[2] Ministry of Labour, *Family Expenditure Survey for 1960 and 1961*, London, HMSO, 1962, p. 1, para. 6.

[3] There have been a number of less significant changes: estimates of imputed weekly income from owner-occupation, based on the net rateable values of dwellings from 1957 onwards, were derived from the gross valuation for income tax purposes under Schedule A in the 1953/4 Survey. In the 1973 Survey, the new and higher 1973 assessments of rateable values were used for this purpose and caused a larger increase in this imputed sum than would otherwise have occurred. In the 1953/4 Survey detailed expenditure records were kept for 21 days; in the subsequent Family Expenditure Surveys for 14 days. The 1957 Survey related to Great Britain, the others to the United Kingdom. There were some further minor changes in the 1973 Survey (see Department of Employment, *Family Expenditure Survey Report for 1973*, p. 4).

[4] Kemsley in CSO, *Statistical News*, November 1975.

about the numbers, ages, economic status, etc. of those in each household, together with details of their incomes and expenditure. From this tape the Department of Health and Social Security derived the tables and grouped data. Results based on this source differ in several ways from those based on published information.

In the first place, we were able to choose some definitions of key variables which we felt were more appropriate for the analysis of poverty than those used in the published *Reports*. Reference is made to these definitions in the relevant chapters: for example, in chapters 4 and 5 it was possible to examine the net income of households, after deduction of income tax and national insurance contributions, rather than gross income. It was also possible to revise the classification of 'retired' and 'unoccupied' persons in the published *Family Expenditure Survey Report for 1971* to take account of 'unoccupied' persons above retiring age. The extent to which we have been able to expand our knowledge of the poor and their behaviour has depended to a large degree on the flexibility which these special arrangements allowed.

The sample of households in our special tabulations is somewhat smaller than the published sample, 7143 households compared with 7239. There were two reasons for this: first – and this is the principal explanation – on grounds of computational convenience the number of adults in each household was limited to four and the number of children to six. Secondly, a few more households were eliminated because their returns appeared to be particularly unreliable. No attempt was made to adjust estimates based on the 1971 special tabulations for these deficiencies, as they are too small to detract significantly from our findings (1·3 per cent of households containing 3·1 per cent of individuals in the Survey were excluded).

A second important difference between the special tabulations and published data concerns the distinction between an 'adult' and a 'child'. In the published *Reports* (until the raising of the school-leaving age) a child was simply defined as a person under 16. In the special tabulations the definition of a 'child' was changed to conform more closely with family relationships: a 'child' was taken to be any person aged under 15, or any person aged 15 to 18 inclusive who was dependent on his parents.[1]

Statistics of tax units in chapter 4 were based on a special analysis in which the individuals in each household were grouped in tax units. For 75 per cent of households the tabulations remained unchanged, since they consisted of a single tax unit; for the remaining 25 per cent the relevant information was allocated to the appropriate tax unit.

---

[1] A child being 'dependent' on his parents if his income was less than £8 per week and/or he was in full-time education.

CHANGES IN POVERTY STANDARDS

The classic social surveys undertaken by Booth and Rowntree at the end of the last century were not the earliest attempts to measure poverty, but their significance lies in the attempt to refine and apply the concept of a subsistence poverty level. For example, Booth's study documented in detail the conditions of life and work of London's working class inhabitants, though his criteria of poverty were essentially intuitive and qualitative.[1]

Rowntree's investigation of the social and economic conditions of the wage-earning classes in York in 1899 attempted to establish a more precise absolute poverty standard, based on the view that there is some minimum subsistence level of consumption necessary for the sustenance of physical health. He distinguished a state of 'primary' poverty, which related to those families in which 'total earnings are insufficient to obtain the minimum necessaries for the maintenance of merely physical efficiency', from a state of 'secondary' poverty, which related to those families where total earnings would be sufficient 'were it not that some portion of it is absorbed by other expenditure, either useful or wasteful'.[2] Thus, Rowntree's poverty line specified a subsistence level of living which required a degree of economy and allowed for no satisfaction of subsidiary needs. This standard was measured by estimating the lowest cost of providing the minimum of food, clothing, shelter, light and fuel necessary to maintain families of specified composition in physical health.

The allowance for food was based on the cost of standard diets required, in the view of nutritionists at that time, to provide individuals with sufficient proteins and calories for maintaining physical efficiency. Rowntree acknowledged a significant element of impracticality in this standard when he observed that 'the poor do not possess knowledge which would enable them to select a diet that is at once as nutritious and as economical as that which is here adopted as the standard. Moreover, the adoption of such a diet would require considerable changes in established customs, and many prejudices would have to be uprooted.'[3]

This appendix has been prepared mainly by P. S. Lansley.

[1] C. Booth, *Life and Labour of the People of London*, London, Macmillan, 1902.
[2] Rowntree, *Poverty*, p. 86.
[3] Ibid., p. 105. The diets used were those of able-bodied paupers in workhouses, since these institutions sought to provide the relevant nutrients at the lowest cost. Workhouse regulations required at least two meat dinners weekly, but Rowntree selected the cheapest proposed rations,

TABLE II.1. *Categories of expenditure[a] in subsistence scales, 1899–1950[b] (£s per week)*

	Rowntree 1899	Bowley 1924	Rowntree 1936	Beveridge 1938	Rowntree 1950
Food	0·63½	1·14	1·02½	1·55	2·36½
Clothing	⎫	0·28	0·40	0·27	1·38½
Fuel and light	⎬ 0·24½	0·20	0·22	0·24½	0·38
Household sundries	⎪	0·20	0·16	–	0·30
Personal sundries	⎭	–	0·37	–	0·57½
Total	0·88	1·82	2·17½	2·16½[c]	5·00¼

Sources: Rowntree, *Poverty* and *Poverty and Progress*; (with Lavers) *Poverty and the Welfare State*; Bowley from G. D. H. and M. I. Cole, *The Condition of Britain*, London, Gollancz, 1937; Beveridge from Treasury, *Social Insurance and Allied Services*.

[a] At current prices, excluding rent.
[b] For a family of two adults and three children.
[c] Includes an allowance of 10p for 'inefficient spending'.

Actual sums paid were taken as the necessary rent expenditure, since Rowntree felt that extravagance in this item was very unlikely. Necessary expenditure on 'household sundries', principally boots, clothes and fuel, was estimated from the views of a sample of predominately low income working people on the very smallest sums needed for these commodities. A nominal figure of 2d per head per week (less than 1p) was allowed for other items such as soap and light. The resulting standard, together with its component elements, is shown for a family of two adults and three children in table II.1, which also presents subsistence scales that have been proposed since Rowntree's original, including the two standards used by Rowntree in his 1936 and 1950 inquiries into working class living conditions in York.[1] To illustrate how the meaning of poverty has changed since the turn of the century, table II.2 compares these standards in real and relative terms; they are converted to constant 1971 prices and also shown as a proportion of average manual earnings currently prevailing. In view of the difficulties involved in measuring average price changes over such long periods of time, this exercise should be treated with caution.[2]

which excluded meat, implying a diet even more meagre than provided in the regulations. The weekly cost of these standard diets was calculated on the basis of prevailing food prices, but excluded any cooking expenses. Modern analyses of the costs of achieving dietary sufficiency (which start from the requirements in terms of calories, vitamins, etc. specified by nutritionists, and then use linear programming methods) have shown that three or four foods, such as milk, potatoes and soya beans, yield an adequate though monotonous diet at minimum cost. Rowntree's diet was not as severe as this.

[1] Rowntree, *Poverty and Progress*; and (with G. R. Lavers), *Poverty and the Welfare State. A third social survey of York dealing only with economic questions*, London, Longmans, 1951.

[2] The official index of retail prices for the period 1914 to 1947, initiated in 1914, was a base-weighted index designed to measure the changing cost of purchasing a 1914 list of essential goods and services. As the range of goods and services actually purchased gradually increased, the reliability of the index as a guide to changes in the cost of living was impaired. Consequently, for the period after 1938 the index used in table II.2 (taken from London and Cambridge Economic Service, *Key Statistics of the British Economy, 1900–1964*, London, Times, 1965) is the estimate of the change in retail prices from 1939 to 1947 made by R. G. D. Allen ('Index num-

Nevertheless, even when allowance is made for the difficulties inherent in price comparisons, it is clear that in real terms Rowntree's 1936 standard was considerably less austere than that for 1899: as the table shows he adopted a basic requirement of £10·26 per week for 1936 compared with £6·93 (both at 1971 prices) for 1899, an increase of about 48 per cent. This rise resulted both from an increase in the number of items included in the standard and from larger allowances for the items in Rowntree's original 1899 list (table II.1).[1] The more generous 1936 standard therefore reflected Rowntree's view that his 1899 subsistence standard of living needed to be modified in response to changes in economic and social conditions since the turn of the century and that, in real terms, the standard appropriate for 1899 was inadequate in 1936. In fact, his minimum tolerable living standard increased slightly more than average earnings.

TABLE II.2.   *The development of minimum living standards,[a] 1899–1973*

Scales		Total expenditure[b] (current prices)	Retail price index (1899= 100)	Total expenditure (1971 prices)		Average male manual earnings (gross)	Total expenditure/ average earnings
				Value	Index (1899= 100=)		
		(£s per wk)		(£s per wk)		(£s per wk)	(%)
Rowntree,	1899	0·88	*100*	6·93	*100·0*	1·44	*61·0*
Bowley,	1924	1·82	*195*	7·35	*106·0*	3·00	*61·0*
Rowntree,	1936	2·17½	*167*	10·26	*148·1*	3·23	*67·0*
Beveridge,	1938	2·16½c	*176*	9·69	*139·8*	3·45	*62·8*
Rowntree,	1950	5·00½	*325*	12·17	*175·6*	7·53	*66·6*
National assistance:							
	1948	3·35	*305*	8·66	*125·0*	6·90	*48·6*
	1953	4·97½	*400*	9·80	*141·4*	9·46	*52·6*
	1963	8·67½	*532*	12·85	*185·4*	16·75	*51·8*
Supplementary benefits:							
	1971	15·95d	*788*	15·95	*230·2*	30·93	*51·6*
	1973	20·20e	*921*	17·28	*249·4*	40·92	*49·4*

Sources: Retail price index from London and Cambridge Economic Service, *Key Statistics for the British Economy 1900–1964*, table C; average male manual earnings from Department of Employment, *British Labour Statistics: historical abstract 1886–1968*, London, HMSO, 1971, and *Department of Employment Gazette* (various issues); scales from same sources as table II.1 and Department of Health and Social Security, *Social Security Statistics 1974*, table 34.01, p. 144.

  [a] For a family of two adults and three children.
  [b] Excluding rent.
  [c] Including an allowance of 10p for 'inefficient spending'.
  [d] Including the long-term addition of 50p.
  [e] The 'long-term' rate.

bers of retail prices, 1938–51', *Applied Statistics*, vol. 1, June 1952). In 1947 the interim index of retail prices, based on weights obtained from the 1937/8 Family Budget Survey, was introduced and used until 1956, when it was superseded by a new index based on weights derived from the 1953/4 Household Expenditure Survey.

  [1] In 1936 household sundries include 8p for insurance; personal sundries include 20½p for contributions to sick and burial clubs, Trade Union subscriptions, travel to work, stamps, writing paper, etc., daily newspaper and wireless, leaving 16½p for 'all else'.

This is not to say that Rowntree's 1936 standard should necessarily be regarded as generous. Indeed, he believed the sum allowed in 1936 erred 'on the side of stringency rather than of extravagance'. The sum allowed for food was based on a report of a committee appointed in 1933 by the British Medical Association 'to determine the minimum weekly expenditure on food which must be incurred by families of varying size if health and working capacity are to be maintained'. The allowance for food thus represented 'the lowest standard which responsible experts can justify'. The sums fixed for other goods included in the budget were equally based on a 'thorough inquiry into the *minimum* expenditure necessary', and were intended to provide merely a subsistence level of living.

To determine the poverty line for his 1950 survey, Rowntree used the 1936 diets modified by the results of a 1950 Report of a Commission of the British Medical Association concerned with nutrition.[1] The allowances for clothing, fuel and light and household sundries were based on the observed expenditure of a small sample of low paid men and women who spent the least on these items. In the case of personal sundries Rowntree used his own judgement, though essentially the items included in 1950 were the same as those included in 1936. Nevertheless, as table II.2 shows, after allowance is made for price changes Rowntree's minimum standard for a family of five in 1950 was some 18 per cent higher than in 1936.

In addition to Booth's study of London and Rowntree's three surveys of York, a number of other inquiries were made into working class conditions in this period.[2] One example was a study of conditions in the four towns, Northampton, Warrington, Stanley and Reading, carried out under the supervision of Professor A. L. Bowley in 1912–13 and repeated in 1924.[3] For both studies Bowley prescribed a minimum living standard; the one for 1924, relating to a family of five, is shown in tables II.1 and II.2. This standard, which covered only the bare minimum expenditure on food, clothing, household accessories, light and coal, was based on Rowntree's 1899 standard, the allowance for clothing, cleaning and lighting being at the same level, but Rowntree's largely vegetarian diet modified by some meat. The sum allocated for fuel was allowed to vary between towns according to cost; actual rent was included in full, but nothing was allowed for items such as travel, private insurance or personal expenses.

There were a number of other surveys of living standards in the interwar

[1] Rowntree and Lavers, *Poverty and the Welfare State*, p. 11. For example, white flour was substituted for wholemeal flour and fresh milk for condensed milk, extra sugar and margarine were added and cheese, bacon and cooking fat reduced.

[2] For a summary of these inquiries see: D. Caradog Jones, *Social Surveys*, London, Hutchinson, 1949; Political and Economic Planning, 'Poverty ten years after Beveridge', *Planning*, vol. 19, no. 344, 4 August 1952.

[3] A. L. Bowley and A. R. Burnett-Hurst, *Livelihood and Poverty*, London, G. Bell & Sons, 1915; A. L. Bowley and M. H. Hogg, *Has Poverty Diminished?*, London, P. S. King & Sons, 1925.

period which used similar methods for establishing a poverty line by setting some minimum standard for food, clothing, fuel and light and household sundries for individuals of different ages and sex. The allowances for food were usually based on contemporary studies of nutrition; standards for other items were generally related to Rowntree's 1899 standard and so allowed for little improvement during the first part of the century.[1]

POSTWAR STANDARDS

Postwar welfare legislation and the associated system of social security were based largely, if not entirely, upon the recommendations of the Beveridge Report of 1942;[2] the value of the national assistance scales in 1948 and certain subsequent years are also shown in table II.2. A principle underlying the Beveridge recommendations was that national insurance benefits should be sufficient to provide a subsistence standard of living, and the Report contained Beveridge's own estimates of these subsistence costs. For this purpose Beveridge drew on the work of Rowntree and the Survey of working class household expenditure carried out by the Ministry of Labour in 1937/8.[3]

Beveridge's estimates of subsistence income were based on the need for food, clothing, fuel and light, household sundries and rent, allowing some small margin for the inevitable difficulty of conforming strictly to the expenditure required in principle by the standard. Food costs were estimated from diets prescribed in the 1936 and 1938 Reports of the League of Nations Technical Commission on Nutrition and by the Nutrition Committee of the British Medical Association in 1933.[4] Estimates of necessary expenditure on clothing, fuel, light and household sundries were based on the 1937/8 Family Budget Survey, being set below the average expenditure on these items observed in the Survey.[5] Estimating a minimum rent was complicated by the fact that this item varies widely between regions and families. Beveridge suggested 50p a week for households and 32½p for individuals, compared with an average weekly rent of 54p revealed by the 1937/8 Survey. Finally, he allowed a margin of 10p a week per couple to cover 'inefficiency in purchasing'.

[1] See for example, PEP, 'Poverty ten years after Beveridge'.

[2] Treasury, *Social Insurance and Allied Services*.

[3] Some results were given in *Ministry of Labour Gazette*, vol. 48, December 1940 and vol. 49, January and February 1941.

[4] *Beveridge Report*, p. 19.

[5] It was felt that actual expenditure was above subsistence requirements and that clothing and sundry needs could be postponed during periods of unemployment and disability. A special scale was established for the elderly on the grounds that their subsistence needs are in some respects below (food and clothing) and in others above (fuel and light) those of younger adults. The various needs of young people of working age and dependent children were calculated in a similar way.

TABLE II.3. *Prewar subsistence scales compared with 1948 national assistance*
(£s per week, 1971 prices)

	Rowntree 1936	Beveridge 1938	National assistance 1948
Single man	6·09	2·80	3·10
Couple	7·53	4·92	5·17
Couple, 1 child	8·99	6·51	6·33
2 children	9·72	8·10	7·49
3 children	10·26	9·69	8·66

Sources: Rowntree, *Poverty and Progress*; Treasury, *Social Insurance and Allied Services*; National Assistance Board, *Report for the year ended December 31st, 1948*, Cmd 7767, London, HMSO, 1949.

Note: Rent excluded from all scales.

The resulting Beveridge scales (at 1971 prices) are shown in table II.3 for different household sizes, along with the Rowntree 1936 standard and the 1948 national assistance scales. The Beveridge scales were below Rowntree's 1936 standard, especially for smaller households, mainly because Beveridge allowed nothing for expenditure on 'personal sundries' and his 'margin for inefficient spending', mainly applicable to food, amounted to only 15–20 per cent of the food expenditure allowance.[1] Table II.3 also shows that the official national assistance scales introduced in 1948 were above the Beveridge subsistence standard for single adults and couples, but below it where there were dependent children. For all types of family they were below Rowntree's 1936 standard. And, although Beveridge recommended that national insurance benefits should be set at the prescribed subsistence levels, in the event they were fixed below national assistance rates when rent is included – a feature that persists to this day.

The principles on which changes in national assistance and supplementary benefit scales have been made in the postwar period have never been precisely formulated. In earlier years the aim appeared to be the maintenance in real terms of the 1948 scales, though the infrequency with which they were changed meant that they sometimes fell below that level.[2] The first explicit statement of objectives appeared in the White Paper announcing the increases for September 1959: it declared that those on national assistance should have 'a share in increasing national prosperity'.[3]

[1] While the household relativities inherent in the Rowntree scales are described as the 'sums necessary to enable families of different sizes to live at the same standard of comfort as an urban family of five spending [£2·17½] (exclusive of rent)', they imply improbably large economies of scale between a single adult and a couple, and between the first and additional children.

[2] For an examination of the changes made to the scales during the 1950s, see T. Lynes, *National Assistance and National Prosperity*, Welwyn, Codicote Press, 1962.

[3] Ministry of Pensions and National Insurance, *Improvements in National Assistance*, Cmnd 782, London, HMSO, 1959.

It was not until 1974 that this was improved upon, when the National Insurance Act provided that long-term national insurance benefits should rise in line with earnings (or prices if they rose more quickly), and short-term benefits, which include ordinary supplementary benefit rates, should rise in line with prices. However, this statutory obligation does not guarantee that the relative position of households receiving supplementary benefits will be maintained, for whilst the principles of revision are now established, their detailed implementation is left undefined.

Table II.2 shows that the national assistance and supplementary benefit scales increased in real terms by 13 per cent between 1948 and 1953, 48 per cent between 1948 and 1963, and 84 per cent between 1948 and 1971.[1] It also presents changes in the value of national assistance or supplementary benefits in relation to average gross earnings of adult manual workers. Since the War, benefits for a married couple with three children have remained approximately constant at about half of average gross manual earnings.

This picture of changes in the relative living standards of those receiving assistance takes no account of changes in the extent and distribution of free and subsidised consumption; nor does it allow for payments of tax and national insurance contributions by working households, nor for income from family allowances. Since the War, the supplementary benefit level has increased steadily as a proportion of net earnings of manual workers, but as shown in chapter 3 net household income of the poor has remained a constant proportion of the median, after allowing for differences in household size and composition. The cause of this divergence of trends lies partly in the increasing proportion of the population dependent on benefits, mainly old people, which has tended to depress incomes in the lower percentiles of the distribution; probably also to the increasing number of working married women and the greater proportion of the labour force now in non-manual, and hence better paid, occupations, both of which have tended to raise incomes at the median.[2]

NUMBERS IN POVERTY

Some historical estimates of the proportion of households in poverty based on early minimum subsistence standards are presented in table II.4.

[1] Since the index of retail prices tends to understate cost of living increases for the poor (see chapter 6), the rise suggested by table II.2 in the real incomes of recipients of benefits may be overstated.

[2] The supplementary benefit rates shown in table II.2 include the 'long-term addition' introduced in 1966 for pensioner households and those who have received benefits for a continuous period of two years or more. In October 1973 this addition was incorporated into a new 'long-term rate', which is substantially higher than the 'ordinary rate' available for other households. The change in the position of households in receipt of the 'ordinary rate' only would be less favourable than indicated by the table.

It would be wrong to assume from the 16·5 per cent for Plymouth in 1935 and the 31·1 per cent for York in 1936 that there was a doubling of the numbers in poverty in a single year. Apart from regional factors, the difference reflects the fact that the 1936 York standard was rather more generous than the 1935 Plymouth standard;[1] it would therefore tend to yield a higher proportion in poverty.

TABLE II.4   *Working class households in poverty, 1899–1950*

Source	Date	Basis of estimates	Town surveyed	Proportion[a] (%)
Rowntree, *Poverty*	1899	Households	} York {	12·7[b]
		Population		15·5[b]
Bowley and Hogg, *Has Poverty Diminished?*, p. 17	1912	Households	Northampton	8·0[c]
			Warrington	12·5[c]
			Stanley	6·0[c]
			Reading	23·0[c]
	1924	Households	Northampton	4·0[d]
			Warrington	7·9[d]
			Stanley	7·5[d]
			Reading	11·3[d]
PEP, 'Poverty ten years after Beveridge', p. 24	1935	Households	Plymouth	16·5
Rowntree, *Poverty and Progress*, p. 451	1936	Population 1936 standard 1899 standard	} York {	31·1 6·8
Rowntree and Lavers, *Poverty and the Welfare State*	1950	Population	York	2·8

[a] Care is needed in comparing these figures because of differences in the methods of the various surveys.

[b] 'Primary' poor.

[c] Those 'certainly' and 'probably' below the standard, based on an assumption of full employment, which was approximately true at that date.

[d] Those 'certainly' and 'probably' below the standard, but without an assumption of full employment.

However, a reasonably direct comparison is possible between the proportions in poverty in York in 1899 and 1936, since Rowntree calculated poverty in the latter year on both his current and his earlier standard. This shows on the 1899 standard a sharp fall in the proportion of the working class population in poverty from 15·5 to 6·8 per cent. Over a shorter period, 1912–24, Bowley's surveys, based on essentially common subsistence criteria, also point to a reduction in poverty; in only one of his four towns, Stanley, did the proportion rise between these years, and then only

[1] Numbers of the poor estimated on the basis of such stringent standards as those of the surveys by Bowley and PEP were almost certainly an underestimate of the extent of poverty and hardship as judged by contemporary standards in the interwar period (see R. F. George, 'A new calculation of the poverty line', *Journal of the Royal Statistical Society*, vol. 100, part 1, 1937).

slightly. The other three towns enjoyed a fall of the order of 50 per cent in the proportion of working class households in poverty; this reflects mainly the application of a static poverty line over a period of rising real wages.

A comparison of Rowntree's prewar (1936) and postwar (1950) surveys of York also points unequivocally to a decrease in poverty judged on the basis of subsistence living standards. Not only is the fall in the proportion in poverty very large, from 31·1 to 2·8 per cent, but the real improvement in Rowntree's standards between these dates means that on his 1936 standard poverty in 1950 would have been even less.

TABLE II.5. *The causes of individual poverty, 1899, 1936 and 1950 (Percentages)*

	1899	1936	1950
Inadequate earnings although in regular employment	74·2[a]	32·8	1·0
Death of chief wage earner	15·6	7·8	6·4
Incapacity of chief wage earner:			
Through illness	5·1	4·1	21·3
Through old age		14·7	68·1
Unemployment or irregular employment of chief wage earner	5·1	28·6	–
Other causes	–	12·0[b]	3·2

Sources: Rowntree, *Poverty; Poverty and Progress;* (with Lavers), *Poverty in the Welfare State.*

[a] The sum of those classified under 'inadequate wages' (52·0 per cent) and 'large family' (22·2 per cent).

[b] Includes inadequate earnings of other workers in casual or self-employment.

These surveys also help to explain changes in the nature of poverty over time. Table II.5 shows that there have been significant changes in the pattern of the apparent causes of poverty. In 1899 the most important cause was low wages in relation to family needs; unemployment was then of minor importance. Low wages were again significant in 1936 – though not to the same extent – and the importance of unemployment had increased. By 1950 low wages and unemployment had been displaced by old age and sickness as the principal causes of poverty in York. However, using a representative sample of all households in the United Kingdom, Abel-Smith and Townsend found that low wages were still an important cause of poverty for perhaps as many as one-third of poor individuals in 1953/4.[1]

LIVING LEVELS AND EXPENDITURE PATTERNS OF THE POOR

There is less information available about living levels and expenditure patterns of the poor than about the numbers in poverty and minimum

[1] *The Poor and the Poorest,* p. 30, table 5.

subsistence budgets. Moreover, the information which is available is often not immediately suitable for comparing actual poverty levels either with earlier subsistence criteria or with the current living standards of those not in poverty.

An early source of such information is provided by an urban working class family budget survey of 1944 families carried out by the Board of Trade in 1904.[1] This showed that average weekly expenditure on food was £1·12½, some 60 per cent of average weekly total expenditure (including rent) of £1·84. Expenditure on food as shown by this survey formed the basis of the weights used in the original 1914 cost of living index.[2] Weights for non-food items were based on less substantial information; they were rent 16 per cent, clothing 12 per cent, fuel and light 8 per cent, and 'other' 4 per cent.

These data are not suitable for an examination of the actual living standards and expenditure behaviour of those in poverty for a variety of reasons. First, the weights are only approximately equal to the proportional distribution of working class expenditure at the time. Secondly, the survey data are not presented separately for different types of household, nor was their average size published, so that a strict comparison with poverty standards is not possible. Thirdly, the survey related in principle to all working class households and not merely to those which, on the basis of some subsistence criterion, were regarded as in poverty. Probably for this reason average household expenditure on food is nearly twice Rowntree's 1899 standard for a family with three children.

In 1937/8 a large scale Family Budget Survey was undertaken by the Ministry of Labour.[3] This helps to show the principal changes in working class living standards and expenditure patterns between the early years of the century and the immediate prewar period. Average weekly expenditure on food in 1937/8 was £1·72, compared with £1·70 (at 1937/8 prices) in 1904. The 1937/8 expenditure pattern was food 40 per cent, rent 12 per cent, clothing 11 per cent, fuel and light 7 per cent, and 'other' 30 per cent; expenditure on rent and clothing had therefore declined somewhat since 1904, but the major shift was away from expenditure on food, which fell from about three-fifths to two-fifths, apparently in favour of 'other' expenditure, which increased from 4 to 30 per cent. Unfortunately, the inclusion of agricultural households in 1937/8 but not in 1904, and uncertainty about the breadth of coverage – in terms of consumers' expenditure – of the earlier survey, mean that the evidence for this apparently sharp change is not conclusive. Moreover, the comparison is not between

---

[1] Information from this survey was reproduced in Ministry of Labour and National Service, *Industrial Relations Handbook*, London, HMSO, 1944, p. 187.

[2] Only fourteen separate items of food were distinguished.

[3] See *Ministry of Labour Gazette*, vol 48, December 1940, and vol. 49, January 1941; also Ministry of Labour, 'Weekly expenditure of working-class households in 1937–38'.

the poor of 1904 and those of 1937/8, but, in a rather rough and ready fashion, between average working class living standards and expenditure patterns in the two years.

TABLE II.6. *The Beveridge standard and actual expenditure, 1937/8*

	Beveridge standard for couples with children:				Actual expenditure by couples with children;			
	0	1	2	3	0	1	2	3
				(£s per week)				
Expenditure on:								
Food	0·75[a]	1·05[a]	1·35[a]	1·65[a]	0·77	0·74	1·11	1·06
Clothing	0·15	0·19	0·23	0·27	0·10	0·12	0·17	0·21
Fuel, light, sundries	0·20	0·21½	0·23	0·24½	0·20	0·20	0·20	0·23
Other items	–	–	–	–	0·33	0·33	0·55	0·40
Total excl. rent	1·10	1·45½	1·81	2·16½	1·40	1·39	2·03	1·90
Rent	0·50	0·50	0·50	0·50	0·30	0·40	0·31	0·36
				(percentages)				
Proportionate pattern[b]								
Food	68	72	74	77	55	53	55	56
Clothing	14	13	13	12	7	9	8	11
Fuel, light, sundries	18	15	13	11	14	14	10	12
Other items	–	–	–	–	24	24	27	21

Sources: Treasury, *Social Insurance and Allied Services; Ministry of Labour Gazette*, vol. 48, December 1940, and vol. 49, January 1941; Ministry of Labour, 'Weekly expenditure of working-class households in 1937–38'.

[a] Including the allowance for 'inefficient spending'.
[b] Excluding rent.

The 1937/8 Survey also facilitates a comparison between actual expenditure behaviour and the hypothetical minimum established by Beveridge. Table II.6 shows the various expenditures allowed for different household sizes in the Beveridge 1938 subsistence budget, as well as actual expenditure by similar households in the lowest total expenditure group of the 1937/8 Survey.[1] Although precise comparisons are not possible because of differences in total expenditure levels, it seems that, whilst the poorest childless couples received an income higher than allowed by Beveridge, they spent on food about the amount required by Beveridge for subsistence (though proportionately less); actual expenditure on clothing was both absolutely and proportionately less than Beveridge's standard, and on 'other items' more. One-child households are more comparable, having similar total expenditures. Their actual expenditure on food and clothing, both absolutely and proportionately, was considerably less than the Beveridge subsistence level, which suggests that resources which Beveridge assumed would be devoted to basic essentials were allocated to 'other items' instead.

[1] The expenditure patterns of households of different sizes are taken from J. L. Nicholson, 'Variations in working class family expenditure'. See also PEP, 'Poverty ten years after Beveridge'.

APPENDIX III

THE METHOD OF ESTIMATING INCOME
DISTRIBUTIONS

UNADJUSTED HOUSEHOLD INCOMES

Table III.1 shows for selected years the distribution of households in the Household and Family Expenditure Surveys by gross weekly income, together with the average number of persons per household in the various income-groups. This information forms the basis of the distribution of households presented in table III.2 in the form of cumulated percentages of households with unadjusted incomes below the specified levels. Values for income levels below which given percentages fell were obtained by interpolation and, where needed, extrapolation. For instance, in 1953/4 5·8 per cent of households had an income of less than £3 per week and 15·7 per cent less than £6 per week, so that to determine the income level below which 5 per cent and 10 per cent of households fall requires extrapolation and interpolation respectively. Linear interpolation is unsatisfactory, since it is known that households are not typically distributed linearly between two income levels; the assumption of piece-wise log-normality is preferable, and graphical estimates were made with the help of log-probability paper.

The reliability of this method can be checked for one year by means of information presented in table 35 of the *Family Expenditure Survey Report for 1971*, which shows certain quantile values for household incomes interpolated linearly but very finely from 170 income intervals. Published values for the 10th, 25th, 50th, 75th and 90th percentiles – £10·64, £20·00, £34·89, £49·63 and £67·62 respectively – compared well with the values interpolated by the above method – £10·80, £20·00, £34·90, £49·60 and £67·90. For 1971 – and also for 1973 – published quantile values have been used in the text.

EQUIVALENT GROSS HOUSEHOLD INCOMES

Estimates of the distribution of income per equivalent household were derived by the following method. The published *Family Expenditure Survey Reports* include tables of income distributions for each type of household.[1] The distributions for each type of household were first adjusted by a set of income equivalence scales appropriate to the type of household in question,

This appendix has been prepared mainly by P. S. Lansley.

[1] For example, Department of Employment, *Family Expenditure Survey Report for 1971*, table 43.

TABLE III.1. *Households classified by income, 1953/4 to 1973*

Households with gross weekly income	No. of households					Persons per household (averages)				
	1953/4	1963	1967	1971	1973	1953/4	1963	1967	1971	1973
£0–£3	747	81	246	622	300	1·15	1·11	1·05	1·11	1·04
£3–£4	1,279					2·01				
£4–£6		203					1·23			
£6–£8	1,437	325	328			2·72	1·92	1·19		
£8–£10	2,031		311			3·14		1·72		
£10–£14	3,425	517	710	679	622	3·40	2·76	2·19	1·81	1·33
£14–£15	2,578					3·75				
£15–£20		660	893	507	461		3·26	2·77	2·31	1·85
£20–£25	1,065	555	1,149	556	380	4·23	3·40	3·24	2·66	2·15
£25–£30		407	1,004	618	393		3·44	3·39	2·88	2·41
£30–£35	271	383	818	652	442	4·40	3·58	3·33	3·23	2·66
£35–£40			574	724	488			3·36	3·16	2·90
£40–£45			699	613	487			3·73	3·40	3·16
£45–£50				494	540				3·50	3·22
£50–£60	78	284	319	700	939	4·21	3·94	3·87	3·57	3·30
£60–£70			335	676	671			3·89	3·61	3·42
£70–£80					474		3·89			3·54
£80–£100				398	473				3·78	3·60
£100 +					456					3·79
All households	12,911	3,415	7,386	7,239	7,126	3·18	3·02	3·00	2·90	2·82

Sources: Ministry of Labour, *Household Expenditure, 1953–54*, table 8; Department of Employment, *Family Expenditure Survey: Report for 1963*, table 2, *Report for 1967*, table 2, *Report for 1971*, table 1, *Report for 1973*, table 1.

TABLE III.2. *Households below specified income levels, 1953/4 to 1973 (Percentages)*

Households with weekly income less than	1953/4	1963	1967	1971	1973
£3	5·8	..	..	..	..
£4	..	2·4	..	..	..
£6	15·7	8·3	3·3	..	..
£8	26·8	..	7·8	..	..
£10	42·5	17·8	12·0	8·6	4·2
£14	69·1	..	..	..	..
£15	..	32·9	21·6	18·0	12·9
£20	89·1	52·3	33·7	25·0	19·4
£25	..	68·6	49·2	32·7	24·7
£30	97·3	80·5	62·8	41·2	30·3
£35	..	..	73·9	50·2	36·5
£40	..	91·7	81·7	60·2	43·3
£45	..	..	..	68·7	50·1
£50	99·4	..	91·1	75·5	57·7
£60	..	..	95·5	85·2	70·9
£70	..	..	..	..	80·3
£80	..	..	..	94·5	86·7
£100	..	..	..	..	93·6

Source: Table III.1.

to yield, for that type, a distribution of households by equivalent income. The equivalence scales used for this purpose, which take account of the results of chapter 7 of this study, are a single adult 0·60, two adults 1·00, an additional adult 0·40 and a child 0·21.[1] It proved impracticable to make any allowance for the varying needs of children and adults of different ages, or for economies of scale not embodied in the above coefficients. Households were then grouped in terms of income per equivalent couple.

In the second stage, the distribution of a given type of household by equivalent income was plotted on log-probability paper. The distribution of each type between standard intervals of equivalent income was then estimated by interpolating directly from the appropriate graph. The results for all types of household were then totalled to yield the composite equivalent income distributions for the whole sample. These distributions relate to the frequencies of households in each income-group; the frequencies of individuals in each group were obtained by multiplying the household frequencies by the number of people in each type of household.

These results are clearly dependent on the accuracy of interpolation between successive income ranges and, more important, of extrapolation at the extremes of the distribution (though, in practice, very little extrapolation was required). Access to ungrouped data for 1971 permitted a check on our methods; this consisted in calculating the equivalent income for each household in the sample (using the original data for 1971 on tape), ranking and grouping households into 30 equivalent income ranges, and plotting the distributions on log-probability paper. From these latter distributions quantile values were obtained which could be compared with those derived from the above composite distributions based on published grouped data. The discrepancies between the two estimates were very small indeed (the largest was 20p for the 25th percentile), encouraging confidence in the method which had to be employed for other years.

Indeed, the similarity of the estimates based on grouped and ungrouped data is all the more reassuring given that certain differences occur inevitably. First, the distributions derived from published grouped data were based on 7239 households, whilst the ungrouped data provided by the Department of Health and Social Security related to the slightly smaller number of 7143 households.[2] Secondly, in the grouped data a child was defined as a person under 16; for the ungrouped source we defined a child as a person under 15 or one aged 15 to 18 'dependent' on his parents. It is of rather more significance that in adjusting the ungrouped data a more refined set of income equivalence scales could be used for children: a child aged 0 to 4, 0·14; aged 5 to 10, 0·21; aged 11 to 18, 0·30.

[1] See table VI.5 below.   [2] See appendix I.

EQUIVALENT NET HOUSEHOLD INCOMES

Estimates of equivalent net household incomes were derived using the method depicted in table III.3 for the 5th, 10th and 50th percentiles. Direct tax payments (income tax and national insurance contributions) were estimated by linear interpolation from published data relating to tax by gross incomes and type of household (converted to equivalent couples).[1] For each percentile in each year, the average direct tax payment was weighted by the appropriate number of households of each type. Since information about direct taxes is provided for only certain types of household, the results can only be approximate. Percentile values of equivalent net income are given in table 3.3.

TABLE III.3. *Derivation of equivalent net household income*

	5th percentile of individuals			10th percentile of individuals			50th percentile of individuals		
	1953/4	1967	1971	1953/4	1967	1971	1953/4	1967	1971
	($£$s per week)								
Gross income	3·90	8·70	11·80	4·65	10·45	14·10	8·20	19·70	27·65
Tax[a] paid by:									
1 adult	..	0·11½	0·07½	0·04½	0·12	0·12	0·33	2·05	3·86¼
1 couple	0·05	0·16	..	0·08½	0·33	0·38	0·51½	2·55	4·24¼
1 couple, 1 child	..	..	..	0·17½	..	0·92	0·38	2·65	4·38
1 couple, 2 children	0·09	..	0·48	0·16½	..	1·05	0·30	2·16	3·91
1 couple, 3 children	0·10½	..	0·63½	0·15½	0·48	1·00	0·24½	1·80	..
1 couple, 4 children	0·08½	..	..	0·14	..	..	..	..	..
1 couple, 5 children	0·11½	..	..	0·13½	..	..	..	..	..
Weighted average tax[b]	0·07	0·14½	0·37	0·11	0·34½	0·58½	0·35½	2·17½	4·09
	(percentages)								
Tax[a]/gross income	1·79	1·67	3·15	2·37	3·30	4·13	4·33	11·04	14·80

Sources: Ministry of Labour, *Household Expenditure 1953–54;* Department of Employment, *Family Expenditure Survey Reports* (various years).

a Tax includes national insurance contributions.

b Weighted for each percentile in each year by the number of households of each type.

The first check on these results was a comparison for 1971 with estimates taken from a special tabulation of the original data, similar to that for equivalent gross income, but this time calculating equivalent net income for each household. The values produced by the two methods were very similar – £11·43 (grouped data) and £11·45 (ungrouped data) for the 5th percentile, and £23·56 and £23·50 for the 50th percentile. A slightly

[1] The information on income tax payments in the 1953/4 Household Expenditure Survey was sometimes incomplete and less reliable than in the Family Expenditure Surveys for later years. This is because it was based on information given in the diaries kept by participating households and not, as since 1957, in answer to direct questions at the interview.

larger difference emerged for the 10th percentile, where grouped data gave £13·51 and ungrouped data£ 13·00.

As a further check, income tax and national insurance contributions were calculated on the basis of the rates in force in each year for three standard households – single adults, married couples, and married couples with a child – with gross incomes equal to those of the quantiles in table III.3. The same calculations were repeated on an equivalent income basis. Also, the results were compared with certain net income distributions for 1963, 1967 and 1971, derived from unpublished data kindly supplied by the Central Statistical Office. Whilst the results of these checks differed in detail, they confirmed the most significant aspects of the main results in chapter 3.

SUPPLEMENTARY BENEFIT SCALES AND MEASURING POVERTY

This appendix sets out the methods and assumptions employed for deriving the estimates of the numbers in poverty contained in chapter 4. The theory of estimating the number of individuals with incomes below a given level is in itself simple but, as explained in that chapter, the practice proves to be quite complex. In part this follows from adopting the supplementary benefit scales as the poverty level, since they vary according to the number and type of persons in each family, and according to other circumstances as explained below.

Two types of estimate were made using data from the Family Expenditure Surveys – those based on individual household records, and those derived from grouped data. First, the principal estimates of numbers in poverty used in chapter 4, as well as the poverty group whose characteristics are examined in chapter 5, were identified from individual household records. A computer program was written to assess a household's needs on the basis which would have been used by the Supplementary Benefits Commission in 1971, and to compare that assessment with the household's income to determine whether or not the household was in poverty in the sense used in chapter 4. A series of special tabulations was then prepared by the Department of Health and Social Security.

Secondly, for the estimates of poverty in chapter 4 relating to tax units, an approximate method based on grouped data was used, which cross-classified tax units by income and composition into groups for which a particular supplementary benefit rate was appropriate. The number of such groups was reduced to thirteen by:

(a) assuming children were of average age rather than distinguishing the five categories in the scales;
(b) adopting an average rent for each type of tax unit, instead of the actual rent allowed in supplementary benefit calculations;
(c) using simple interpolation where the calculated poverty line fell within an income range for a given type of tax unit.

In a test of the reliability of this method, it was found that the results of using grouped data differed little from those derived from individual household records.

This appendix has been prepared mainly by G. C. Fiegehen.

SUPPLEMENTARY BENEFIT SCALES

Under the supplementary benefit system the government tries to ensure a minimum income level for each individual. The scheme is means-tested, so that each additional pound of other income leads in principle to an equivalent reduction in benefit. Certain categories of people are ineligible irrespective of their incomes; they include those in full-time employment, young people staying on at school and people able to work but not 'signing on'. People in part-time employment are not excluded. Provided a person is not ineligible, the next step is to compare his income with his entitlement; if his income is less than his entitlement it is supplemented to that level.[1] The levels of entitlement laid down by the government are the supplementary benefit scales; they consist of three main elements – the scale rate, 'net rent' and certain discretionary additions.

The scale rate is the amount allocated for each person to cover most everyday needs apart from rent. It varies with marital status (strictly 'cohabitation' status), with whether the claimant is regarded as a 'householder', a 'non-householder' or a 'boarder', and with the number and age of his or her dependent children. Until July 1974 a separate allowance known as the 'long-term addition' was given to claimants who either were over retiring age, or had been receiving supplementary benefits for two years or more. Since then this addition has been superseded by a system of separate scales for short-term and long-term beneficiaries, and at the same time additional categories of people have been reclassed as 'long-term'. Since estimates of the number of poor in chapter 4 were based on the rates and allowances applicable in 1971, a 50p long-term addition was added to the entitlements of pensioner units (single persons and married couples counting as one unit), but in other cases the long-term addition was ignored. The relevant 1971 supplementary benefit scales are shown in table IV.1.

Housing costs, provided they are reasonable,[2] are added in full to the claimant's scale rate as part of the standard entitlement; these costs – or 'net rent' – comprise rent, rates (less rebates or allowances) and mortgage interest repayments. It proved impossible to distinguish mortgage interest and mortgage capital payments in the household expenditure records, so we were obliged to consider alternative procedures for determining 'net rent'. Two options were available. The first consisted in treating the housing expenditure of owner-occupied (and rent-free) households in the same manner as in the published Family Expenditure Survey tables:

---

[1] Strictly the income of a family is considered, so that a wife's income is added to her husband's and she may not normally claim in her own right.

[2] Although the Supplementary Benefits Commission can reduce the entitlement where 'net rent' is considered unreasonable, no attempt was made to do this in the present exercise.

TABLE IV.1. *Supplementary benefit scales, 1971 (£s per week)*

	Up to 19 September	From 20 September	Weighted average
Couple	8·50	9·45	8·77
Single householder	5·20	5·80	5·37
Non-householder			
Aged 16–17	3·05	3·60	3·20
Aged 18–20	3·50	4·05	3·65
Aged 21 or over	4·15	4·60	4·28
Long-term addition[a]	0·50	0·50	0·50
Children			
Aged under 5	1·50	1·70	1·56
Aged 5–10	1·80	2·00	1·86
Aged 11–12	2·20	2·45	2·27
Aged 13–15	2·40	3·00	2·57
Aged 16–17	3·05	3·60	3·20
Aged 18–20	3·50	4·05	3·65

Source: Department of Health and Social Security, *Annual Report for the Year 1971*.

[a] Payable to each pensioner unit.

namely adding an imputed rent to both income and housing costs of these households, since accounting logic requires that the imputed rent be regarded as part of the households' needs. Alternatively, the full mortgage repayments of those buying their houses could be counted as part of their needs. Using the first option the risk of poverty amongst households with mortgages was 1 per cent, and using the second 2·6 per cent; thus the first method tends to understate the extent of poverty in this group, and the second to overstate it. In the event, the first method was adopted in chapters 4 and 5, with a consequent understatement of 0·2–0·5 per cent of households in poverty.

There are two kinds of discretionary additions to supplementary benefit scales: supplements to the weekly entitlement to allow for exceptional circumstances, such as special dietary or laundry requirements, and lump sum payments designed to meet, for example, purchases of clothes that are damaged or missing. Account has been taken of neither kind of addition in our calculations. Most families benefiting from them would be receiving supplementary benefits above the standard level.

Supplementary benefit scales are in practice not applied to families with working members, but in using these scales to determine the needs of such families it seemed appropriate to make some allowance for the additional costs of employment – fares, clothing, etc. We had no direct evidence on such costs and, for want of a better figure, based our calculations on those in *Two Parent Families*.[1] In that study a sum of 50p a week was

[1] Department of Health and Social Security, *Two Parent Families: a study of their resources and needs in 1968, 1969, and 1970* by J. R. Howe, London, HMSO, 1971.

allowed in 1970 for each working member of the household; we allowed 55p for 1971.

Supplementary benefit entitlements are fairly complex to calculate and, as stated, we have not been able to follow all the rules that are laid down. There are other regulations, however, which can be quite important in determining whether families receiving supplementary benefits have incomes above or below the standard level. First, some sources of income are 'disregarded' partly or in full in the calculation of benefits due. Thus (in 1971) the first £2·50 of a wife's weekly earnings were generally ignored, and certain special benefits – for example, educational maintenance allowances and the £10 Christmas Bonus – were disregarded completely. A certain amount of income from capital is also ignored; for small amounts of capital, up to £325 in 1971, no income is assumed, but thereafter interest is included on the basis of a standard tariff and this, not the actual rate of return, is taken into account. The effect of such 'disregards' is that a family's income may be higher than its supplementary benefit entitlement, even though it is receiving supplementary benefits.

Disregarded income complicates comparisons over time when entitlements are raised with inflation but the values of 'disregards' are not. 'Disregards' have been adjusted at longer intervals and it has been suggested that they have lagged behind entitlements. If so, the movement of the scales and the apparent incomes of beneficiaries relative to incomes generally may be misleading indicators of the true position.

On the other hand, entitlement may be less than the prescribed level. Where the claimant was unemployed but not sick, his total income from supplementary benefits and other sources (total entitlements plus 'disregards') was not (in 1971) allowed to exceed normal take-home earnings when last in employment (after allowance for deductions, but inclusive of family allowances and any family income supplement). This was known as the 'wage-stop'[1] and was one reason why families receiving supplementary benefits had incomes below the supplementary benefit level.[2] Less than 1 per cent of supplementary benefit cases were wage-stopped at any one time, and many of them would have been receiving supplementary benefits for less than thirteen weeks, so that in terms of 'normal' income they would have been classified as receiving earnings rather than supplementary benefits.

SUPPLEMENTARY BENEFITS AND THE FAMILY UNIT

The supplementary benefit scheme is administered on the basis of the

[1] It was terminated in July 1975.

[2] Another case is that of single people without dependants who are unemployed but not sick. There are a number of rules and procedures to encourage this group to find employment; one of these is the limitation of benefits to four weeks provided employment is available.

family unit, which is similar to the tax unit and to the concept of the 'inner family'. In administering the scheme, rules have been evolved to define the family unit and to attribute responsibility for maintaining dependent children and spouses.[1] However, using supplementary benefit scales in conjunction with the Family Expenditure Surveys to yield estimates of the numbers in poverty gives rise to a number of problems when the estimate is based on the broader concept of the household; this happens quite frequently, since a quarter of households in our sample contained two or more tax units.

Two kinds of problem arise. First there is the conceptual question of whether the incomes of all family units living in shared accommodation should be taken into account when measuring poverty; this is discussed in chapter 4.

Practical problems also arise – one being the distinction between householders, non-householders and boarders made in the supplementary benefit scales.[2] Since information collected in the Family Expenditure Surveys does not allow us to follow supplementary benefit rules, we have been obliged to adopt our own conventions in calculating the entitlement for each household in the Family Expenditure Survey separately. These were – all married couples are householders; single persons are householders only if they are the head of the household, or they are unrelated to the head of their household, otherwise they are non-householders. The category of boarder was ignored.

Another practical problem concerns housing costs or 'net rent' for tax units sharing accommodation, since in the Family Expenditure Surveys housing costs are computed for the household as a whole. Where the household is the basic unit no problem arises, but when we base our estimates on family units housing costs must somehow be allocated between units sharing accommodation. Since information from the Family Expenditure Survey to which we had access does not permit such a division, in estimates for tax units we employed the following approximation. We used information on average net rents by size of family contained in the November 1970 survey of supplementary benefit cases,[3] but raised them by 6 per cent to correspond to the increase in the housing component of the index of retail prices between November 1970 and mid-1971; the resulting average rents for each family type were then used as 'net rents' of tax units. A test of the reliability of this method distinguished tax units which shared households from those which did not, and yielded results

1 Perhaps the most controversial of these is the 'cohabitation' rule, by which a man and woman who are living together are regarded as man and wife for purposes of supplementary benefit entitlement.

2 It is possible for a household in the Family Expenditure Survey to have two supplementary benefit 'householders'.

3 Unpublished data kindly supplied by the Department of Health and Social Security.

that were close to housing costs calculated for each household separately, except in the case of single-person tax units sharing households, where it appeared that their needs may have been overstated. Allowing for this would have reduced the number of people in poverty by about $\frac{1}{2}$ million.

CHANGES IN SCALES WITHIN A YEAR

In each recent year there has been at least one increase in the supplementary benefit scales; when this occurs the poverty line changes abruptly. In estimating the extent of poverty such changes in the scales can, in principle, be accommodated in several ways. The extent of poverty might be measured in a particular week or month during which supplementary benefit scales were unchanged, but this would reduce the sample available for analysis.[1] A second possibility would be to convert household incomes to a common base date by means of price or wage indices. This method has been used by J. R. Howe; he converted earnings to a value at the end of the year by means of the change in earnings in the appropriate industry, and raised benefits by any increase since the interview; supplementary benefit scales in operation at the end of the year were then taken as the poverty line.[2] However, one assumption entailed by this method is that earnings of all employees in each industry rise with the average rate of increase. We felt that this was not a good assumption to make in measuring poverty.

The method we chose for the exercise in chapters 4 and 5 required no such wholesale revision of the original data. We compared household incomes with the supplementary benefit scale in operation at the time the household was interviewed for the Survey. The poverty line for households interviewed in the first part of the year was therefore lower than for those interviewed after the scales were increased.

DISPERSION ABOUT THE SUPPLEMENTARY BENEFIT LEVEL

We have seen that there are a number of reasons why the incomes of households in the Family Expenditure Survey receiving supplementary benefits will not necessarily be identical with the supplementary benefit level as we calculated it. Since we are using 'our' supplementary benefit scales as the poverty level, it is appropriate to examine the distribution of households in relation to their supplementary benefit entitlement. This is shown in table IV.2.

---

[1] The Family Expenditure Survey for a year is based on a changing sample of weekly incomes from January to December.

[2] Department of Health and Social Security, *Two Parent Families*. The same method is also used for estimates of low income in CSO, *Social Trends*.

TABLE IV.2 *Distribution of households about the supplementary benefit level, 1971*

Net normal income of households as a proportion of supplementary benefit entitlement[a]	Number of households	Households receiving supplementary benefits		
		One tax unit	Two or more tax units	All recipients
Under 50 per cent	25	–	–	–
50–74 per cent	44	2	2	4
75–89 per cent	133	22	4	26
90–99 per cent	304	154	7	161
100–109 per cent	529	322	32	354
110–124 per cent	443	93	32	125
125–149 per cent	745	19	41	60
150–199 per cent	1711	7	82	89
200–299 per cent	2287	4	70	74
300 per cent and over	922	–	8	8
All households	7143	623	278	901

Source: Special tabulations of 1971 Family Expenditure Survey.

[a] Supplementary benefit entitlements taken as the scales in force on the date each household was interviewed.

Incomes of households receiving supplementary benefits may differ from our calculations of their entitlement because one household may contain two or more supplementary benefit tax units or because of disregarded income, discretionary additions to the basic scale, the 'wage-stop' (and 'rent-stop')[1] and measurement error. Table IV.2 enables us to assess the numerical importance of households containing more than one supplementary benefit tax unit; as many as 44 per cent of households receiving supplementary benefits are of this type. They are concentrated towards the upper end of the distribution of supplementary benefit households and account for almost nine-tenths of supplementary benefit households with incomes over 125 per cent of their entitlement. That so many households appear to have incomes considerably in excess of their supplementary benefit entitlement can thus be largely explained by the fact that they contain more than one tax unit. Among households consisting of one tax unit only we find a much narrower dispersion about the supplementary benefit level. Of such households receiving supplementary benefits, 76 per cent had incomes within ± 10 per cent of their calculated supplementary benefit entitlement, compared with 57 per cent if households with two or more tax units are included.

The table suggests that the effect of disregarded income and discretionary additions is to cause the average income of supplementary benefit households to be above the basic supplementary benefit level. The median income of supplementary benefit households containing one tax unit is

[1] 'Rent-stop' accounts for very few cases.

equivalent to 104·2 per cent of the calculated supplementary benefit entitlement.

Since in 1971 less than 1 per cent of supplementary benefit claimants were wage stopped,[1] the rest of the dispersion of households receiving supplementary benefits about the calculated supplementary benefit level is attributable to measurement error of one form or another – misreporting by households, changes in circumstances between the last supplementary benefit assessment and participation in the Survey, and any mis-specification in our program.

[1] Department of Health and Social Security, *Annual Report for the Year 1971*, tables 116 and 126.

HOUSEHOLD CHARACTERISTICS AND THE DEFINITION OF POVERTY

This appendix assesses how similar are patterns of poverty when different definitions of poverty are used and when different assumptions are made in their application.

To examine the effect of alternative definitions of poverty we first ranked households in the 1971 Family Expenditure Survey by the ratio of their net normal income to their supplementary benefit entitlement. This is similar to ranking households by income per equivalent household, since the supplementary benefit scales vary with household size and composition. We then compared the characteristics of the lowest 10 and the lowest 20 per cent of households with the characteristics already described in chapter 5 of households with incomes below the supplementary benefit level. Only 7·1 per cent of households had incomes below the supplementary benefit level; the maximum income of the lowest 10 per cent was 104 per cent of the basic supplementary benefit entitlement, and of the lowest 20 per cent just under 125 per cent of the entitlement.

In table V.1 we show, for each of the three definitions of poverty, the risk of low income for households with certain characteristics, and the proportion of all low income households which possess each characteristic (its accountability). The characteristics of the lowest 10 per cent are very similar to those below supplementary benefit level and the share of poverty accounted for by each category is not very different, indicating only small differences in relative risks.

When the lowest 20 per cent of households is considered, some change in pattern emerges. There is a rise in the proportion of poor households with employees as heads and with male heads of about 5 percentage points. The importance of households with two adults and where income from employment is the main source rises by about 6 points, but the proportion of poor households with heads aged over 75 drops by about 2½ points. It is noticeable, however, that the overall pattern of the characteristics associated with poverty remains largely unaffected.

It is also possible to vary the allowance made in the poverty level for the needs of different types of household, for example, by raising or reducing the needs of children relative to those of adults. Indeed, part of the difference between the estimates of the proportion of people with low incomes in

This appendix has been prepared mainly by G. C. Fiegehen.

TABLE V.I. *Characteristics of alternative poverty groups, 1971 (Percentages)*

	Below supplementary benefit level		Lowest 10 per cent of households		Lowest 20 per cent of households	
	Risk[a]	Account-ability[b]	Risk[a]	Account-ability[b]	Risk[a]	Account-ability[b]
Adults in household:						
1	20·4	*57·2*	28·8	*57·1*	52·0	*50·0*
2	4·4	*38·7*	6·2	*38·7*	14·7	*44·3*
3 or 4	1·7	*4·2*	2·4	*4·2*	6·5	*5·6*
Status of head of household:						
Aged: 16–24	6·6	*4·9*	8·1	*4·2*	17·4	*4·5*
25–34	2·9	*7·1*	4·0	*6·8*	8·9	*7·5*
35–44	1·8	*4·3*	2·9	*5·0*	8·0	*6·7*
45–54	2·3	*5·9*	3·2	*5·7*	6·8	*5·9*
55–64	5·8	*15·2*	7·7	*14·2*	16·1	*14·5*
65–74	16·6	*37·1*	24·4	*38·5*	49·9	*38·1*
75 and over	24·4	*25·4*	34·7	*25·6*	63·9	*22·8*
Male	4·3	*47·7*	5·9	*46·7*	12·2	*52·0*
Female	18·0	*52·3*	25·5	*53·3*	48·2	*48·0*
Employee	1·3	*11·6*	1·8	*11·2*	5·2	*16·2*
Unemployed[c]	20·2	*4·5*	24·5	*3·9*	45·3	*3·5*
Self-employed	5·6	*6·3*	7·4	*5·9*	15·3	*5·9*
Retired	19·0	*41·2*	27·7	*42·3*	56·3	*41·9*
Unoccupied						
Under retiring age	19·0	*12·6*	27·0	*12·7*	51·0	*11·6*
Over retiring age	26·5	*23·7*	38·0	*24·0*	68·6	*21·0*
Main source of household income:						
Employment or self-employment	1·2	*12·4*	1·6	*11·8*	5·0	*17·8*
Investment, property, etc.	5·1	*3·9*	6·2	*3·4*	14·0	*3·7*
Social security benefits	29·1	*79·3*	42·1	*81·2*	81·0	*75·8*
Other	26·2	*4·3*	30·6	*3·6*	45·7	*2·6*

Source: Special tabulations of the 1971 Family Expenditure Survey.

  [a] Proportion of households with specified characteristics in poverty by the appropriate standard.

  [b] Households with the specified characteristics as a proportion of all households in poverty.

  [c] Defined as 'out of work, but seeking employment'.

1971 made in chapters 3 and 4 arose from giving less weight in chapter 3 than in chapter 4 to the economies of scale that larger households derive from sharing accommodation. Consequently a greater proportion of large households fell within the low income group in chapter 3 than in chapter 4 – the average number of persons in poor households was 2·5 instead of 2·0.

When total expenditure is used as well as, or instead of, income to measure each household's resources, there are considerable differences in the proportion in poverty and their characteristics. The group of households where both total expenditure and net normal income are below supplementary benefit entitlement – the 'dual criterion' group, which has greater consistency in its recorded incomes and expenditure – has a higher proportion of households with retired heads (including unoccupied and over retiring age) than the group where income alone falls below the supplementary benefit entitlement – 78 instead of 65 per cent. The importance of households with heads in other economic categories falls correspondingly: employees from 12 to 6 per cent, self-employed from 6 to 3 per cent, and heads unoccupied and under retiring age from 13 to 9 per cent. Only households with unemployed heads comprise the same proportion of both groups.

The dual criterion group also reveals a higher proportion of one-person households (60 instead of 50 per cent) and a higher proportion of households for whom social security benefits are the main source of income (90 instead of 80 per cent). Our analysis suggests, therefore, that, amongst less well off households, elderly people living by themselves with social security benefits as their main source of income are those most likely to have consistent levels of income and expenditure, and that they do not draw to any great extent on savings to maintain living standards in retirement, spending a high proportion of their income within the week it is received.

Had we chosen to ignore income altogether and compared a household's total expenditure alone with its supplementary benefit entitlement the composition of the poverty group would again have been somewhat different. Of poor households 18 per cent would have had employees as heads, rather than the 12 per cent we found using income, and the proportion of households with heads in other categories, except the unemployed, would have fallen correspondingly. We would have found 5 per cent fewer poor households had children (15 instead of 20 per cent), and 2–3 per cent more would have been owner-occupiers – both those buying and those who were outright owners – but there would have been a reduction in the number who rented furnished accommodation. In relation to our discussion of the life-cycle, the risk of poverty for households with heads aged under 25 would have been 2·3 per cent instead of the 7·0 per cent we found using income. No doubt fluctuations in expenditure from week to week, the omission of certain items from 'total expenditure' and the failure to record all income received explain much of the differences found. But again, except for the 381 households with heads aged under 25, the broad pattern of the characteristics associated with poverty remains substantially unaltered.

Our final comparison was between the low income group and those households within it who did not receive supplementary benefits, since there may be grounds for believing that those who received supplementary benefits and were classified as poor on the basis of their income had understated their actual income in the Family Expenditure Survey. The effect of this exclusion from the poverty group is, of course, to reduce the importance of those characteristics most closely associated with the receipt of supplementary benefits, old age and living alone. Thus, the proportion of households with retired and unoccupied heads is 12 per cent lower (66 instead of 78 per cent), and the proportions of one-person households and of households with social security benefits the main source of income are 10 and 12 per cent lower than for the whole group. In contrast, the proportion with employees as heads rises from 12 to 19 per cent, and with self-employed heads from 6 to 10 per cent.

Bearing in mind the overlap between all the various categories of the poor we have considered, the overall degree of conformity between the patterns, in terms of both risk and accountability, seems reasonably satisfactory.

THE METHOD OF ESTIMATING EXPENDITURE PATTERNS

ESTIMATES BASED ON GROUPED DATA

The method used for estimating expenditure patterns of the poor and the non-poor on the basis of published data from the Family Expenditure Surveys, and after allowances for variations in household size and composition, was similar to that described in appendix III for tracing changes in comparative incomes, although certain additional difficulties were encountered. To obtain expenditure distributions in each year, ideally we should first rank and group all households in the sample on the basis of their income per equivalent couple. However, for several reasons only approximations to these distributions can be obtained from the published tables. In the first place, information on expenditure patterns by type of household and income is not provided for the whole sample; for example, in 1971 such an analysis was published only for households accounting for 74 per cent of the total (table VI.1). Apart from single-parent households it is the larger heterogeneous households which are excluded. These categories tend to have above-average equivalent incomes, so that their exclusion tends to understate contrasts between the expenditure patterns of the poor and other families. With the trend towards smaller households and the declining frequency of larger households, the proportion of the sample included rose from 65 per cent of households in 1953/4 to 74 per cent in 1971. Consequently estimates for the latter year may reflect contrasts in expenditure patterns more closely than those for the former. The sharp rise between 1971 and 1973 in the proportion covered results from the change in definition of a child in 1973, which, by raising the age at which a person ceases to be considered a child from 16 to 18, reduced the proportion of households with three or more adults. The change in definition may have a considerable impact on comparisons between 1973 and earlier years, since it leads to the inclusion of households with 16 and 17 year olds at work, and these households may have very different spending patterns to households where all the children are in full-time education.

Secondly, the published data from which we derived these expenditure distributions are presented in the form of group means for each gross income cell. To obtain the expenditure distributions therefore requires a slightly different procedure from that adopted in appendix III for deriving

This appendix has been prepared mainly by P. S. Lansley.

TABLE VI.1.   *Households included in estimates of expenditure patterns*

		1953/4	1961	1971	1973[a]
Households containing:		(no. of households)			
Adults	*Children*				
I	—	1306	494	1248	1345
1M, 1F	—	3093	939	2032	2065
1M, 1F	1	1665	394	683	767
1M, 1F	2	1447	370	835	866
1M, 1F	3	571			419
1M, 1F	4	181	248	562[b]	220[c]
1M, 1F	5+	115			
Total included		8378	2445	5360	5682
		(percentages)			
Proportions included[d] of:					
Households		64·9	70·1	74·0	79·7
Individuals		54·4	61·2	65·9	73·4

Sources: Ministry of Labour, *Household Expenditure 1953–54;* Department of Employment, *Family Expenditure Survey Reports* (various years).

[a] Definition of a child changed from 'under 16' to 'unmarried and under 18'.
[b] Any two adults and three or more children.
[c] Any two adults and four or more children.
[d] Proportions of total in Survey.

the income distributions. The group means for each type of household were converted separately into equivalent couple units, using the same set of equivalence scales as in appendix III for each expenditure item and for total expenditure. On the basis of the results for each type of household, the groups were then re-ranked according to their equivalent total expenditure. A percentile ranking was then obtained by assuming that the respective group means correspond with the expenditure of the household at the mid-point of that group – a slightly different assumption from that implicit in the procedure adopted to obtain income distributions in appendix III. Expenditure breakdowns at other points on the scale were obtained by linear interpolation.

This process inevitably involves some misordering of households in the ranking procedure. Starting with separate group means for each type of household, converting them and combining them is likely to give somewhat different percentile ordering from that obtained by converting, ranking and grouping each household individually. This is because the groups for each type of household contain a range of household incomes which, if separately converted to equivalent units, might place them in a different group.

Another result of operating with group means of particular types of household is that derivation of standard percentile points may involve interpolating between two different types of household whose expenditure patterns are influenced by differences in their composition as well as in their equivalent total expenditures. This potential source of error was reduced by considering average expenditure patterns of a wide group of households lying around the relevant quantiles, rather than focusing attention on the pattern of the particular type at the relevant quantiles. Thus the expenditure pattern attributed here to the 5th percentile is based on the average pattern of the bottom 10 per cent of families. Similarly the pattern of the lowest 10th percentile is based on the average pattern for families between the 5th and the 15th percentiles, and the expenditure pattern of the median family on the average pattern for families between the 45th and 55th percentiles.

TABLE VI.2.   *Household expenditure at current prices,[a] 1953/4 to 1973 (£s per week)*

	5th percentile[b]				10th percentile[b]				Median[b]			
	1953/4	1961[c]	1971	1973	1953/4	1961[c]	1971	1973	1953/4	1961[c]	1971	1973
Housing	0·65	1·11	2·74	2·87	0·60	1·07	2·34	3·16	1·04	1·27	3·20	4·09
Fuel, light and power	0·57	0·93	1·86	2·00	0·44	0·78	1·52	1·95	0·57	0·74	1·68	1·75
Food	2·07	2·77	4·64	5·85	2·22	3·07	4·92	6·17	2·88	4·15	6·31	8·17
Clothing	0·35	0·41	0·81	0·91	0·41	0·51	0·99	1·06	0·91	1·20	1·71	2·68
Alcoholic drink	0·10	0·17	0·26	0·46	0·11	0·19	0·45	0·52	0·19	0·33	0·96	1·40
Tobacco	0·19	0·32	0·45	0·66	0·34	0·47	0·75	0·87	0·44	0·75	1·13	1·26
Durables	0·20	0·26	0·64	0·77	0·21	0·34	0·74	0·86	0·59	0·86	1·76	2·24
Other goods and misc.	0·36	0·49	0·96	1·18	0·39	0·55	1·14	1·39	0·65	0·98	1·81	2·42
Transport and vehicles	0·14	0·22	0·64	1·05	0·19	0·39	1·03	1·07	0·43	1·13	2·82	4·58
Services	0·35	0·49	1·35	1·27	0·28	0·47	1·04	1·31	0·66	0·81	1·99	2·61
Total	4·98	7·17	14·35	17·02	5·19	7·84	14·92	18·36	8·36	12·22	23·37	31·20

Sources: As table VI.1.

[a] Expenditure per equivalent couple.
[b] Households ranked by equivalent gross normal income.
[c] Based on a small sample.

Our estimates of expenditure patterns for the historical comparisons are given in table VI.2.

EXPENDITURE PATTERNS IN 1971

Table VI.3 presents the basic data from which the expenditure patterns contained in table 6.4 were derived. The general nature of the series contained in this table has been described in chapter 6; further details about the methods used to obtain them are given below.

Differences between the first and second columns of the table show the impact on expenditure patterns of ranking households by equivalent total expenditure rather than by equivalent gross income. It was shown in chapter 6 that this modification affects observed expenditure patterns

TABLE VI.3. *Expenditure, 1971, by households ranked by different methods (£s per week)*

	Equivalent total expenditure, using common scales and whole sample[a]	Equivalent gross income		
		Using common scales		Using specific scales[c] and whole sample[a]
		Whole sample[a]	Dual criterion sample[b]	
5th percentile				
Housing	2·31	2·47	2·09	2·23
Fuel, light and power	1·31	1·70	1·62	1·65
Food	3·99	4·69	4·29	4·82
Clothing	0·23	0·98	0·36	1·02
Alcoholic drink	0·16	0·29	0·22	0·35
Tobacco	0·44	0·48	0·53	0·58
Durables	0·23	0·44	0·24	0·42
Other goods and miscellaneous	0·79	1·07	0·84	1·08
Transport and vehicles	0·31	0·68	0·34	0·66
Services	0·74	1·27	0·73	1·32
Total	10·51	14·07[d]	11·26	14·13[d]
10th percentile				
Housing	2·44	2·64	2·50	2·34
Fuel, light and power	1·38	2·40	1·65	2·34
Food	4·72	4·90	4·47	5·03
Clothing	0·45	0·76	0·52	0·75
Alcoholic drink	0·28	0·45	0·25	0·51
Tobacco	0·64	0·51	0·41	0·64
Durables	0·30	0·78	0·36	0·76
Other goods and miscellaneous	0·86	0·92	0·91	0·92
Transport and vehicles	0·60	1·05	0·47	1·03
Services	0·81	1·03	0·87	1·05
Total	12·48	15·44[d]	12·41	15·37[d]
Median				
Housing	3·06	3·19	2·94	3·09
Fuel, light and power	1·59	1·46	1·51	1·54
Food	6·60	6·47	6·54	6·47
Clothing	1·82	2·13	1·84	2·10
Alcoholic drink	1·02	1·04	0·93	1·23
Tobacco	1·10	1·05	1·09	1·24
Durables	0·91	1·69	1·13	1·61
Other goods and miscellaneous	1·70	1·93	1·77	1·90
Transport and vehicles	2·60	2·97	2·62	2·83
Services	1·69	2·00	1·64	1·92
Total	22·09	23·93	22·01	23·93

Source: Special tabulations of the 1971 Family Expenditure Survey.

[a] 7143 households, about 99 per cent of the full sample.

[b] 46 per cent of the full sample of households with a ratio of total expenditure to gross income in the range 0·75 to 1·25.

[c] Equivalence scales calculated separately for each type of expenditure.

[d] In principle these totals should be the same in the two columns; the discrepancies are due to rounding in the estimation of equivalence scales.

more than any other. The effect of this on the proportion in poverty was also found to be considerable in chapter 4, where it was shown, *inter alia*, that when households are classified by income, their average total expenditure tends to exceed average income at low income levels and be less than income at higher income levels. Conversely, when households are classified by total expenditure, incomes tend to be greater than expenditure at low total expenditure levels, and less than expenditure at higher total expenditure levels.

The series in the second column from special tabulations of the 1971 Family Expenditure Survey is based on percentile values relating to households ranked by gross income, with equivalent income and expenditure values obtained by using income equivalence scales. The principal difference between this series and that for 1971 in table VI.2 is that, because of the limitations of the published grouped data, the latter is based on about three-quarters of the full sample of households covered by the Family Expenditure Survey, whilst the former relates in effect to the full sample. Another difference is that separate income equivalence scales for children of different age-groups, which could not be applied to data from the published Family Expenditure Survey tables, were used in the case of the special tabulations for 1971. Also the ranking in table VI.2 was based not on individual households, as in the case of the special tabulations, but on group means. Otherwise the method used to derive the expenditure data is the same; that is, expenditure levels at each percentile were obtained by linear interpolation from grouped expenditure data, assuming that the group income in each case corresponds with the expenditure of the household at the mid-point of the group, and in both cases each expenditure level is a weighted average based on the group of households which straddle the particular percentile. The results using grouped published data give a remarkably close fit to those derived from the ungrouped data.

TABLE VI.4. *Distributions of equivalent household incomes and total expenditure, 1971*

| | Households ranked by gross income | | | | Households ranked by total expenditure | |
| | Gross income | | Total expenditure | | Total expenditure | |
	Value	Propn. of median	Value	Propn. of median	Value	Propn. of median
	(£s per wk)	(%)	(£s per wk)	(%)	(£s per wk)	(%)
5th percentile	11·50	*41·3*	14·07	*58·8*	10·51	*47·6*
10th percentile	13·10	*47·0*	15·44	*64·5*	12·48	*56·5*
25th percentile	18·30	*65·7*	19·13	*79·9*	16·32	*73·8*
50th percentile	27·85	*100·0*	23·93	*100·0*	22·10	*100·0*
75th percentile	39·45	*141·7*	30·81	*128·8*	30·56	*138·3*
90th percentile	54·00	*193·9*	36·82	*153·9*	42·56	*192·6*

Source: Interpolated from special tabulations of the 1971 Family Expenditure Survey.

For 1971 the situation is summarised in table VI.4. The first and third columns of this table show gross income and total expenditure respectively for the specified percentiles of households ranked by equivalent gross income; the fifth column shows total expenditure for the specified percentiles of households ranked by equivalent total expenditure.

The second column of table VI.3 reveals differences in expenditure behaviour between the poor and the non-poor when households are ranked by gross income, that is in expenditure patterns corresponding to the total expenditures shown in the third column of table VI.4. This is likely to yield results which fail to indicate the full extent of the difference between expenditure patterns of the poor and the non-poor, for a comparison of the fourth and sixth columns of table VI.4 indicates that total expenditures for 5th and 10th percentiles households ranked by gross income are significantly nearer the median (58·8 and 64·5 per cent respectively) than are the total expenditures of 5th and 10th percentile households ranked by total expenditure (47·6 and 56·5 per cent respectively). It was to gauge the effect of this distinction that in the first column of table VI.3 expenditure patterns were presented for households ranked by equivalent total expenditure.

The third column of table VI.3 gives expenditures of poor and non-poor households when the latter are designated by means of a 'dual criterion'. For this purpose households with a large discrepancy between total expenditure and income – with a ratio of total expenditure to gross normal income outside the range 0·75 to 1·25 – have been discarded. Possible explanations of wide discrepancies between household incomes and expenditure are considered in chapter 4. The reason for their exclusion in the present context is that the expenditure behaviour of households within the specified range is likely to be more representative of actual household expenditure at specified income levels. Application of this dual criterion leads to the retention of 3302 households, about 46 per cent of the total sample, and again these were ranked by equivalent gross income.

The equivalent expenditure values in the first three columns of table VI.3 are based on income equivalence scales that are identical for each expenditure item. In contrast, the figures in the fourth column were obtained from the set of specific equivalence scales in table VI.5. They accord reasonably well with estimates produced in chapter 7 of this study. The effect of using different scales for each item rather than a common scale is to increase the equivalent expenditure of households on items for which that household has a lower specific scale than an overall income scale, and vice versa. The effect on households with a high proportion of young children, for example, is to increase equivalent expenditure on alcohol and tobacco, for which the specific needs of children are assumed to be zero. In other words the extent to which this change in statistical

TABLE VI.5. *Specific and income equivalence scales*

	Single adult	Two adults	Each additional adult	Each child aged		
				0–4	5–10	11–17
Housing	0·73	1·00	0·35	0·20	0·26	0·24
Fuel, light and power	0·66	1·00	0·25	0·16	0·16	0·17
Food	0·56	1·00	0·40	0·12	0·23	0·33
Clothing	0·52	1·00	0·48	0·05	0·27	0·42
Alcohol and tobacco	0·50	1·00	0·50	–	–	0·05
Durables	0·60	1·00	0·40	0·24	0·30	0·38
Other goods and misc.	0·56	1·00	0·44	0·13	0·24	0·38
Transport and vehicles	0·60	1·00	0·40	0·20	0·26	0·39
Services	0·55	1·00	0·46	0·16	0·25	0·43
Income scale[a]	0·60	1·00	0·40	0·14	0·21	0·30

Source: Modified from some preliminary estimates provided by L. D. McClements, Department of Health and Social Security.

[a] Weighted average of the specific sales, with weights the estimated budget shares of the commodities.

method alters the contrasts in expenditure patterns of the poor and the non-poor depends on the ways in which family composition of poor and non-poor households differs (see chart 3.1). Of individuals in median households 35 per cent are under 16 years old, compared with only 25 per cent in 5th percentile households. In median households only 6 per cent are over 65, compared with 42 per cent in the 5th percentile household and 34 per cent in the 10th percentile household. Elderly persons undoubtedly have distinctive consumption needs, but whilst this may have a significant implication for individual items, as stressed in chapter 6, the overall effect of the adjustment is small.

EQUIVALENCE SCALES: A METHODOLOGICAL REVIEW

The most systematic attempt to measure equivalence scales using family budget data was that undertaken by Prais and Houthakker more than twenty years ago.[1] In their approach, the Engel curve is cast in the general form:

$$\frac{E_{ij}}{\Sigma_h c_{ih} n_{hj}} = f_i\left(\frac{Y_j}{\Sigma_h c_{oh} n_{hj}}\right) \tag{1}$$

where:

E_{ij} is expenditure on the i-th commodity by the j-th household;

Y_j is total net income of the j-th household;

n_{hj} is the number of persons of type h in the j-th household;

c_{ih} is the specific equivalence scale for the i-th commodity and h-th type of individual

and c_{oh} is the income equivalence scale for a person of type h.

This equation expresses expenditure on the i-th commodity per equivalent adult (using the relevant specific equivalence scales c_{ih}) as a function of income per equivalent adult (using income equivalence scales c_{oh}). It can be shown that the income equivalence scale for any given type of individual, h, can be expressed as a weighted average of that type's specific equivalence scales:

$$c_{oh} = \frac{\Sigma_i w_i c_{ih}}{\Sigma_i w_i} \tag{2}$$

Prais and Houthakker suggested an iterative procedure for estimating both specific and income scales based on equations (1) and (2) which can be summarised as follows. Certain initial values for the income equivalence scales are assumed *a priori* and used to standardise incomes on to an

This appendix has been prepared by N. C. Garganas.

[1] See S. J. Prais, 'The estimation of equivalent-adult scales from family budgets', *Economic Journal*, vol. 63, December 1953, which formed the basis of chapter 9 of Prais and Houthakker, *The Analysis of Family Budgets*. The earliest attempt at this approach is to be found in paper by E. Sydenstricker and W. I. King, 'The measurement of the relative economic status of families', *Journal of the American Statistical Association*, vol. 17, September 1921. (A discussion of this and other references to earlier works are to be found in *The Analysis of Family Budgets*, pp. 126 and 131–3.) A recent account of earlier methods has been given by J. L. Nicholson, 'An appraisal of different methods of estimating equivalence scales and their results', *The Review of Income and Wealth*, series 22, March 1976.

equivalent adult basis in order to estimate specific equivalence scales from equation (1). The resulting specific scales are then combined using equation (2) to re-estimate the income equivalence scales. The procedure is repeated until the estimates converge. In their investigations based on the 1937/8 Family Budget Survey, Prais and Houthakker implemented only the first step of their proposed method; they estimated specific equivalence scales on the assumption that the income equivalence scale for all types of individual was unity. The limited electronic computing facilities available were the main reason for the restriction on the scope of this study. Grouped household averages, prepared by a punched-card tabulator, were fed into an early electronic computer, which carried out the complex iterative regression analysis. The method was applied in full only twenty years later, using modern electronic computers, in investigations by Singh and Nagar, and by McClements.[1]

As a consequence of further work based on the 1953/4 Household Expenditure Survey, Forsyth argued that specific equivalence scales cannot be fully identified by such an approach. This is because there are insufficient independent parameter estimates in the set of Engel curves that can be fitted to each commodity and family type to allow a determinate solution. In other words, specific and income equivalence scales can be simultaneously determined only if some *a priori* restrictions are placed on certain of the values which they can assume.[2]

That this objection is not universally valid can be shown by theoretical illustration. Let us consider the Engel curve for a particular commodity specified separately for two distinct family types, the first family type, say a couple with no children, being taken as the standard, with unit coefficients for all scales. For this family assume the Engel curve is of the semi-logarithmic form and so may be written as

$$E_i = a_i + b_i \log Y \qquad (3)$$

where a_i and b_i are the parameters of the underlying Engel curve, assumed common for all households. For the second family, with k children, we then have

$$\frac{E_i}{1 + kc_i} = a_i + b_i \log \frac{Y}{1 + kc_o} \qquad (4)$$

where k represents the number of children in the family, c_i is the relevant

<hr />

[1] B. Singh and A. L. Nagar, 'Determination of unit consumer scales', *Econometrica*, vol. 41, March 1973; L. D. McClements, 'Equivalence scales for children' (unpublished paper presented at an SSRC Conference on Consumer Behaviour, April 1975).

[2] Forsyth, 'The relationship between family size and family expenditure'. See also J. S. Cramer, *Empirical Econometrics*, North-Holland, Amsterdam, 1969, for a simplified analysis of the problem.

specific equivalence scale for a child, and c_o is the child's income scale relative to a couple.

Equation (4) can be transformed to show the relation between household expenditure and household income, as

$$E_i = [(1 + kc_i)a_i - (1 + kc_i)b_i \log(1 + kc_o)]$$
$$+ (1 + kc_i)\, b_i \log Y \qquad (5)$$
$$= A_i + B_i \log Y \qquad (6)$$

where A_i and B_i are constants for that particular type of family. The problem is to estimate the coefficients a_i, b_i, A_i and B_i, and to derive from them estimates of the scales c_i and c_o.

It can be seen from equations (3) and (5) that, if separate Engel curves are fitted to two family types, consisting respectively of a couple with no children and a couple with k children, then, denoting by $\hat{a}$ the least-squares estimator of a, etc.:

$\hat{a}_i$ provides an estimate of a_i $\qquad (7)$

$\hat{b}_i$ provides an estimate of b_i $\qquad (8)$

$\hat{A}_i$ provides an estimate of
$\qquad (1 + kc_i)a_i - (1 + kc_i)b_i \log(1 + kc_o) \qquad (9)$

and $\qquad \hat{B}_i$ provides an estimate of $(1 + kc_i)b_i$ $\qquad (10)$

From which, with some manipulation, estimates of the c_i and c_o scales may be obtained. Thus, taking (8) and (10) together yields:

$$c_i = \frac{\hat{B}_i - \hat{b}_i}{k\hat{b}_i} \qquad (11)$$

$$c_o = \frac{\exp(\hat{a}_i/\hat{b}_i - \hat{A}_i/\hat{B}_i) - 1}{k} \qquad (12)$$

It can be seen from equation (11) that the specific commodity scale for a child will depend on the estimated coefficients of the Engel curves for the different family types, and will normally vary between commodities. It is also worth noting that for c_i to be positive the curves for larger families must have steeper slopes than those for smaller families (i.e. $\hat{B}_i > \hat{b}_i$), which will generally be true in the case of the semi-logarithmic form – as a comparison of (8) and (10) shows. The income scale c_o, on the other hand, should be identical for all commodities within the margins of sampling error. An appropriate statistical significance test would reveal whether differences between the c_o coefficients obtained for the various commodities are significant.

The crucial point to be observed in relation to equations (11) and (12) is that they permit the equivalence coefficients for both the income and the specific scales (c_0 and c_i) to be expressed in terms of the observed parameters of the two Engel curves, that is, in terms of their constants and slopes. There is no shortage of equations to determine the required number of unknowns; on the contrary, there is an excess of equations in relation to the income scale, since a separate estimate can be obtained on the basis of each commodity analysed. It is a matter to be determined by the facts whether such estimates are sufficiently similar to enable the varying patterns of consumption by households of different types to be subsumed in terms of the simple hypothesis (1), or whether there is need for a more complex approach.

The above argument is concerned merely with the principle of the matter, that is whether income and specific scales can be distinguished conceptually. We see that earlier doubts on this matter are not justified in principle; nevertheless Forsyth's objection suggests that in practice caution is required. In the above theoretical example a determinate solution was obtained only when the full restrictions imposed on the coefficients by the precise non-linear form adopted were considered. But the variability of the data and the limited size of the samples available may not permit a sufficiently precise determination of the appropriate non-linear form; it would then be necessary to look for other restrictions to permit a determinate solution.[1] That the method outlined above requires exceptionally large samples will be apparent from equation (12), which is based on the difference between two ratios of values all subject to sampling error and all of which cumulate.

After a number of exploratory trials the simpler method explained in chapter 7 was eventually adopted. This directs attention to consumption levels about the mean income where sampling errors are lower; it is also less sensitive to the precise degree of non-linearity in the relationship between consumption and income. In addition, it affords a simple test for determining whether the scales vary with income levels. Adoption of this method is not intended to suggest that the full iterative process described earlier is inappropriate, but that at this stage certain basic issues can be fruitfully explored with a simpler approach.

Some observations are merited on an alternative method that has been proposed for deriving income equivalence scales from expenditure surveys. The method in question is based on the assumption that households devoting an identical proportion of total expenditure to a given basic necessity or group of necessities, such as food, enjoy an identical standard of living. By fitting Engel curves for the chosen expenditure category to

---

[1] The method described above in terms of a semi-logarithmic Engel curve could be recast in terms of a linear form and certain other – but not all – functional forms; it could not be used if the Engel curve adhered precisely to the double logarithmic form.

households with and without children it is possible to identify the income at which the proportion of expenditure on food in a household with children is the same as that in a two-adult household with a specified income. By assumption the ratio between these two income levels provides an estimate of the income equivalence scale for children.[1] The advantages of this method are that the income equivalence scale can be isolated and measured in a comparatively simple manner and that, in principle, it allows the estimates of the income equivalence scale to vary with levels of income.

Nevertheless, it has two crucial weaknesses. First, the central assumption that the percentage of household expenditure devoted to food provides a basis for comparing living standards of families in different circumstances is unlikely to be substantially true. At a given standard of living (however defined) the percentage of total expenditure devoted to a particular commodity by households of different composition will depend on the specific requirements of the various members of the household for that commodity; accordingly this percentage cannot be used directly as an indicator of comparable living standards. Secondly, the approach tacitly assumes that economies of scale in consumption, associated with variations in family size, are the same in the case of both food and non-food items. In fact the scope for such economies varies between categories of expenditure – for example, they are usually larger for housing and heating than for food and clothing. Income equivalence scales derived from a group of necessities that includes food, housing, etc., would suggest that children have a smaller impact on family requirements than those based on food alone. In other words the choice of the standard commodity inevitably introduces into the analysis an arbitrary element of some significance. Conceptually this method bears a generic resemblance to that employed by Nicholson and Henderson,[2] which involves equating levels of expenditure on commodities consumed exclusively by adults, rather than the expenditure share of food, as a basis for measuring equivalent standards of living.[3]

Finally, more recent attempts to construct models for estimating household equivalence scales have been associated with work on the estimation of complete systems of demand equations. The idea on which such systems are based is that variations in household composition play a role analogous to that of price changes. This has led Barten to suggest that price elasticities

[1] This method was originally proposed by M. Friedman, 'A method of comparing incomes of families differing in composition', in National Bureau for Economic Research, *Studies in Income and Wealth*, vol. 15, New York, 1952. It has recently been revived by J. J. Seneca and M. K. Taussig, 'Family equivalence scales and personal tax exemption for children', *Review of Economics and Statistics*, vol. 53, August 1971.

[2] Nicholson, 'Variations in working class family expenditure'; Henderson, 'The cost of children'.

[3] See chapter 7; also J. A. C. Brown and A. S. Denton, 'Models of consumer behaviour: a survey', *Economic Journal*, vol. 82, December 1972.

might be estimated from family budgets alone,[1] an approach further explored by Muellbauer, who has shown how, at least in principle, the procedure could be used to yield estimates of equivalence scales.[2] Though the technique has the appearance of great analytical power, it has yet to justify itself empirically.

[1] A. P. Barten, 'Family composition, prices and expenditure patterns' in P. E. Hart, G. Mills and J. K. Whitaker (eds.), *Econometric Analysis for National Economic Planning*, London, Butterworth, 1964.

[2] J. Muellbauer, 'Household composition, Engel curves and welfare comparisons between households. A duality approach', *European Economic Review*, vol. 5, August 1974.

INDEX

PUBLICATIONS OF THE
NATIONAL INSTITUTE OF ECONOMIC AND SOCIAL RESEARCH

published by
THE CAMBRIDGE UNIVERSITY PRESS

Books published for the Institute by the Cambridge University Press are available through the ordinary booksellers. They appear in the five series below:

ECONOMIC & SOCIAL STUDIES

* At present out of print.

OCCASIONAL PAPERS

* At present out of print.

STUDIES IN THE NATIONAL INCOME AND EXPENDITURE OF THE UNITED KINGDOM

Published under the joint auspices of the National Institute and the Department of Applied Economics, Cambridge.

NIESR STUDENTS' EDITION

* At present out of print.

REGIONAL PAPERS

1   *The Anatomy of Regional Activity Rates* by JOHN BOWERS, and *Regional Social Accounts for the United Kingdom* by V. H. WOODWARD. 1970. pp. 192. £2·60 net.

2   *Regional Unemployment Differences in Great Britain* by P. C. CHESHIRE, and *Interregional Migration Models and their Application to Great Britain* by R. WEEDEN. 1973. pp. 118. £2·60 net.

3   *Unemployment, Vacancies and the Rate of Change of Earnings: A Regional Analysis* by A. E. WEBB, and *Regional Rates of Employment Growth: An Analysis of Variance Treatment* by R. WEEDEN. 1974. pp. 114. £2·60 net.

THE NATIONAL INSTITUTE OF ECONOMIC AND SOCIAL RESEARCH

publishes regularly

THE NATIONAL INSTITUTE ECONOMIC REVIEW

A quarterly analysis of the general economic situation in the United Kingdom and the world overseas, with forecasts eighteen months ahead. The first issue each year is devoted entirely to the current situation and prospects both in the short and medium term. Other issues contain also special articles on subjects of interest to academic and business economists.

Annual subscriptions, £10·00 (home) and £14·00 (abroad), also single issues for the current year, £3·00 (home) and £4·00 (abroad), are available directly from NIESR, 2 Dean Trench Street, Smith Square, London, SW1P 3HE

Subscriptions at the special reduced price of £3·50 p.a. are available to students in the United Kingdom and the Irish Republic on application to the Secretary of the Institute.

Back numbers are distributed by Wm. Dawson and Sons Ltd., Cannon House, Park Farm Road, Folkestone, price £3·00 each plus postage. Reprints of issues which have gone out of stock are available from the same address, price £4·00 each plus postage.

Also available directly from the Institute

THE IVTH FRENCH PLAN

By FRANÇOIS PERROUX, translated by Bruno Leblanc. 1965. pp. 72. 50p net.

Published by Heinemann Educational Books

AN INCOMES POLICY FOR BRITAIN
Edited by FRANK BLACKABY. 1972. pp. 260. £4·00 net.

THE MEDIUM TERM: MODELS OF THE BRITISH ECONOMY
Edited by G. D. N. WORSWICK and FRANK BLACKABY. 1974. pp. 256. £4·80 net.

THE UNITED KINGDOM ECONOMY
By the NIESR. 1976. pp. 144. £1·25 net.

Available from booksellers.